CHEVY/GMC TRUCKS 1967–1972

HOW TO BUILD & MODIFY

Jim Pickering

S-A DESIGN

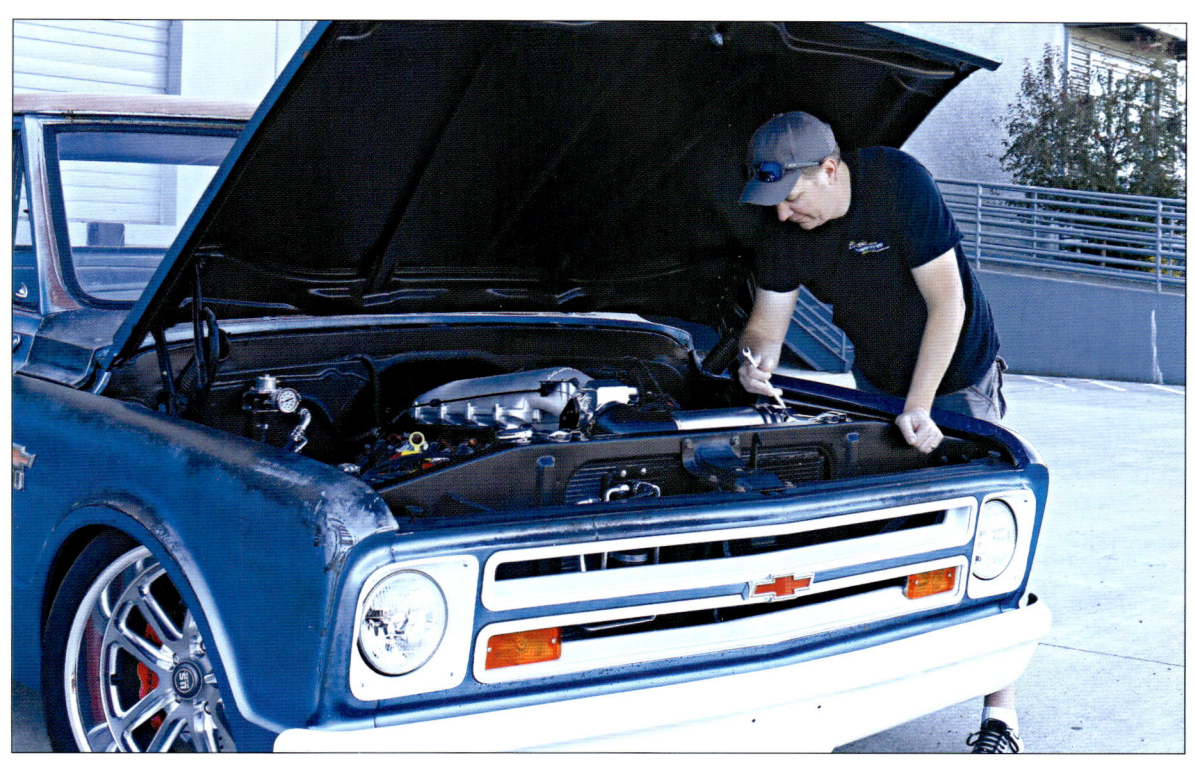

CarTech®

CarTech®

CarTech®, Inc.
6118 Main Street
North Branch, MN 55056
Phone: 651-277-1200 or 800-551-4754
Fax: 651-277-1203
www.cartechbooks.com

© 2023 by Jim Pickering

All rights reserved. No part of this publication may be reproduced or utilized in any form or by any means, electronic or mechanical, including photocopying, recording, or by any information storage and retrieval system, without prior permission from the Publisher. All text, photographs, and artwork are the property of the Author unless otherwise noted or credited.

The information in this work is true and complete to the best of our knowledge. However, all information is presented without any guarantee on the part of the Author or Publisher, who also disclaim any liability incurred in connection with the use of the information and any implied warranties of merchantability or fitness for a particular purpose. Readers are responsible for taking suitable and appropriate safety measures when performing any of the operations or activities described in this work.

All trademarks, trade names, model names and numbers, and other product designations referred to herein are the property of their respective owners and are used solely for identification purposes. This work is a publication of CarTech, Inc., and has not been licensed, approved, sponsored, or endorsed by any other person or entity. The Publisher is not associated with any product, service, or vendor mentioned in this book, and does not endorse the products or services of any vendor mentioned in this book.

Edit by Wes Eisenschenk
Layout by Connie DeFlorin

ISBN 978-1-61325-747-0
Item No. SA528

Library of Congress Cataloging-in-Publication Data Available

Written, edited, and designed in the U.S.A.
Printed in China
10 9 8 7 6 5 4 3 2 1

CarTech books may be purchased at a discounted rate in bulk for resale, events, corporate gifts, or educational purposes. Special editions may also be created to specification.
For details, contact Special Sales at 6118 Main Street, North Branch MN 55056 or by email at sales@cartechbooks.com.

All photos are courtesy of Jim Pickering unless otherwise noted.

DISTRIBUTION BY:

Europe
PGUK
63 Hatton Garden
London EC1N 8LE, England
Phone: 020 7061 1980 • Fax: 020 7242 3725
www.pguk.co.uk

Australia
Renniks Publications Ltd.
3/37-39 Green Street
Banksmeadow, NSW 2109, Australia
Phone: 2 9695 7055 • Fax: 2 9695 7355
www.renniks.com

Canada
Login Canada
300 Saulteaux Crescent
Winnipeg, MB, R3J 3T2 Canada
Phone: 800 665 1148 • Fax: 800 665 0103
www.lb.ca

CONTENTS

Dedication 4
Acknowledgments 4
Introduction 5

Chapter 1: The Action Line............ 6
A Modern Look........................... 6
From Muscle to Utility and Back.. 8
The Basics.................................... 8
Other Items to Note..................... 9

Chapter 2: Getting Started........... 14
Setting a Budget and Making
  a Plan 15
Tools and Workspace 15
Finding a Truck 17
What to Look for and
  What to Avoid 17

Chapter 3: Body Disassembly, Fixes, and Modifications.................... 22
Front-End Removal.................... 22
Keeping Track of Parts............... 24
Bed Removal and Teardown Tips.. 25
Cab Removal............................... 26
Rust Repair................................. 26
Building a Short-Bed out
  of a Long-Bed 30

Chapter 4: Suspension 41
Front Suspension....................... 41
Rear Suspension........................ 42
Lowering the Truck 45
Getting Low with Leafs 47
C-Notches 48
Drop Spindles............................ 49
Complete Suspension Kits 49
Coilover Conversions................. 50
Air Suspension 50
Installing RideTech's Coilover
  Kit on a C20............................ 52
How Low Can You Go? 60

Chapter 5: Brakes and Steering .61
Brakes 61
Steering 74
Converting a C20 into a Corner
  Carver 75

Chapter 6: Engine Basics 77
Available Engines 78
Common Power Upgrades 79
Engine Swaps............................. 85
Intake Manifolds 90

Chapter 7: Installing an LS in a C10 92
Engine Mounts........................... 93
Oil Pans..................................... 95
Fitting the Engine in the Truck ... 95
Engine Accessories 98
Exhaust...................................... 99

Chapter 8: Fueling, ECU, and Cooling System................ 102
Fueling 102
Fuel Lines................................ 107
ECU... 110
Cooling System 112

Chapter 9: Transmissions.......... 114
Manual 114
Automatic................................ 115
Upgrades 117
Transmission Swaps 118
Manual Swaps 121
Hydraulic Clutches.................. 127
Driveline 128

Chapter 10: Rear Axle 129
Axle Identification 129
Heavy-Duty Axles.................... 130
The 12-Bolt.............................. 130
5-Lug versus 6-Lug.................. 131

Checking Gears........................ 132
Two-Tire Fire 133
Other Options......................... 134
Selecting the Right Parts.......... 134
Selecting Gears 136
Breaking in New Gears............ 144

Chapter 11: Interior and Air Conditioning 145
Seats 145
Other Seats 146
Sound 146
Other Interior Components 147
Air Conditioning 153

Chapter 12: Wiring and Lighting................................... 157
Alternator 157
Adding Big Power.................... 158
Lighting................................... 159

Chapter 13: Finishing Touches .. 165
Common Body Modifications... 165
Roll Pans and Bumpers 166
Cleaning Up and Matching
  Original Paint....................... 168
Reassembly Tricks 171
Bed Installation 171
Wheels..................................... 172
Tires.. 174

Source Guide 176

Dedication

For my friend Paul.

Acknowledgments

No truck project is ever completed alone, and neither is a book that requires a truck build to be finished on a deadline. It takes many people to make something like this work, especially when a global pandemic and resulting parts-supply issues throw a big wrench into the plan.

I have to thank Chester Allen for supporting me throughout this process, along with the team at Audrain Motorsport and *Linkage* magazine. Thanks to fellow CarTech author and GM truck expert Kevin Whipps for suggestions, images, and general support; Jeff Stites for his illustration work; and B. Mitchell Carlson for his image assistance.

Thanks to Brian Baker for lending me his welder when I was first starting out and to Jim Fahey for his metal inert gas (MIG) expertise and tools. Without those, none of this would have been possible. Professional painter Alistair Case deserves special recognition for his expertise and willingness to chase down an ideal patina finish and for smoothing out the metal that I warped when I got too excited with Fahey's welder. Recognition also goes to Rick Redmond of AIR Automotive for his seat restoration tips and to Jay Harden for making time to help with some heavy parts lifting.

Ben Schwisow needs credit for the ideas used in my smooth bumper section and for talking trucks with me endlessly, both before and during this project.

For parts information and support, particularly in the midst of supply issues, thanks to Blane Burnett and Steve Sparkman at Holley, Alan Rebescher at Summit Racing, Gabe Flores at Classic Industries, Rick Love at Vintage Air, Jason Brady at RideTech, Tim King and Rick Elam at Baer Brakes, Chris Plump at US Mags, Jeff Kauffman at Silver Sport Transmissions, Jason Chandler and Mike Gray at Auto Metal Direct, Ben Silverstein at Dapper Lighting, Matt Criswell at Carolina Truck Shop, and Shari Arfons at McCullough Public Relations. Thanks to Dan Stafford of Dan's Garage (dansgarage.net) for selling me a great starting-point truck.

A special thanks goes out to Wes Eisenschenk and Bob Wilson from the CarTech editorial team for rolling with me as my deadlines moved based on COVID-impacted parts needs.

Thanks to my wife, Kristina, and my daughters Katie and Emma, who made time for this project in their lives and encouraged me to keep going despite the time commitment that it required.

Finally, thanks to my father, James M. Pickering, for his dedication to this project, his ability to problem-solve his way out of any situation, and for his hands-on help in nearly every section of my build. I couldn't have done any of this without him.

Introduction

During my college days at Pacific University in Forest Grove, Oregon, I was one of two students on campus who drove an old truck. Mine was a 1975 Chevrolet C20. The other was an orange and white 1971 C10 that was fitted with a custom flatbed and was clearly fresh from the farm. During that first semester, this other truck owner and I made a habit out of parking next to each other. I think we both assumed safety in numbers was a viable protection plan for our old rigs.

We eventually figured out that we were neighbors in the dorms as well and became great friends. Ryan went on to be the best man at my wedding, and he's the godfather to my daughter. Nearly 20 years later, he still has that truck too.

So goes the classic truck world. You can't drive one of these things anywhere without making a friend or two. But here's the rub: if you want to drive a classic truck often, you'll eventually get tired of slow steering, finicky drum brakes, truck-like ride and handling, a behind-the-seat fuel tank, and dim lighting. Eventually, you will want to upgrade your truck, either in terms of style or performance.

Fortunately, you can gain that modern performance while keeping the classic look and feel of your 1967–1972 C10 or C20. Thanks to GM truck engineering, these are great projects for both beginners and for expert builders alike. That's where this book comes in. From mild to wild, you can do tons of things to a classic GM truck to make it faster, handle better, and more comfortable than it was when it was new, all while keeping the charm that makes people stop and want to say hello. It is my goal to show you what's available and how to complete these tasks.

Putting together a book like this can be done in one of two ways. The first is to find many different truck projects and owners and to document the work they're doing. Go to a shop that specializes in these rigs and stand by with a camera in your hand and questions on your mind. The other way is to get your hands dirty and do it yourself by turning the wrenches, putting in the build time, and working out your own solutions to problems you wouldn't have thought of otherwise.

Both methods produce a fine product, but for me, getting involved adds depth to the content. There are aspects of a build that people don't consider until they're knee deep in it. That level of detail and the kinds of questions that pop up only when you're doing the work makes a difference in the final product. I hope that carries through to you as you read this book.

My goal with the truck was to build something that's both fast and fun and well equipped for extensive use, even in modern traffic. Of course, what I chose to do in my how-to sections represents one direction among thousands of possibilities, but the basics apply no matter what modifications you choose to tackle with your own project or how many of them you decide to do to your own truck.

GM's 1967–1972 trucks continue to appeal to just about every demographic. The aftermarket has really embraced them as the modern hot rods and customs that they truly are with more parts on the market that make them turn, stop, accelerate, and sound better than they ever did in stock configuration. The key for you as a builder is to get your truck there. I hope that this book helps you reach that goal.

CHAPTER 1

THE ACTION LINE

There's something special about GM's Action Line 1967–1972 trucks. Maybe it's their unique mix of utility, usability, style, and relative simplicity. Maybe it's nostalgia, as many of us remember riding around in them with parents or grandparents when life seemed simpler.

These trucks are among the most popular classic rigs in America today. They've played a lot of different roles in many peoples' lives over the years. Thanks to that, everyone seems to have some sort of connection to them—from good old Americana to the most modern custom trend. It doesn't matter where you're from or how old you are. Regardless of the demographics, these trucks always seem to be part of the show and are often front and center.

This book is about how to find, build, and modify these classic trucks into something you'll want to drive and show off. Before I dive into that, it's important to understand some of the factors that have driven the popularity of these trucks over the years, as that gets to the heart of why you might want to choose one for your next build.

A Modern Look

Throughout the late 1950s, the American truck world evolved. The days of stark utility were waning, as Americans looked for more comfort and convenience items in their vehicles. The typical American buyer wanted a truck to drive everywhere versus just to the job site. By the dawn of the 1960s, GM decided that it was time to develop a utility rig

GM's Action Line trucks have been popular for decades. There's no limit to what can be done with one—from complete factory restorations through total custom builds. This 1968 example is a desirable short-bed with good options.

CHEVY/GMC TRUCKS 1967–1972: HOW TO BUILD & MODIFY

THE ACTION LINE

The plan for a more comfortable truck began with the Cameo Carrier in 1955. The 1967 model year expanded on some of the ideas that the Cameo launched. (Photo Courtesy B. Mitchell Carlson)

Starting in 1971, Chevrolet added disc brakes (indicated by this tailgate decal) as standard on its light-duty truck line. Disc brakes were a major improvement over the fade-prone drum brakes that came before.

that had both style and comfort as part of its basic features.

Along with the rest of the Big Three manufacturers (General Motors, Ford, and Chrysler), GM worked to refine and streamline its utilitarian trucks with the hopes of grabbing onto the changing market. It was a lofty goal, but at GM, this was familiar territory.

Chevrolet styling department head Chuck Jordan had played with the idea of a flashy, comfortable truck about a decade prior, which led to the launch of the 1955 Chevrolet Cameo Carrier and GMC Suburban Carrier. Both the Cameo and Suburban Carriers came with styled fiberglass bedsides, chrome trim, V-8 engines, wraparound rear glass, and car-like appointments inside. It was just the thing for a farming family to take to church on Sunday, but it wasn't a particularly hot seller. Only 5,220 Chevrolets and about 300 GMCs were sold that year. While both of these trucks seemed like the answers to a question that America had not yet asked, they served as a road map for the future of American utility. It was a watershed moment for GM, and it paved the way for the more comfortable and better-equipped trucks of the 1960s, 1970s, and beyond.

By 1964, GM was working on the design for what became the 1967 Action Line trucks. These trucks were the second generation of C/K rigs and featured simple, clean lines throughout with a cohesive design that looked more car-like than any GM truck that had come before.

Style was important, but key to the experience were some of the available features: V-8 power, power steering and power brakes, air conditioning, AM/FM radios, tachometers, speed warning systems, bucket seats, tinted glass, upscale trim packages, disc brakes, Positraction axles, trailing-arm rear suspension, tilt columns, etc. The net result was a truck that was just as tough as any that GM had built prior but with a new era of comfort and convenience. That car-like style didn't hurt either.

By the time these trucks were on dealer lots in 1967, buyers could order a rig that was completely basic in nature (as they had been able to do since the end of WWII) or one could be ordered with all kinds of car-like options to suit frequent or daily use. Many fell somewhere in the middle. For today's buyers, this was important because one of the most compelling things about these pickups is the way they drive compared to the way they look.

The available comfort options, even the most basic ones, make these trucks drive a lot better than the uninitiated might expect. They look like classic trucks with clean, simple lines, but when fitted with the right options, they give that old truck look and feel without an overly harsh ride or the limited niceties that are the hallmarks of many other classic trucks. That's the heart of what makes these special today, alongside a long history of reliable service that tends to endear them to those who remember the days of two-tone

CHEVY/GMC TRUCKS 1967–1972: HOW TO BUILD & MODIFY

CHAPTER 1

This 3/4-ton is a range-topping Custom model from 1967 that consisted of special bright trim around the windshield, at the beltline, and around the grille and headlights. It also had nicer interior appointments.

When the muscle-car world pushed Camaros and Chevelles out of the reach of typical muscle-car people, many turned to trucks, such as this one. Many of the practices used in muscle-car customization and restoration carried over. This 1972 has big-block power, Rally wheels, and red-line tires.

paint, all-metal construction, and DIY tune-ups.

These trucks still look, sound, feel, and smell like the good old days, but they're modern enough for daily use. That, combined with their continuing popularity, makes them the perfect basis for restoration and/or modification with use in mind.

For every top-level Cheyenne Super with air conditioning and a big-block, there were many 6-cylinder workhorses built without any options at all. That's great for truck builders today, as even the most basic example can serve as a great canvas for customization.

From Muscle to Utility and Back

This book is about custom trucks, but American muscle cars have a role in the Action Line's popularity today too.

The original American muscle car era that raged through the early 1960s and into the 1970s had wound down by the 1980s. Within a decade, muscle-car owners realized what they had lost, and the drive to restore and modify muscle cars started a new boom that has evolved and grown in the years since. That reinvigoration of muscle had an interesting impact on GM's Action Line trucks.

With so many of these trucks built over the six-year run of the model, they were cheap, available, and often nicely equipped. They also had a lot of the same attributes as a Chevelle or Camaro: small- or big-block power, a stout transmission and axles, and more. In addition, an important fact was that many states didn't require emissions testing on rigs built prior to 1973. As such, it didn't take long for muscle-car and hot-rod enthusiasts to begin working on their trucks too. These started to be seen as muscle cars as well but in a truck-shaped body that could double as a parts hauler.

That simple factor meant that these rigs took on a new role in the 1990s and 2000s. Around that time, with muscle-car values on the rise, more people, specifically younger people, began to modify these trucks beyond daily utilitarian roles. That movement has grown and evolved with industry tastes in the years since.

Today, you'll find top-level 1967–1972 GM rigs everywhere from SEMA to Barrett-Jackson Scottsdale, often equaling or bettering both the restored and custom cars around them in craftsmanship and creativity. The aftermarket has risen to the occasion as well, with everything from small trim pieces to complete cabs available to resurrect even the rattiest, rustiest rig. The key for builders is to source a good truck to start with and figure out a plan for what to do with it.

The Basics

Action Line trucks were available in a few different lengths, depending on what the buyer ordered. Generally speaking, there are three wheelbases

8   CHEVY/GMC TRUCKS 1967–1972: HOW TO BUILD & MODIFY

THE ACTION LINE

In the 1960s, Scott-Bilt, a company in Oklahoma, produced custom crew-cab trucks using front doors in both the front and rear locations. Not many were built, and most were used by the railroad and the US Forest Service.

If this Blazer looks a little strange, it's because it has a 1967 nose married to a 1969-or-later Blazer chassis. This kind of swap is relatively common and pretty easy to accomplish, so keep that in mind while looking at trucks for sale.

available: 115 inch (short-bed), 127 inch (long-bed), and 133 inch (Longhorn). The short-bed rigs had a 6-foot, 6-inch-long bed; the long-bed trucks had an 8-foot bed; and the Longhorn (available starting in 1968 and only in two-wheel-drive C20 configuration) had an 8-foot, 6-inch bed. All but the Longhorn were available in either fleetside or stepside configurations. Long stepside beds measured 9 feet long.

The trucks were available as 1/2 ton (C10/1500), 3/4 ton (C20/2500), and 1 ton (C30/3500), with the short-beds limited to half-ton capacity.

These trucks were only offered from the factory in single-cab form, but some builders (such as Scott-Bilt and the Alton Company) produced crew-cab variants in the period. Custom builders have risen to the challenge of building their own quad-cab and extended-cab versions using Suburban doors and custom touches in the rear. If you find a GM truck from this era with more than two doors, someone other than the factory built it.

Other Items to Note

You'll often find big-block 4x4 trucks from this era for sale, but GM never built any. All 4x4s in this era were fitted with 6-cylinder engines or small-block V-8s. Anything with a big-block must've been swapped at some point, so keep that in mind.

GM never built a Longhorn 4x4 at the factory. Some builders made their own, but if you run across one, GM didn't do it.

Many parts are interchangeable throughout the Action Line run, but some key pieces are not. For example, 1967 and 1968 Chevrolet fenders don't have the proper nose contour for the 1969-and-later grille surround. GMC fenders and Chevrolet fenders don't interchange past 1968, as the GMC grille never received the full perimeter trim that the Chevrolet did starting in 1969. You can use any 1967–1972 GMC fender on a GMC regardless of the year.

The 1967 and 1972 doors are unique: the 1967 for the way the exterior door handle mounts and the 1972 for its exposed upper screw as well as longer door latch and window-regulator actuators to match the thicker, molded door panels. Keep the year of your truck in mind when hunting parts at your local swap meet.

Tilt columns from vans fit with some slight modifications. While a tilt column is a relatively rare option, the market for aftermarket replacements is bigger than you might assume.

CHAPTER 1

Action Line Pickups by Year

If you've decided to hunt down an Action Line truck to build, it's important to understand the differences because these trucks changed over the years. Here's a quick rundown of each model year with a look at what makes each one special.

1967

Production		
Type	Wheelbase	Production Total
1/2-ton C10	short	92,336
1/2-ton C10	long	194,972
1/2-ton K10	short	2,307
1/2-ton K10	long	3,452
3/4-ton C20	long	60,582
3/4-ton K20	long	3,399
1-ton C30	long	18,566
Chevrolet Total: 375,614		
GMC Total: 130,659*		
*GMC production records were lost. Detailed totals from this era are not available.		

This was the debut of the Action Line for both Chevrolet and GMC. The quickest way to spot a 1967 of either make is to note the lack of side markers, which didn't become standard until 1968. Small back windows were standard for 1967, with big back panoramic glass available as a special-order option. Medium-duty trucks kept the small back window through 1972.

The '67 is special in that it doesn't have the side reflectors mounted in the fenders or in the bed that are seen on 1968 models. It's also the only year that offered the small back window (as seen here). This truck is wearing later square side mirrors, which are more often seen on 1971 and 1972 models.

Three trim levels were available at Chevrolet: Base, Custom, and Custom Sport Truck (CST). At GMC, they were offered as Deluxe, Custom, and Super Custom. Standard features included safety belts, padded sun visors, two-speed electric wipers, rubber floor mats, a dome light, padded dash, left-hand mirror, reverse lights, turn signals, and four-way flashers.

Unique 1967 parts include the available 283-ci V-8, vent wing-window latch knobs, interior door handles and window cranks, exterior door handles, an ashtray, ignition-switch bezel, glove box latch button, and dash gauge cluster surround. Some of those items were carried over from the previous-generation GM truck, and some were carried on into early 1968.

GMCs had a unique grille with stamped letters in 1967. Power steering on both Chevrolet and GMC in 1967 was a ram style, so there's no clearance in the frame at the steering-box mount for a larger integrated-style power-steering box as was used in the later trucks. The 1967 and 1968 models feature a hand-operated parking brake and have tip-forward bench seat backs.

Uncommon options for 1967 included a tachometer, speed-warning gauge clusters, overdrive, and the CST trim level.

1968

Production		
Type	Wheelbase	Production Total
1/2-ton C10	short	95,540
1/2-ton C10	long	239,934
1/2-ton K10	short	3,198
1/2-ton K10	long	4,911*
3/4-ton C20	long	79,208
3/4-ton K20	long	6,617*
3/4-ton C20 Longhorn	long+	1,902
1-ton C30	long wheelbase	18,269
Chevrolet Total: 449,579		
GMC Total: 148,479		
*Incomplete records		

By 1968, GM added front and rear side markers to both Chevrolet and GMC trucks to comply with new federal safety regulations. If you see a Chevy truck with side markers, the sloped early hood, and a twin rectangular grille opening, it's a 1968.

Note that in 1968, these side markers were reflectors (not lights). That changed in later years, and it still confuses

10   CHEVY/GMC TRUCKS 1967–1972: HOW TO BUILD & MODIFY

THE ACTION LINE

This 1968 Chevrolet C10 has the Anniversary Gold paint scheme and features CST equipment. This truck has an automatic transmission, factory air conditioning, power steering, and power brakes. It features sidesaddle fuel tanks and later squarebody hubcaps.

many builders today because the aftermarket offers the same front and rear lighted side markers/reflectors for all of these trucks regardless that the original 1968 wiring harness had no provisions for side-marker lights.

A new 307-ci V-8 replaced the 283-ci engine option, and the larger rear window became standard. The biggest change was the addition of the Longhorn truck that was offered with a 133-inch wheelbase and an 8.5-foot bed. It was only available on 3/4-ton trucks and only in two-wheel-drive models.

Chevrolet celebrated its 50th anniversary with a special two-tone white and Anniversary Gold truck that required a fleetside box and a gold and Parchment interior. It was offered as option code 551, and it was available on pickups, panel trucks, Suburbans, and vans.

At GMC, the grille emblem moved up to the leading edge of the hood like it was on Chevrolets.

Uncommon options included bucket seats, a center seat-belt, air conditioning, 396-ci 2-barrel and 4-barrel engines, CST equipment, a tachometer, and overdrive.

This was a pivotal design year for GM trucks because they lost some of their svelte appearance in favor of a more upright hood and grille treatment to make the truck look tougher and more truck-like. This year also marked the debut of the popular K5 Blazer at Chevrolet, which turned the truck platform into an off-road powerhouse and stole the thunder from Ford's hot Bronco.

The majority of 1969's changes are in the nose of the truck. The Chevrolet bowtie was moved from the grille to the leading edge of the hood, and the grille was changed to include a bright center bar and egg-crate inner sections. Headlight buckets were painted black, and turn signals were mounted in the grille on either side of embossed "Chevrolet" letters.

Side markers gained lights, and the 327-ci V-8 was dropped in favor of the 350 that we all know and love. Inside, the truck's parking brake was shifted to a floor pedal from the previous under-column handle, and a new two-bar steering wheel was introduced.

Side trim also changed, as both upper and lower trim were now available (as opposed to the earlier lower-only over-the-wheel designs).

1969

Production		
Type	Wheelbase	Production Total
K5 Blazer	N/A	4,935
1/2-ton C10	short	105,701
1/2-ton C10	long	307,163
1/2-ton K10	short	3,405
1/2-ton K10	long	5,493*
3/4-ton C20	long	95,939
3/4-ton K20	long	8,296
3/4-ton C20 Longhorn	long+	8,797
1-ton C30	long	20,821
Chevrolet Total: 560,550		
GMC Total: 150,180		
*Incomplete records		

For 1969, a new grille, fenders, and hood gave the truck a more upright look. It's hard to differentiate between a 1969 and a 1970, as the main differences are in the grille itself.

CHAPTER 1

Action Line Pickups by Year *continued*

Front fenders and hoods interchange between 1969-and-later Chevrolet trucks, but note that by 1971, the hood-mounted Chevrolet emblem was moved back into the grille, so there will be two stud holes to fill if you run an earlier hood on a later truck.

At Chevrolet, trucks were still available as Standard, Custom, and Custom Sport Truck (CST). GMC offered base, Custom, and Super Custom options. Both Sierra and Sierra Grande debuted in as options groups this year.

Uncommon options included CST equipment, a chrome rear bumper, roof marker lamps, and a tachometer.

1970

Production		
Type	Wheelbase	Production Total
K5 Blazer 4x2	N/A	985
K5 Blazer 4x4	N/A	11,527
1/2-ton C10	short	83,592
1/2-ton C10	long	269,335
1/2-ton K10	short	4,247
1/2-ton K10	long	7,838 *
3/4-ton C20	long	87,291
3/4-ton K20	long	8,200
3/4-ton C20 Longhorn	long+	5,821
1-ton C30	long	18,516
Chevrolet Total: 497,352		
GMC Total: 121,833		
*Incomplete records		

In 1969, new side trim debuted, and it was carried over for 1970. This truck is a good example of how restoration parts can be added or subtracted to make something unique, as it wears 1972 Cheyenne Super wood-grain lower trim.

Neither Chevrolet nor GMC made many changes for the 1970 model year, but among the more important changes was the Chevrolet grille. It was similar but not exactly the same as the 1969. It utilized a different paint scheme to accentuate horizontal fins rather than the egg-crate look used the year before. Some restoration parts sources claim these can be interchanged. While they do, they are visually not the same, so keep that in mind if you want a stock look.

Tilt wheel became available in 1970, and the 396-ci big-block was replaced with a 402-ci engine that was called a 400 in the truck's side badging. A bedside toolbox was optional for the long-bed and the Longhorn, and it was mounted on the passenger's side of the truck. These toolbox doors rusted quickly and are coveted today.

The Chevrolet Blazer gained a sibling in the GMC Jimmy, which was offered for the first time in 1970.

K-series 4x4 trucks gained a new open-knuckle Dana 44 front axle that replaced the closed-knuckle units. This is unique to 1970 due to its drum-brake setup, which was dropped the next year. Out back, the 12-bolt rear-axle housing gained about an inch of width partway through the model year, which is an important distinction for builders looking to swap over to later 5-lug-axle setups. Earlier and later axle shafts do not interchange due to this difference in housing width, and earlier axles only came with six-lug configuration.

Uncommon options for 1970 included two-wheel-drive Blazers, the Powerglide transmission, 4-speed manual transmission, and tachometer.

1971

Production		
Type	Wheelbase	Production Total
K5 Blazer 4x2	N/A	1,277
K5 Blazer 4x4	N/A	17,220
1/2-ton C10	short	53,382
1/2-ton C10	long	224,115
1/2-ton K10	short	4,506
1/2-ton K10	long	11,406
3/4-ton C20	long	72,940
3/4-ton K20	long	11,858
3/4-ton C20 Longhorn	long+	3,331
1-ton C30	long	20,684
Chevrolet Total: 420,719		
GMC Total: N/A		

For 1971, Chevrolet shifted its trim-level designations. The base level was now known as the Custom, the Custom

12   CHEVY/GMC TRUCKS 1967–1972: HOW TO BUILD & MODIFY

THE ACTION LINE

The Cheyenne Super package launched in mid-1971, but this truck wears the standard Cheyenne blackout trim, which suggests it may have not been a Super from the factory. However, it does have RPO P01 full wheel covers and a big-block engine. Note the rearview-mirror arm mounted to the roof panel and the egg-crate grille that together denote 1971.

Deluxe took over for the Custom, and the CST became the Cheyenne. Later in the year, a Cheyenne Super option became available, complete with wood-grain side trim and nicer interior appointments.

At GMC, the Sierra served as the top trim level. Beyond that, the main change came with the addition of a new grille and front bumper. The grille returned to the egg-crate design surrounded with a black stripe set within the grille surround. The Chevrolet badge moved back to the center of the grille, while the turn signals moved down into the bumper for the first time. Headlight buckets were bright aluminum.

Other changes included the addition of sport mirrors to the options list, as well as AM/FM radios. Cabs gained a vent in the doorjamb that was used to assist with closing the door when the windows were rolled up. Also unique to the year was a raised pad in the cab roof sheet metal for the rearview-mirror mount. Steel throttle arms were dropped for 1971 in favor of a safer cable-actuated throttle and a matching cowl-mounted throttle pedal.

Functionally, the most important change was the addition of front disc brakes, which became standard in 1971. To highlight this, a special 1971-only "Disc Brake" decal was fixed to the upper driver's side of the tailgate.

At GMC, the changes were much more limited. The grille carried over from 1970 but with black paint applied around its perimeter.

Uncommon options included the 396-ci engine, bucket seats, an oil-bath air cleaner, the LPG engine package, Cheyenne Super package, and Powerglide transmission.

1972

Production		
Type	Wheelbase	Production Total
K5 Blazer 4x2	N/A	3,357
K5 Blazer 4x4	N/A	44,266
1/2-ton C10	short	63,412
1/2-ton C10	long	299,009
1/2-ton K10	short	7,805
1/2-ton K10	long	21,976
3/4-ton C20	long	109,682
3/4-ton K20	long	22,461
3/4-ton C20 Longhorn	long+	3,328
1-ton C30	long wheelbase	28,051
Chevrolet Total: 603,347		
GMC Total: 132,243		

For 1972, the Chevrolet's grille lost its black border accent, but the nose of the truck was otherwise unchanged.

The inside, however, featured several changes, including a new glued-on-windshield rearview mirror, which is the quickest way to spot a 1972. Other changes included a new molded door panel with an integrated armrest that required a slightly longer door latch and window regulator crank as well as handle mounts to match. A reinforcing screw mounted in the upper section of the inner door just under the wing-window frame is also a 1972-only feature.

Uncommon options for 1972 included the Cheyenne Super package, a tachometer, AM/FM radio, bedside toolbox, bucket seats, extreme-bend 4x4 tow hooks, and LPG engines. ∎

The rearview mirror here is glued to the windshield, which suggests that this K20 is a 1972, but that's one of the only real tells. This one's been given a mostly stock restoration, aside from a small lift and larger-than-stock tires.

CHEVY/GMC TRUCKS 1967–1972: HOW TO BUILD & MODIFY   13

CHAPTER 2

GETTING STARTED

Over the six years that GM built the Action Line trucks, nearly four million examples rolled off the assembly line. That's good for you as a builder because it means there are still plenty of trucks out there to be found. The key, of course, is finding a good one, which can mean different things to different people.

Before you decide what a good starting point might be for you, it's important to first think about what exactly you intend to do with your truck. You need to come up with a plan for your build because that plan will dictate what kind of truck you should be hunting and in what condition.

Are you looking to build a mostly stock rig with some nice options? Are you going to remove the engine, transmission, and drivetrain in favor of more modern parts? Will the interior be stock or stock-ish by the time your truck is on the road, or will you be tossing the factory interior in favor of a modern seat setup and a digital dash?

None of this may seem like a big deal, but considering the prices that these trucks bring in today's market, it could end up being a waste of money for you to buy a complete truck if you intend on removing most of the stock components. In some cases, you might be better off buying a bare cab and frame (with title, of course), rather than a complete, functional original.

Just because a truck looks stock doesn't mean that it hasn't been upgraded. Modern upgrades (such as shocks, brakes, fuel injection, and an overdrive transmission) can make a truck like this drive much better than it did originally without changing much of the original appearance.

The other side of the coin is a full-tilt build with everything from aerodynamic add-on parts to modern LS power. Many of the parts shown here are custom, but there are many aftermarket C10 parts available, including full carbon-fiber panels, flush-mount glass, and more.

14 CHEVY/GMC TRUCKS 1967–1972: HOW TO BUILD & MODIFY

The chances are good that if you've come this far, you already have an idea for the truck you want to build. However, in case you're not sure, go to some car shows to help you determine which style of truck you like. The 1967–1972 GM trucks are well suited to every style of customization—from drag trucks to body-dropped slammed machines on air suspension.

Understanding your direction can save you a lot of time and money right out of the gate, so do your homework before turning any wrenches. The most expensive way to build a project truck is to change your mind partway through the process and do things over again.

Social media can be your friend here. Facebook and Instagram are fantastic places to see what the current trends are in the truck world. Trends change quickly, so stay up to date on what's going on by staying connected. It's also a great place to see what neat tricks other builders have come up with for their own trucks, which can help you develop custom touches for your rig.

Setting a Budget and Making a Plan

One of the most important aspects of any classic car or truck build is the money it takes to build it. Regardless of how much work you can do yourself, every old truck costs money to build. The key to success here is to understand how much money it's going to take and to build a plan to keep things rolling along so that your project doesn't end up stalled in the garage for years on end.

Even the most basic engine rebuild will cost a few thousand dollars with machining. Performance modifications increase the price from there, sometimes well beyond $15,000 in the case of turbocharged or supercharged engines that have been properly set up for boost—and that's just the engine. You still have to consider the transmission, rear axle, suspension, brakes, interior, and other little details. Some of this will undoubtedly remain stock on your own build (and therefore be comparatively cheap), but there is still a lot to consider before diving in.

I didn't mention this to scare you out of a build. Yes, this kind of thing can be expensive, but if you know what you're getting into before you start taking things apart, you can plan your order of operations, which can have a huge impact on your overall experience throughout the process.

Remember that the best projects are the ones that keep you interested, and being able to drive your project as you go is a lot more fun than diving into a complete restoration, unless that's your plan. It may make sense to start out slow and complete one piece at a time if your budget is limited. That way, you can still drive the truck while you're building it. On the flip side, it may be smarter to buy pieces to make a whole truck or to convert a cheaper C20 into a C10.

The best bet is to start by making a list of the things you intend to change from stock. From there, I like to go to Summit Racing (summitracing.com) to price out as much of the build as I can. I make a spreadsheet during the process (complete with part numbers and current prices) that I can refer to later on.

This information helps with your order of operations (what you're going to do now and what you're going to do later) and provides a good picture of the overall direction of the project.

As I mentioned, there's no more expensive build than one that changes directions partway through. This step, while it may seem silly, is a good way to force yourself to really consider what you want before you pick a direction, as well as balance out the reality of the truck you want versus the truck you can realistically afford.

For most of us, the project we complete will be a compromise between those two things as well as a prompt to learn some new skills.

Tools and Workspace

Your truck is never smaller than it is the day you buy it. As soon as you start taking it apart, you'll have bits and pieces everywhere, so consider where you're going to be doing the work and where you're going to store parts during the project.

Work in a well-lit area that's out of the weather both in summer and winter. A garage is ideal, and it doesn't need to be fancy. It just needs to be dry, well-lit, and lockable.

While you can build one of these trucks in sections while you continue to use it, there are projects that take multiple days or weeks to complete from start to finish. This requires a secure, dry place for you to keep it while it's apart. It's important to be able to walk away from the project when you've had a frustrating moment or two, as distance and time can help you approach problems from a different perspective.

Your workspace should have decent power too. Make sure you have a few healthy electrical circuits for running electric tools. It is helpful to have a good, decent-sized workbench with a bench vise as well. Additionally, a decent floor jack with at least two pairs of jack stands, a dedicated Shop-Vac, a good air compressor that has enough capacity to run air tools, and a shop stereo system are necessary.

Other nice things to have include an engine hoist, engine stand, shop press, MIG welder, pressure washer, angle grinder, and a pair of sawhorses for holding doors or bedsides while you're working on them. Of course, this is just some of what you'll need. I'll cover more as we move through the following chapters.

In terms of hand tools, GM trucks from this era don't require much beyond a standard SAE set of wrenches and sockets ranging from 5/16 inch to 1 inch. It's helpful to have ratcheting wrenches if they're available, and it's also nice to have some short "stubby" wrenches as well as some oddball-angled units, as some bolts are in tight places. If you're swapping to LS or LT power, you'll need a metric set of wrenches, as all modern GM fasteners are metric.

You'll want a good 3/8-inch ratchet with the normal extensions of various lengths as well as wobble extensions. A good selection of both Phillips and standard screwdrivers is also needed. You should also have a few good hammers, a few punches, a decent drill, and good drill bits. In terms of air tools, a die grinder is a helpful tool, as is an air chisel, especially if you're going to be removing frame rivets or dealing with rusty bolts.

One of my favorite tools is DeWalt's 1/2-inch-drive 20-volt impact, which is powerful enough to break off rusty bolts and can set up a crush sleeve in a 12-bolt Chevrolet axle, which is not an easy task, even for a good pneumatic impact.

Finally, when plumbing the fuel or brake lines, it's nice to have access to a high-quality double flaring tool with 45-degree dies for standard fittings and 37-degree dies for AN-style junctions.

Beyond that, the most important tools are reference books on these trucks. Classic Industries carries

Garage space is important if you intend on working on a truck year-round, but it's not vital. The most important aspects are good lighting and a way to lock things up, and a one-car garage is enough to handle that.

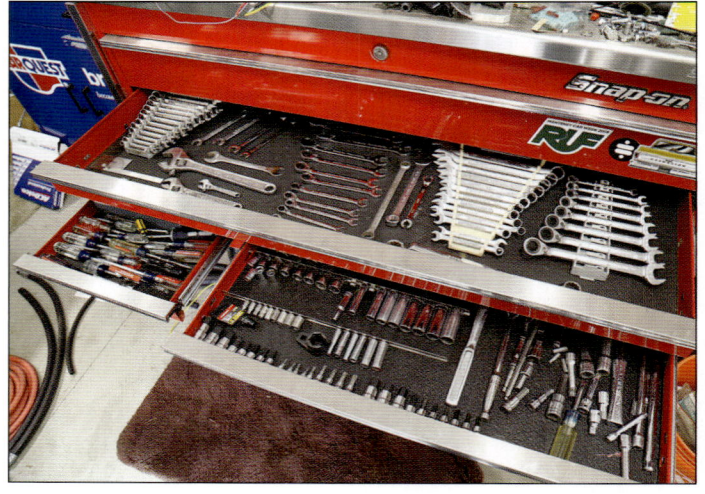

It is important to have a complete set of SAE wrenches, sockets, and a variety of extensions and other hand tools for basic maintenance. Generally, custom work requires more specialized equipment.

A good welder is important, especially if you intend to cut a long-bed truck into a short-bed. This is an older Lincoln 140 that runs on 220-volt power. It's powerful enough to handle welding on a frame and can also tack together sheet metal.

GETTING STARTED

Cordless impact technology has come a long way in a few short years. Something like this DeWalt 1/2-inch impact is a real bonus for dirty work. This, plus a set of impact sockets, will make quick work of any fastener (from suspension to body bolts) on your C10.

original reprints of the factory service manuals for each year of 1967–1972 GM trucks. They're handy in that they describe everything from how to assemble and disassemble certain components with the original torque specifications and special tools required. How things are disassembled isn't always clear, so this information can save you all kinds of trouble and will help you not damage original pieces that you might want to save and reuse.

Finding a Truck

With so many of these trucks built over the run of the bodystyle, many are available. So, where should you start? Craigslist is a good place to look, as is Facebook Marketplace, your local paper's classified ads, and any event with a car corral, such as a swap meet or car show. Garage sales are also often a good source. Local swap meets will undoubtedly have a few available, as will auction sites, such as Bring a Trailer and eBay Motors.

Before you buy any other book on C10s, pick up a copy of GM's service manual for the year of your truck. These books include just about everything you need to know about body gaps, wiring, torque specifications, special tools, and more. (Photo Courtesy Classic Industries)

When hunting for a rig on the web, search for as many applicable model names as possible. Search for "C10," "C-10," "C20," "C-20," "Cheyenne," "Sierra," "truck," and "pickup," and create alerts for those models. Remember that search functions aren't always accurate, so sometimes it's best to be as general as possible to cast the widest net. I've had good luck searching by model year and leaving the rest blank. It can lead you to trucks that would have otherwise been missed.

Just as important as the search is you being ready to make a deal. Time isn't always on your side when it comes to buying a popular model of collector car or truck, as there will always be a number of people ready to jump in right behind you. You need to be committed to making a buy, including convincing your significant other that it's okay to do so before you dive in.

What to Look for and What to Avoid

Finding a truck to buy is the easy part. The next part is more difficult. You have to know what to look for, and what to avoid. When it comes to 1967–1972 GM trucks, there's a good bit to know.

Rust

Are you comfortable tackling a lot of rust repair before you dive into the fun stuff? Would you rather find a solid body and pay a little (or a lot) more for it? It's helpful to understand your skill set, available time and tools, and ability to learn new things.

These trucks are known for rust. Almost all of them need rocker-panel and cab-corner repairs from years of being used in all kinds of weather.

CHEVY/GMC TRUCKS 1967–1972: HOW TO BUILD & MODIFY   17

CHAPTER 2

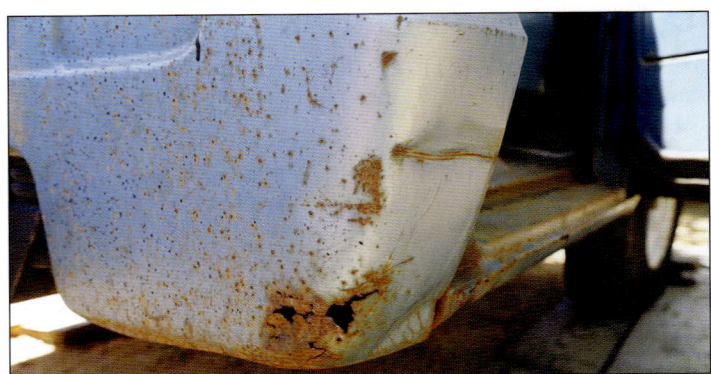

Many rust problems on this generation of GM truck begin in the windshield area. This is an extreme case. If you find rust this bad, it's better to find another cab.

Cab corners are just as quick to rust as the rocker panels, but this isn't a deal-breaker. Instead, look underneath at the floor supports, especially in the areas where they contact the inner rocker panel. There are four floor supports: one on each side in the front and one on each side in the back. If your floor supports have rust, you can buy replacements.

Ideally, you'll find rocker panels that look like the blue truck on the right instead of the truck with the white panel on the left. Outer rockers should be considered wear items, and they're not hard to replace. The bigger challenge is repairing the panels around them, which is much harder when the truck looks like the one on the left.

They often have rust in the cab around the windshield seal and in the upper parts of the cowl. Rust is often found at the seam that happens to run right above the factory fuse box on the driver's side and above the glove box on the passenger's side. Rust around the windshield seal leads to water inside the cab, which over time rusts out the rockers and parts of the outer floor. The cab supports under the floor are often thin or Swiss cheese–like, and the lower front fender sections are often rusty as well.

Another typical rust area to check is the battery box, the inner fender below it, and the core support that holds it up. Battery acid speeds up rust, so otherwise-solid trucks often have issues here.

When looking at a truck you want to buy, the first thing to check is the condition of the rocker panels on the outside of the truck, inside the doorjamb, and underneath. While underneath, look at the front and rear cab supports where they meet the inner rocker. If all that looks okay, sit in the driver's seat and look at the seal above the windshield. You should be able to pull it down a little to see the metal flange inside. If bits of rust fall out, you have cause for some concern. Fixing windshield rust can be a serious job, but it's not a deal breaker.

GETTING STARTED

If the truck has carpet, check to see if it has been wet. Look up at the fuse box from below with a flashlight to check the seam in the cab above it. If you see rust, adjust your offer accordingly.

The goal is to find a cab that is solid in all of these spaces. Regardless, it's likely the truck you find will need some fixes in this department, either to solve visible issues or redo some ham-fisted work that came before you.

Bring a magnet and flashlight with you, and don't be too afraid of what you might find. Note that all of the panels for these trucks are available from companies such as Auto Metal Direct (AMD) and Classic Industries. Some companies, such as Premier Street Rod, offer complete aftermarket cabs, which is a great solution if the rust is serious and your budget allows.

Solving rust is only a matter of time, money, and skill. With that being said, it's likely a lot cheaper to go on a road trip to somewhere dry than it is to mess around with a lot of rust repair from a truck you found nearby.

In places where road salt is common, check the frame for any serious rust issues or other damage. Replacement frames are available, but swapping frames can lead to problems with registration later on due to a mismatch of vehicle identification numbers (VINs). Different states have different rules regarding that potential issue, but it's still something to consider.

Look in Dry Places

When looking for a truck to buy, be sure to check the dry areas around your hometown. For me, that's eastern Oregon, eastern Washington, Idaho, and northern California. It's also helpful to get away from population centers and into the rural communities, as there are more trucks in those areas of the country.

A road trip can pay off if you find a solid rig. The truck I bought for this book came from Dan's Garage, a wrecking yard in Kennewick, Washington.

Check Those Rivets

With rust being a longstanding issue with 1967–1972 GM trucks, cab swaps have been a popular fix over the years. The problem is that swapping cab VIN plates doesn't sit well with our pals at the state or federal level.

Starting in 1965, GM began to use what's known as rosette rivets to affix VIN tags to the doorjambs of their trucks. These rivets were tightly controlled by the factories that built the trucks, as they were intended to help identify VIN tampering.

In many cases, truck owners that swapped their cabs with less-rusty examples did so without the benefit of government approval or the proper rivets. Why? For years, these trucks weren't anything more than basic utility rigs. The collector car world didn't yet care, and sales over state lines weren't much of a consideration yet.

Today, it's a different story. In some states, pop rivets in the place of original rosettes are no big deal, but in others, the wrong rivets can mean that you end up with a bonded title or no title at all.

If you choose to buy a truck that you know had a swapped cab and has the incorrect round pop rivets holding the plate to the jamb, understand that you're taking a risk in doing so, even if the swap was completely legitimate. The government doesn't know if your swap was legitimate or not, and it won't take your word for it.

If your VIN plate looks like it's been removed and replaced sometime in the past, it can cause trouble when you register your truck. All 1967–1972 Chevy and GMC trucks had these rosette-style rivets from the factory. If you find a truck with pop-rivets here, you may have title and registration issues.

Having all the paperwork for both the original truck and the swapped cab is important, as it can help you get a state-issued VIN that will solve the problem. An even better idea is to keep looking for a truck that still has the rosettes in place. ■

CHEVY/GMC TRUCKS 1967–1972: HOW TO BUILD & MODIFY 19

Rust can be fixed, or you can skip the work and buy a complete cab from Premier Street Rod in Lake Havasu City, Arizona. These cabs are fully licensed by GM and built in the US with better-than-OEM gaps and fit. They come complete with doors and a dash, and they're customizable. (Photo Courtesy Premier Street Rod)

This is my C20 on the day that I collected it. This truck was a factory flatbed with no options from the factory, including no cigarette lighter or radio and only one sun visor. What it did have was generally solid metal for one of these rigs, particularly in the trouble spots.

Dan has a number of generally solid rigs out that way, as it doesn't rain much there and they don't salt the roads in the winter. This one was especially good around the windshield. I bought it without an engine, transmission, or pickup bed. I considered everything but the missing bed to be a time-saving bonus, as someone else had already pulled and sold the original 6-cylinder engine and 3-speed transmission. Look for old wrecking yards in out-of-the-way places and give them a call. You might be surprised by what you find sitting in plain sight.

Mechanicals

It's important to remember that most of these trucks lived long lives as worker bees. Even the newest Cheyenne pickup from this generation of trucks is 50-plus years old as of this writing, and 50 years of hard labor can do a number on anyone, even a rig that was built for it. Assume that any truck you find will have mechanical issues that you'll need to sort out, but remember your plan. For example, if you're planning on an LS swap, you don't need to buy a truck with a running engine. If you're picking up a C20 and your

The trip up to Washington required a day's worth of driving twice—first to go look at the truck, and later to return with a trailer to collect it. The payoff is in the solid nature of the cab, most notably around the windshield and in the floor area.

20   CHEVY/GMC TRUCKS 1967–1972: HOW TO BUILD & MODIFY

GETTING STARTED

Chevy's V-8s are really hard to beat for longevity as well as power per dollar. If a truck you're looking at has sat for any length of time and isn't running, the first thing to do is check to make sure the engine isn't stuck. Then, move on from there. If the engine turns, you have a reasonably good chance of getting it to run.

plan is to make it into a C10, it doesn't matter if the heavy-duty rear axle is leaky and noisy. This can save you both time and money.

Checking the Drivetrain

When it comes to the engine, it's smart to check the obvious things, such as compression and oil consumption, especially if you intend on using or upgrading the powertrain.

Does the truck's coolant look clean and full? Does the oil look clean? Does it idle smooth? Was it already warmed up when you came to look at it? If so, ask why.

Many of these trucks had engine swaps over the years, so try to verify what's under the hood. The best way to do this, at least in terms of a V-8, is to check the engine stamping on the pad forward of the passenger-side cylinder head. There is a two- or three-digit suffix code at the end of a string of numbers, and that code helps you determine what you're looking at. An online search of the suffix will tell you what the engine is and if it's original or not.

A running engine can be a bonus even if you don't intend on using it. A small- or big-block Chevrolet engine is a saleable piece that you can use to fund other aspects of your build.

Look for leaks from the transmission and rear axle and check the condition of the brake fluid in the reservoir. Ideally, everything will be relatively clean and generally full, but expect some leaks, especially from TH350 automatics and 12-bolt axles.

If the truck runs and drives, pay attention to the brakes, steering, and the ride. Steering boxes and linkages can wear out to the point of wandering, and brakes can range from grabby to theoretical. All of these things are fixable, but you need to be realistic about what you're really buying and how much you're paying for it.

Look for previous accident damage. Look at tire wear on all four tires to help determine if something is out of alignment. If you see a lot of alignment shims on the upper A-arms, dig deeper to find out why. Check body-panel gaps and look for the cab-to-bed alignment. It should be generally even on both sides of the truck. Note that you'll often find rough bed floors (both steel and wood) from years of truck duties. Trucks that had slide-in campers when they were new are usually the best when it comes to bed condition, so if you find one with a camper or with a bed cap in place, consider that a bonus, especially if it was there when it was new.

The goal here is to find the best truck you can for the best (but maybe not cheapest) deal possible. Finding and buying a good starting point will pay off when you get deeper into the project.

Build Theory: 1967 C20 Project Truck

C10s are great, but when it comes to 1967–1972 GM rigs, the cheapest way into the market is to buy a 3/4-ton two-wheel-drive truck. If you've been on the hunt for long, you already know this. However, the key is that many parts interchange, and the parts that don't interchange can be easily swapped out.

The bodies of the two trucks are exactly the same. The differences are in the frames and running gear, but even that can be completely swapped out or converted from the heavier-duty components to the aftermarket-friendly C10 items. For this book, I chose to start with a C20 and turn it into a 1/2-ton C10.

I will detail my reasoning behind the parts I chose to use, but it all follows one main theme: to bring a classic truck up to and beyond modern daily driver standards so that it's turn-key ready for anything from cross-country drives and Sunday car shows to daily commuting and runs to the local Home Depot.

I can't stress this enough: you don't need to do all the things in this book to make your classic truck into a great driver, but each of them will make your classic truck more fun to drive. I'll show you how I did them so you can pick and choose what you might want to do with your own rig. ∎

CHAPTER 3

Body Disassembly, Fixes, and Modifications

The trucks that GM built in the 1960s are fundamentally very simple, and that makes disassembly fairly easy. You only need a few good wrenches and sockets to tear down a truck most of the way, and most of the bolts are easy to find and in accessible locations.

But why tear a truck down? Some builders may choose not to, and that's perfectly fine. When it comes to adding items (such as an LS engine) or trying to tackle rust repair, it's a lot easier to work with the truck in pieces versus the truck assembled. Access is best achieved by removing the front fenders, hood, bed, and cab.

The main consideration is where you're going to put all these pieces once the truck has been disassembled because they add up quickly and take up a lot of space. On top of that, a lot of these pieces are heavy and slightly awkward to handle if you don't have help readily available. Consider getting a spare set of hands to help while you're removing pieces and moving them around.

Also, make sure that you're not tripping over parts, such as the fenders and hood, when you're working around them. It's really easy to damage sheet-metal components when you're in a tight space that's serving as both a workshop and a storage area.

Front-End Removal

If you intend to upgrade the front suspension or do a complete engine swap, plan to take the front sheet metal off the truck. There is an order of operations that makes the process relatively easy. Having a helper pays off in this situation, so get another set of hands before getting too far into the project.

The bigger the goals, the more teardown is required. This 1970 Longhorn will be a lot easier to modify once the bed, hood, and fenders have been removed.

22   CHEVY/GMC TRUCKS 1967–1972: HOW TO BUILD & MODIFY

BODY DISASSEMBLY, FIXES, AND MODIFICATIONS

Front-End Teardown

1 The first step in the teardown process is to remove the truck's hood. It's held to the hood hinges with four bolts. Set a few moving blankets on the cowl so that you can slide the hood down the hinges and onto something soft while preparing to lift it out of the way without damaging the paint.

2 With the windshield wipers out of the way, the cowl is next. There are four 1/2-inch bolts that hold it to the cab, including two in the doorjambs. Don't forget the row of Philips-head screws across its face.

3 With the cowl removed, you can reach the upper fender bolts. There are two per side, along with one at the bottom under the cab. Remove all of these but leave the rearmost one threaded in place to hold the fender while you work.

4 You'll find a few bolts holding the fender to the core support and/or the grille, depending on the year of your truck. These are most easily reached with the headlights removed.

5 There's a row of inner fender bolts that run every few inches over the top of the wheel. Expect that some of these will break, as they've been exposed to the elements over the years. Hit them with rust penetrant and let them sit for an hour or so before you try to turn them.

CHEVY/GMC TRUCKS 1967–1972: HOW TO BUILD & MODIFY 23

CHAPTER 3

Front-End Teardown *continued*

6 It's smart to remove the front bumper before you try to remove each fender. Next is the grille assembly, which is attached to the hood latch and the core support. With all of that out of the way, you can pull each fender.

7 The last piece of the front end is the core support. Don't be surprised if yours is rusty under where the original battery was mounted. Keep at least one side of the original mounting hardware, and reassemble it the same way it was removed as a roadmap for reassembly.

Keeping Track of Parts

Do you think you can remember where 500 different fasteners go? Maybe you can if you're reassembling something that you took apart yesterday, but that's not realistic for a truck project. The solution is bagging and tagging.

This is a simple solution that requires two things: 1) a box of plastic sandwich bags and 2) a permanent marker. Every set of bolts gets its own bag and is marked with the pen so that you'll remember where those bolts go in a few months or years.

Keeping track of your truck's various fasteners is as simple as packing them up in cheap sandwich bags. Be sure to mark each one clearly so that you can find your parts during reassembly.

Even if it may seeem like a waste of time, it's not. Don't skip this step. In fact, overkill here is better because organization will help you immensely when it's time to put things back together. Do this right, and you'll end up with a box full of nicely organized nuts and bolts that

24   CHEVY/GMC TRUCKS 1967–1972: HOW TO BUILD & MODIFY

BODY DISASSEMBLY, FIXES, AND MODIFICATIONS

are all labeled by where they came from. While you're waiting for parts delivery, grab one bag a time and clean them up with a wire brush so they'll be ready when you are.

Bed Removal and Teardown Tips

There are a lot of good reasons to remove a bed, from installing a Blazer-style tank to cutting down a long-bed into a short-bed.

Two people can handle a short-bed fairly easily, but it's much better with four. You'll need that help for sure if you have a long-bed. You also need to have a solid plan for where you're going to place the bed when it's free from the truck. I don't recommend setting it on the ground because doing so damages the lower bedsides. Use a few fabricated wood blocks or some heavy-duty sawhorses for this task.

A long-bed is held to the frame with eight square-shank round-head bolts that pass from the bed floor down through brackets in the frame. Simply remove the nuts from underneath, and the bed will be free. However, pull the tailgate and back bumper first. Also, disconnect the factory wiring harness at the back of the frame.

My truck originally came with a factory flatbed, so I sourced this 1968 C20 bed locally. It had carried a slide-in camper for years, which meant it was out of the weather and almost completely rust free.

The beds themselves are easy to dismantle into a front panel, two bedsides, the bed floor, and tailgate. This is key if you intend to cut a long-bed into a short-bed because working on the bedsides is much easier to do with the bed itself in pieces. Note that each bedside is bolted in place, but they are also spot welded at the rear and underneath each taillight. These welds need to be cut to get each bedside free.

The biggest challenge you'll face is rust, especially on the bolts that hold the bedsides to the bed floor.

 **Find a Helper**

Have a friend stand in the bed and step on each bed bolt as you work to loosen it. This helps keep the square shank fixed in the square hole and allows you to get the nuts off without the bolts spinning and potentially hogging out the bed-floor holes. ■

Once the header panel bolts and all of the bed-floor bolts are loose, the bedside can be removed—but not until you cut the weld at the rear that's underneath the taillight. It's best to take the bedside and the wheel housing off together, as it's easier to get to the bolts that hold the wheel housing in place once the bedside is on the ground.

CHEVY/GMC TRUCKS 1967–1972: HOW TO BUILD & MODIFY   25

CHAPTER 3

Stubborn Bed Bolts

If you find a bedside bolt spinning in its square bore when you try to remove it, the best option for quick success is to break it off rather than fight with it.

This is where the DeWalt impact mentioned in Chapter 2 comes in handy. One quick tightening zip on each one will break it off before it has a chance to spin in its bore, and you'll have your bedsides off in no time. Simply replace it when it's time to reinstall. ■

Cab Removal

If your cab has rust (and even the best cab probably will), you'll need to gain access to repair it. One of the best ways to do so is to pull the cab off the frame. While it seems like a lot of work, it's not challenging. Getting the cab free from the frame makes tasks (such as shortening a long-bed into a short-bed) a lot easier and provides access to clean and paint the chassis and bottom of the cab floor, replace cab mounts, and more.

The most challenging part of the process is figuring out a good way to lift the cab. If you have a two-post car hoist, this is a no-brainer. If you don't have a hoist, you'll need to get creative to accomplish this task.

First, figure out where the cab is going to go once it's off the body. Building a wooden cart works well, especially if you have access to heavy-duty casters to roll the cab around while you're working on it.

Next, it's a matter of finding a safe and controlled way to lift the cab from the chassis and getting it high enough so that the chassis can be rolled out from underneath. There are many ways to do this: using a lift, using custom-fabricated parts and an engine hoist, or calling friends over to try and manhandle it. I've had good luck using a crib pile (as a machinery rigger would do) along with a beam and a bottle jack to control the ascent and the descent.

Whichever method you use to lift the cab from the frame, remember that with the glass in place, the cab is nose-heavy, so it will try to tilt forward on you. The best bet is to go slow, have a lot of help on hand, and think through each move before you try it. The last thing you want to do is drop your cab and damage it or yourself.

Rust Repair

If you have a 1967–1972 cab that came from anywhere where rain ever fell from the sky, you probably have some rocker-panel rust. It's a common issue that's not very difficult to solve, especially if you source the right tools and parts for the job.

Even my cab, which came from a dry environment, needed both outer rocker panels, a section of floor, kick-panel repairs, and one cab corner. I sourced all the parts from Auto Metal Direct (autometaldirect.com) because the company has a great reputation for quick delivery and parts that have great fitment. Here's a quick look at how to tackle these basic issues.

Scan this QR code with your smartphone to go directly to autometaldirect.com.

If you don't have a lift, the most effective way to remove the body is to jack up the entire truck and secure it, remove the four cab-mount bolts, and then use fabricated blocks and a beam as a crib pile to secure the cab. Then, lower the chassis away from the body, remove the rear wheels for clearance, and roll the chassis out from under the cab on a floor jack. Be careful. With the windshield in place, the cab is nose-heavy.

BODY DISASSEMBLY, FIXES, AND MODIFICATIONS

Replacing a Fender Extension

1 The passenger-side lower fender extension is a common rust area on this era of C10. Auto Metal Direct sells a complete replacement lower section as part number 204-4067-R (both an inner and outer panel already spot welded together) to solve this problem.

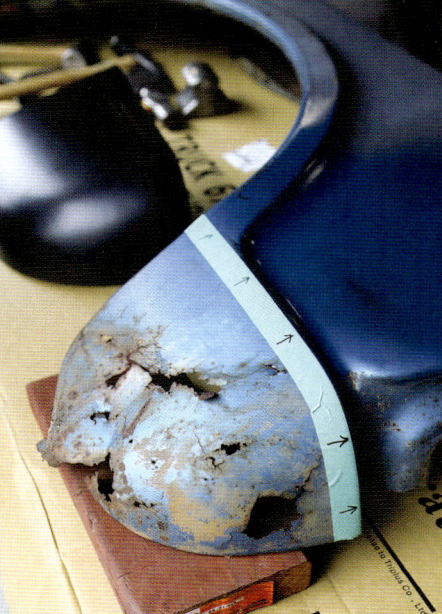

2 The goal is to remove enough metal to eliminate the trouble spots in such a way to limit the amount of bodywork needed, especially if you're attempting to save the factory paint. Cutting right against the body line with a cutting wheel provides a consistent edge on both the new and old panels and helps minimize intrusion into the higher areas of fender.

3 Getting the fitment right is the trickiest part, but AMD's panels are close to stock in how they fit. Once the fitment is right, it's time to spot weld the panel in place, recheck fit, and work across it with spot welds until it's completely tacked in place. Then, grind the welds smooth, add fill where it is needed, prime, and paint. Be careful to spread out the heat when both welding and grinding to minimize warping.

Fixing Rocker Panel and Cab-Corner Rust

1 C10 cabs from this era are known for this kind of rot, but don't let it get you down. Solving this problem is easier than it looks.

2 The floor section on the passenger's side consists of an outer rocker panel, inner rocker panel, and a cab corner. These parts are from Auto Metal Direct.

CHEVY/GMC TRUCKS 1967–1972: HOW TO BUILD & MODIFY 27

Fixing Rocker Panel and Cab-Corner Rust *continued*

3 Before cutting, take a large carpenter's square, place it on the rocker-panel lip, and measure up 12 inches at both the A-pillar and the B-pillar. Mark these spots for reference because you'll use them to ballpark your rocker-panel alignment later.

4 Use a good drill bit and a spot-weld cutter (like this one) to remove the factory spot welds at the front and back of the rocker panel. You might need to take a grinder to the spot-weld areas to help locate them. Once you've found them, center punch them, drill a hole, and use the spot-weld cutter to grind through each spot weld.

5 With the spot welds removed at the front, back, and along the lower lip, the outer rocker can be removed. Now's the time to poke around to see what kind of rust you have underneath it, as that will tell you how much metal you'll need to replace. Here, the entire upper section of the inner rocker and floor is rusted through, so it needs to be replaced.

6 Mocking up the floor section requires removing parts of the lower A-pillar and B-pillar where they meet the floor, but they can be reattached later. Before doing so, add some bracing to the cab to keep things from moving around while you work. When things are out of the way, set the new panel over the old one, scribe a line on the rusty floor where the new panel will sit, and use a cutoff wheel to remove the original rusty section.

7 Sheet-metal clamps are fantastic for this kind of work, as they'll hold your panels in place while you weld them back together. Here, we played with the fitment, made adjustments, and are ready to burn in the new metal from AMD using stitch welds to try and eliminate shrinkage and warping of the steel.

BODY DISASSEMBLY, FIXES, AND MODIFICATIONS

8 With the outer floor/inner rocker section stitch welded in place, the inner section of the B-pillar can go back in its original location. We removed the rusty section of cab corner up to the body line on the truck. The replaced section will be ground smooth and painted with weld-through primer prior to fitting the outer rocker panel.

9 Up front, I elected to replace the lower section of the cowl piece with a replacement section from AMD, as the OEM steel was thin in spots. This is a simple cut-to-fit and weld-in-place operation, but it needs to be handled before the rocker can be reinstalled.

10 The 12-inch reference mark is helpful to set the rocker height, but you also need to refit the door so you can check the gap at the rocker panel. Adjusting the door around the cab needs to be done now before the rocker goes into place.

11 The last step before fitting the rocker panel to the truck is to drill a few holes for new spot welds in the factory locations. Then, slide it into place, fit it to the door, and use Vise-Grips and self-tapping screws to hold it in place while you burn it in with new spot welds.

CHEVY/GMC TRUCKS 1967–1972: HOW TO BUILD & MODIFY

CHAPTER 3

Fixing Rocker Panel and Cab-Corner Rust *continued*

12 With the rocker replaced, the cab corner is next. It was cut to fit only the sections of original steel that were rusty. I marked the cab and used a cutting wheel to remove the original rusty areas, and then cut the new panel to match. Test fit it along the way before you finally burn it in.

13 All that's left is to seam seal the corners, finish grinding the welds smooth, and tackle the bodywork to make this look like it never happened.

Building a Short-Bed out of a Long-Bed

As mentioned in Chapter 1, GM made C10s in both 115-inch and 127-inch wheelbases. The shorter trucks have become all the rage in the aftermarket these days. If you want a short-bed and all you have access to is a long-bed, you don't have to buy a different truck. You can build a short truck yourself out of your long-bed C10 or C20—assuming that you're handy with a cutting wheel and a welder and aren't afraid of ruffling the feathers of purists.

Cutting the truck to make it shorter requires three different things to be cut: 1) the bed, 2) the chassis, and 3) the running gear.

Regarding the bed, you can buy

If you'd rather not go through the trouble of cutting down your own bed, Auto Metal Direct has complete bedsides and complete beds ready to go. It also offers wider-than-stock wheel wells and narrower bed floors to match for those who want to install wider rear rubber. (Photo Courtesy Auto Metal Direct)

Original tailgates tend to be fairly well beaten, but good replacements are available. This one is a GM Restoration part sourced through Auto Metal Direct, and it's a good, heavy reproduction of an original. AMD has all the hardware needed to mount a tailgate, including latches, rods, and the OEM-style handle.

BODY DISASSEMBLY, FIXES, AND MODIFICATIONS

an original short-bed or you can source all new short-bed panels from Auto Metal Direct, complete with a new bed floor, bedsides, a header panel, tailgate, and wheel tubs.

If you have a nice bed that already matches, you can choose to cut it down. The difference between a long bedside and a short bedside is 20 inches overall. Long-beds have 12 inches more metal ahead of the wheel well and 8 inches more metal behind it, so turning a long-bed side into a short-bed side is as simple as removing those dimensions from the side and welding everything back together. The same measurements need to come from the bed floor (either steel or wood) as well. After the cuts have been made and the parts have been stitched back together, your long-bed will now be a short-bed.

Some builders choose to cut their beds with the bed still assembled, but I've found that it's more complex that way. Plus, having the bed torn apart for this work makes it easier to realign the pieces to be welded back together, as the sections are smaller and easier to manipulate.

The chassis follows the same basic math as the bedsides: 12 inches out of the front and 8 inches out of the rear. It's typically done with an aftermarket plating kit that helps reinforce the area where the frame must be welded back together. This makes the entire operation safe and generally simple. Although, you'll have an easier time tackling it with the truck torn apart (complete with the cab off the frame) because the frame cut falls under the cab and not the bed.

Don't forget the mechanicals, which add cost to the job. The driveshaft needs to go to a shop to be cut down and rebalanced or swapped outright for a one-piece unit. The brake lines and emergency brake cable need to be shortened, and you'll likely need to visit an exhaust shop to have the original system chopped or a new one fabricated.

Bedside Cuts

There are a few different ways to cut down your bedsides, and each method has its pros and cons. It is important to understand your capabilities before diving in. Cutting a bed and stitching it back together requires some finesse and a time commitment, so factor those in as well.

The first method is to straight cut both the front and the rear bedsides and remove a straight 12-inch section up front and an 8-inch section out back. However, if you've looked at the bedsides, you've probably noticed that the body line slopes down as you get closer to the taillight, so you need to account for this as you cut.

The straight-cut method requires the builder to use a small flathead screwdriver to tweak the body lines on each panel and line them back up as the rear sections are welded back together. This works, but the results aren't always as clean as they could

These panel clamps, otherwise known as butt-weld clamps, work by holding two panels together at a fixed, narrow distance that allows you to butt two panels against each other and weld them together. I bought these from Harbor Freight Tools.

There's no right or wrong way to shorten a bedside, but some ways look better than others. This method is a more-or-less straight cut, minus the area around the marker light. The original slope of the body line isn't as pronounced due to removing 8 inches of metal at the rear.

CHEVY/GMC TRUCKS 1967–1972: HOW TO BUILD & MODIFY   31

CHAPTER 3

MetalOx Fab has a helpful how-to video available on its website that you must watch if you're considering taking on this job yourself. The video includes excellent, intensive step-by-step instructions and all the detailed measurements of the company's proprietary method.

be. You'll likely have more bodywork to complete with this type of cut.

The second method is the one pioneered by truck metal expert Kyle Oxberger of MetalOx Fab in Peoria, Arizona. He figured out a method that jogs the rear cut across the curve of the body line, which allows it to slide back together and maintain its factory look. It also pushes the seams relatively far forward and aft, which are visually more appealing. In the case of the front, it's easier for welding, as the material is doubled over at the front of the bed.

Keep in mind that Kyle at MetalOx also cuts down beds for customers, which could be a good option if you don't want to try this yourself.

Cutting the Bedside

1 Here's how the front cut lays out. Note how it compensates for the stake pocket, which you'll want to keep. Everything between the tape lines is to be removed. Once it's been cut out, the front of the bed can slide back and meet the remaining section of the bedside. The measurement between the tape lines is exactly 12 inches.

2 The rear cut is more complex with a jog that accommodates the downward slope of the factory body line. Everything between the tape lines will be removed, including the side-marker light. For a 1967, that's perfect, but you can add the marker back in for 1968–1972 trucks. This represents 8 inches of metal removal.

BODY DISASSEMBLY, FIXES, AND MODIFICATIONS

Cutting the Bedside *continued*

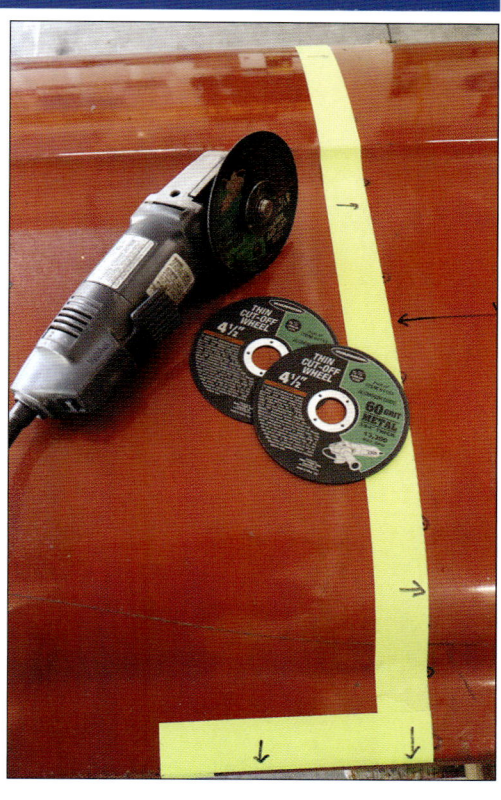

3 The inside of the bed needs to be cut the same amount as the outside, but since it's generally flat, straight lines are enough here. This is 8 inches of removal in the rear and 12 inches in the front, following the tape lines from the front cut where they wrap over the top of the bedside.

4 The key to making this all work is to use a thin cutting wheel, either on an electric angle grinder or a pneumatic die grinder. The thinner the wheel, the better. Wear suitable protection, including heavy gloves, a shirt, and a face shield because you're going to throw a lot of sparks. Watch closely to be sure you're cutting straight and right up against the tape line but not into it.

5 With the inner and outer cuts complete, the pieces are fit together to check fitment prior to removing the tape. This is a good time to use a grinder to clean up your cuts if need be, but do so with the tape in place so that you still have a reference point for the original cut lines.

6 The short-bed proportions are now clear. If you plan on keeping the side-marker lights, this is a good time to cut them out and mock them up in their new location.

CHEVY/GMC TRUCKS 1967–1972: HOW TO BUILD & MODIFY

CHAPTER 3

Cutting the Bedside continued

7 Before you can weld things back together, you need to remove a bit of paint to keep from burning it. This is a basic Harbor Freight paint-removal wheel on a die grinder, but you can use anything that will bring the panel down to bare metal.

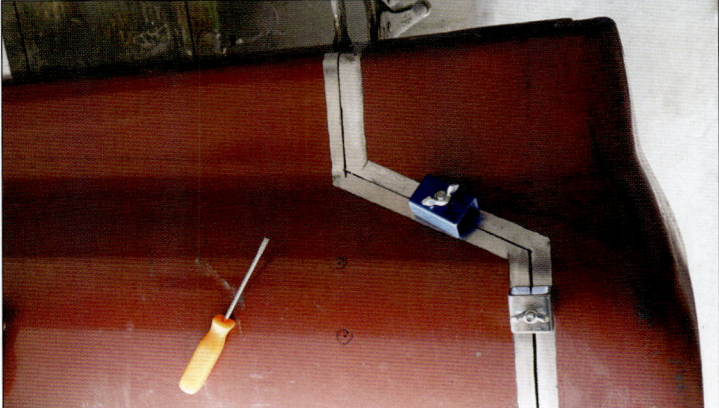

8 Refitting the panels is the most time-consuming part of this process because you need to verify that everything lines up both on the face of the panel and on the back side. You may need to grind, bend, or tweak your setup to get the fitment you want. A little flathead screwdriver works wonders for alignment here, as do panel-alignment clamps.

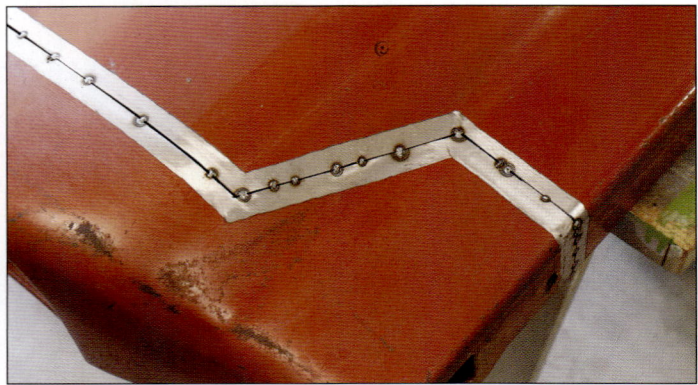

9 Once you're happy with the fitment, start stitching the panel back together. The key is to try to spread out the heat from the welder by moving it around. Too much work in any one area will shrink the material and cause warping.

10 The lower rear section will not line up perfectly, as the bed tapers down in height from the front to the rear. The best method to solve this is to walk the panel around the corner with a pair of Vise-Grips and tack weld it as you go to follow the curve of the taillight section. Then, cut off the excess with a cutting wheel.

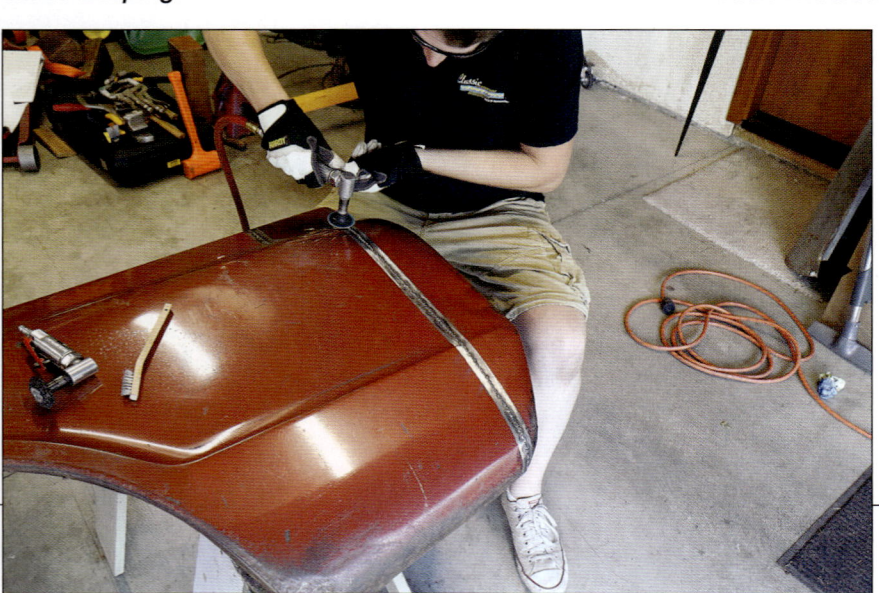

11 Once all of the stitch welding is complete (front and back and inside and out), the next step is to grind the welds smooth with the surface of the bedside. From there, you can choose to leave the scars or paint over them.

BODY DISASSEMBLY, FIXES, AND MODIFICATIONS

12 *If you measured carefully, cut straight, and kept a close eye on alignment, both of your bedsides should come out exactly the same length as a set of factory short-bed sides.*

Bed Floor Cuts

Cutting a bed floor is a relatively straightforward process, and it's much simpler with a wood bed than it is with a steel one. Still, either can be accomplished. If you already figured out how to cut down a bedside, the floor will be no problem.

As with the sides, 12 inches must be cut out of the front of the bed and 8 inches out of the rear. For wood beds, you will simply cut the plank or install a new floor kit. For steel beds, the key is cutting the floor in the right places to allow you to maintain all the factory spacing for the bedside mounting bolts that run up and down each side of the bed floor. If you do this right, everything will bolt together like it would have from the factory.

If you're working on a bed floor, particularly a wood one, check out CarTech's *Truck Beds: How to Install, Restore and Modify* by Kevin Tetz. The book features an in-depth look at the processes required for wood floors, and it's full of helpful info that pertains to 1967–1972 GM trucks.

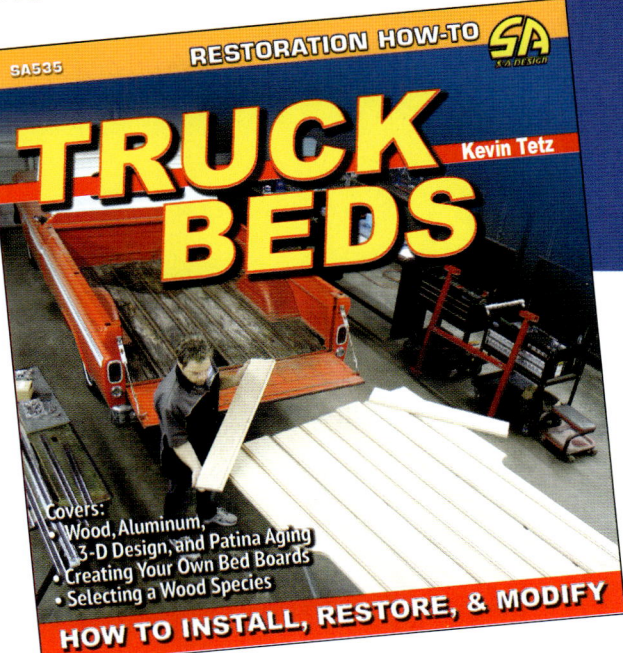

Scan this QR code with your smartphone to buy *Truck Beds: How to Install, Restore & Modify* (SA535) by Kevin Tetz.

CHEVY/GMC TRUCKS 1967–1972: HOW TO BUILD & MODIFY

CHAPTER 3

Cutting a Metal Bed Floor

1 The first step, once your floor is separated from the sides and the header panel, is to locate all the factory spot welds at the rear crossmember and drill them out. A wire wheel helps to find them.

2 Next, measure from the rear of the bed floor up 8 inches, follow the original contour of the floor, and then mark back 1/2 to 3/4 inch at the tailgate side of the line, which represents the metal that you'll bend over the crossmember when you reassemble the floor section. Once you're happy that the lines are straight and measured correctly, zip it off with a cutting wheel.

3 Note the cut here on the tape line at the stakes and 3/4 inch long at the tailgate area. This allows for the floor to be folded over the crossmember. This is a good time to run a permanent marker along the tape line for later reference, as you'll need to remove the tape for spot welds later.

4 Up front, there are a few options. You can cut the front of the bed and butt the corrugated section against the header panel, but I prefer saving the factory tapered front section of the floor so that it looks correct. My first tape line is set at 14 inches from the nose, and the second one is 2 inches, which makes up the 12-inch cut. The section between these two tape lines is to be removed.

36 CHEVY/GMC TRUCKS 1967–1972: HOW TO BUILD & MODIFY

BODY DISASSEMBLY, FIXES, AND MODIFICATIONS

5 This cut runs right along the edge of the crossmember underneath. If you cut straight, you won't damage it. Once you have both pieces cleaned up and ready to weld, butt-weld clamps can hold it together while you tack it back in place.

6 A quick mockup shows the bolt-hole alignment at the front of the bed. Note how saving the front 2 inches of metal kept the original floor taper and square holes for the header panel. Once you're happy with the fitment, stitch weld the floor section completely, and then grind down the welds.

7 Out back, make some space for the rearmost bedside stake pocket mounting flange, which won't sit flat. This is as simple as cutting a slot, working the panel flat, and welding it back up in the area where the flange will bolt.

8 Next, refit the rear crossmember, which requires factory-style spot welds. Do this by drilling holes and then welding through them to the crossmember underneath. You can see the marker showing the original 8-inch line that we pulled with our tape to mark where the edge of the crossmember will need to sit.

CHEVY/GMC TRUCKS 1967-1972: HOW TO BUILD & MODIFY

CHAPTER 3

Cutting a Metal Bed Floor *continued*

9 Once the crossmember is spot welded in place at the 8-inch mark, take a big hammer and roll the remaining bed-floor section around the crossmember. Then, reassemble the bed and install it on the truck.

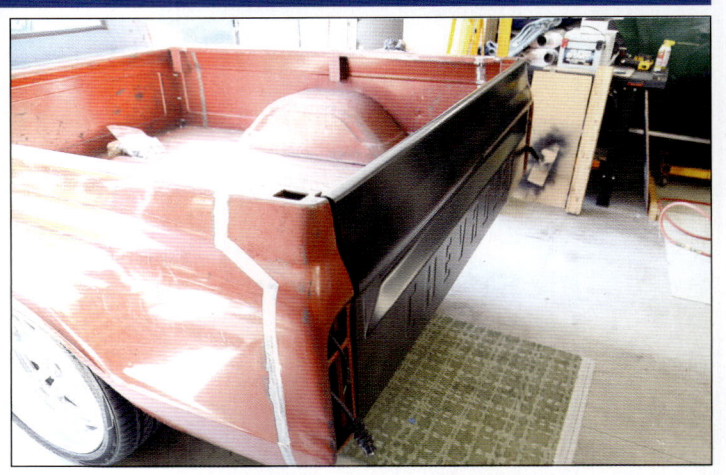

10 With a new bed-bolt kit, you can reassemble the bedsides, the header panel, and more. The tailgate is a good guide to line up the bedsides before you spot weld them back to the rear crossmember.

Frame Cuts

The final piece of this puzzle is the frame itself, which must follow the same rules as the bed and the bed floor: 12 inches is removed from the front and 8 inches from the rear.

The most challenging part is measuring everything to be sure that the cuts are square and both frame rails end up even and true when welded back together. Several companies make frame-shortening kits, including MetalOx and Brothers Trucks. In reality, these kits only sell you peace of mind and a shorter turnaround. You can make your own kit with some 1/4-inch plate and a tape measure if you're confident in your skills.

Cutting the Frame

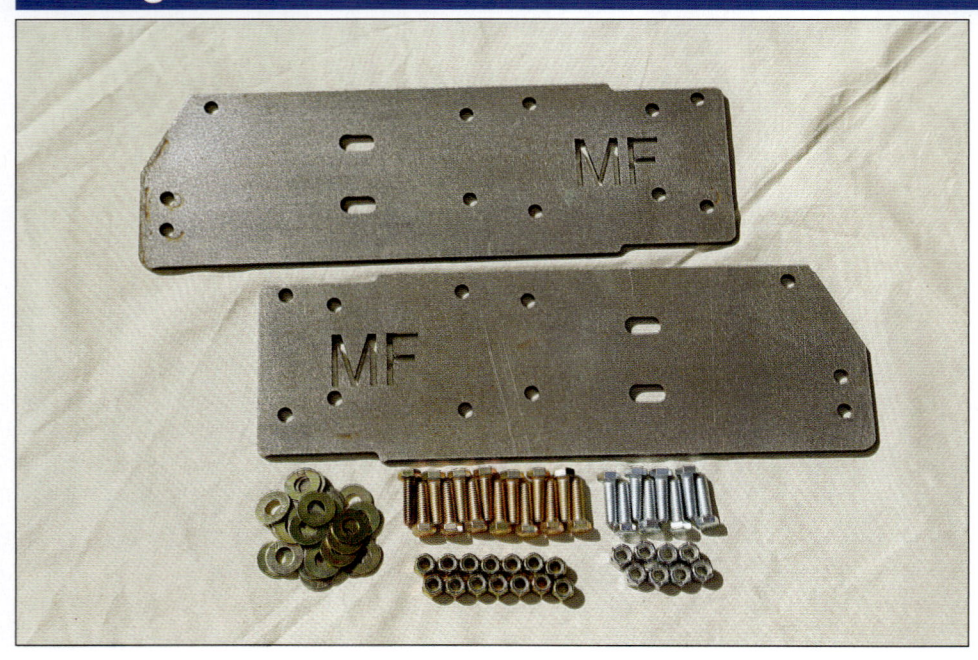

1 This is MetalOx Fab's 1967–1972 frame plate kit that comes with two heavy-duty steel plates, new Grade 5 and Grade 8 hardware, and all of the proper instructions. This kit makes the job a lot easier, as it locates most of the 1/2-ton holes for you.

BODY DISASSEMBLY, FIXES, AND MODIFICATIONS

Cutting the Frame continued

2 *You don't have to remove the cab for this job, but you need to at least remove the bed to gain access. Once that's out of the way, the rear cab mount must come off the frame, as it needs to be relocated 12 inches back. I like to center-punch the rivets and drill them out. You'll need to remove the front-most bed stands on the left and right sides of the frame. Short-beds don't use them.*

3 *MetalOx's plates bolt to the outside of the frame using the cab mount holes, which provide marking locations for the rear cut that you'll make. Measure 12 inches forward from that mark, which gives you this 12-inch section to remove. Using a carpenter square helps verify that your lines are straight.*

4 *Next, move the cab mount back 12 inches. Use a square to mark the centerline of the original holes and measure 12 inches back from that line. Then, drill the two rearmost cab mount holes and install the mount using it as a template for its front two bolts. The levels are to verify that the frame and mount are parallel. Note that I retained the 3/4-ton mount height, which is lower on the frame than a 1/2-ton.*

5 *After supporting the frame with jack stands, the cut is next. A reciprocating saw makes quick work of a thick 3/4-ton frame. The key here is to cut straight and true with any mistakes erring away from the tape line rather than into it. You can grind for fitment later, but you don't want to make the section of frame that you remove wider than 12 inches because if you do, the finished frame will be too short.*

6 *Once both sides are cut, the next step is to chamfer the edges of the frame with a grinder to prep for welding. The MetalOx plates can install (loosely) inside the rear section of frame rail using the original cab mount bolt holes. From there, the front and rear sections of the frame can come together, bolt together loosely, clamp together, and be checked to confirm they are true.*

CHAPTER 3

Cutting the Frame continued

7 *If you're happy with all of your measurements and have verified that the frame is level and square, you can tack weld the frame sections, tighten all of the plate hardware, and weld the frame rails back together. Call a professional if you're not comfortable with this type of welding.*

8 *It's important to weld the plate in several sections (see arrows) around the inside of the frame rail. Weld the plate at the front and rear as well as at the top and bottom, and plug-weld any holes in the plate that pass through to the frame behind it. These welds, along with the bolts supplied in the kit, make the plate part of the frame.*

9 *The final step before reassembly is to cut 8 inches off the rear of the frame, which will bring the overall length of the frame to short-bed specs. All that's left is to clean up all the welds, grind everything smooth, and paint. Then, the cab mounts can be reinstalled, followed by the bed.*

40   CHEVY/GMC TRUCKS 1967–1972: HOW TO BUILD & MODIFY

CHAPTER 4

Suspension

When it comes to building a great truck that you'll want to drive often, a fundamental system to upgrade is its suspension. This is what sets the overall stance of your rig, and it can make or break how it handles, which will impact how much you want to use the truck.

If the goal is to build something you want to drive all the time, your truck's suspension should be one of the first things you consider upgrading—even ahead of the engine, transmission, and rear axle. Fortunately, these trucks are popular enough that the aftermarket has everything you could possibly need to make yours handle better, regardless of whether you're planning on a stock-style revamp or a down-in-the-weeds look on airbags or coilovers.

Front Suspension

Every light-duty two-wheel-drive C-series truck built from 1967 to 1972 used GM's independent front suspension system that consists of an upper A-arm and a lower A-arm that connect to a spindle via an upper and lower ball joint. This system used a live coil spring that was captured between a spring pocket in the front

Style and function go hand in hand. Lowering your truck can give you improved handling over stock and a better look—if you go about it the right way. How low you go is up to you.

crossmember and the lower control arm with a shock mounted outside of it (and to the rear of the truck behind the A-arms). Some trucks had sway bars when they were new, but many did not.

This system was used both in half-ton (C10) and larger (C20 and C30) rigs, and the heavier trucks used different lower control arms. These lower control arms featured uprated cross-shafts and larger ball joints as well as a different upper control-arm cross-shaft that was retained to the frame with larger 9/16-diameter studs compared to the 1/2-ton's 1/2-inch units. Fundamentally, all of these trucks used the same basic design and were simply uprated for carrying heavier loads when needed

CHAPTER 4

Every C10 through C30 carries the same basic front suspension system, albeit with heavier-duty components on the heavier-duty models. This is a fundamentally sound system that provides a good ride, but you can bet that after 50 years, these components are tired.

by using heavier springs and bigger components.

Common wear points include the ball joints, tie-rod ends, and shocks. Wear is often progressive over time, which means the owner may not notice how worn a front suspension system has become until he or she starts replacing parts.

If the original parts are to be reused, it's important to look everything over very closely for loose components, excessive play, and wear. At the very least, plan on new ball joints, tie-rod ends, and shocks.

Factory Upgrades

Note that the front crossmember on these trucks is removable, complete with the front suspension and coil springs as part of the assembly. If your engine has already been removed, you can remove a handful of bolts, and the entire front suspension will slide out from under the frame. This is handy for later-model OEM-style swaps.

In 1971, GM revised its front suspension and brake systems slightly, so 1971 and 1972 systems are generally good upgrades if a complete unit can be found. Additionally, later 1973–1987 front crossmembers generally bolt in with a little bit of work, so you can swap in a complete later unit and gain 5-lug disc brakes while keeping everything GM. You don't have to swap crossmembers to gain those parts. The 1973–1987 squarebody spindles all bolt onto the original 1967–1972 A-arms if you swap over to the proper ball joints to match the spindle, which is handy if you don't want to remove the engine to gain the newer front-suspension system. The exception to this rule is swapping from 3/4-ton to 1/2-ton, but more details on that will follow.

It's important to note that the engine stands for squarebody trucks from 1967–1972 are different because the frames are different, so swapping crossmembers likely means that there will be some irregularities with these parts when everything is bolted back together. This can be solved by drilling new holes in the later crossmember for the factory 1967–1972 engine stands.

The main benefit of swapping the entire unit is cost. You can source a complete used front-suspension and steering setup from a squarebody truck for less than the aftermarket conversion parts for your 1967–1972. However, keep in mind that any used front-suspension parts are going to need the same basic inspections and component replacement as the original parts.

Rear Suspension

Out back, GM used two different suspension systems in its 1967–1972 trucks. The most commonly found suspension in Chevrolet trucks is referred to as the trailing-arm system. It used two long lower control arms connected to the frame via a crossmember located behind or under the cab.

This system is known for its mild ride. These trucks were among the smoothest, best-handling rigs of their era because of this system, so it's a good thing to have in your classic truck. It's also similar to the systems that NASCAR used in its race cars until 2021.

Common wear points include rubber control-arm bushings, shocks, and coil springs. The lower control arms can and do rust, so keep that in mind if you're looking at a truck or chassis from an area where it snows.

The 1/2-ton and 3/4-ton units were generally the same. Although, the heavier-duty rigs featured reinforced control arms with added steel plates riveted on the bottom

CHEVY/GMC TRUCKS 1967–1972: HOW TO BUILD & MODIFY

SUSPENSION

The trailing arm suspension system offered from the factory is a fantastic setup that offers great ride and limited wheel-hop in performance applications. These were available in both Chevrolet and GMC applications throughout the 1967–1972 model years.

and increased frame reinforcements around the spring mount area to help spread out the load. Additionally, the springs for the 3/4-ton trucks were heavier-duty to allow for more payload capacity.

The other system, generally found in GMCs, is a standard leaf-spring system that utilizes a pair of leaf springs mounted directly to the axle and the frame. This is a simple and effective setup, especially for handling heavy loads. Common wear points include spring eye bushings, shocks, and the leaf springs themselves, especially after years of hauling heavy loads. Some trucks have extra springs (known as overloads) that help in extreme situations. You might also find a set of air shocks to help keep things on the level.

The truck frames are the same between the two styles of suspension, but they have different crossmembers and different reinforcements, depending on which suspension system was used. They have different bed mounting brackets as well. Considering that, you can swap between styles if you want, but it will be a lot of work for not much gain. It makes more sense to upgrade what's already there.

Upgrades

The stock suspension systems available in these trucks work relatively well, especially on trucks that had the rear long-control-arm rear setup when they were new. With that being said, you can do many things to make a classic GM truck handle a lot better than it did when it was new.

Shocks

If you think of your suspension as a living system, the shocks are the brains of the operation. They dampen and help eliminate unwanted motion. A good set of shocks make a bigger difference in your truck's overall handling than any other suspension component, so this is a good place to start.

Considering that, it's important to select the proper shock for your application—preferably something with a bit of adjustment that allows you to dial in the amount of rebound. Modern shock technology has come a long way in the past decade. A good, adjustable monotube replacement shock is not particularly expensive these days, and it will work wonders on the ride and handling of an otherwise-stock rig with air shocks that were probably installed when Reagan was still in office.

If you're looking to replace shocks as a first step in the project, and if that project involves lowering your truck later, consider a cheap factory-replacement-style shock and save the adjustable unit for after you correct your truck's ride height. Lowered trucks often require shocks with a shorter operating range, which means less compression and extension,

If you're looking to improve handling without changing your truck's stock suspension configuration, the best bet is to source a good set of aftermarket adjustable shocks, such as these HQ-series single-adjustable shocks from RideTech. These allow for several different rebound settings and for you to dial in the type of ride that you want. (Photo Courtesy RideTech)

CHAPTER 4

The best bang for your buck, at least in terms of instant improvement, is to install a front sway bar on your C10 or install a larger one than stock. Many aftermarket companies make bigger sway bars for C10s. This one is from RideTech and is designed to work with factory control arms. (Photo Courtesy RideTech)

so it makes sense to buy these once versus twice.

Sway Bar

A sway bar isn't something you'll always find on a truck, mostly because trucks were built to haul weight versus handle well. There wasn't much point in fitting them from the factory unless the truck was a higher-option version.

A front sway bar is nothing more than a torsion spring that links both lower control arms together across the front of the truck. A sway bar limits motion and flattens out a truck's body roll under heavy cornering, which makes a big difference in how a truck responds to quick steering input.

OEM-style sway bars can be found for 1967–1972 GM trucks, but it's much better to source something aftermarket. With sway bars, bigger is almost always better. The thicker the bar, the less deflection will occur and the flatter the truck will run through the corners.

You can also find rear sway bars that operate in much the same way. The two sides of a truck's suspension are linked together and to the frame to help keep the truck flat through the corners.

It's important to note that running flat (level) through corners does not always mean a truck will handle those corners better. It won't lean quite so much when navigating around. For daily driver use, the feeling that a good front sway bar offers is worth the work of installing one. In performance applications, consider a rear bar—but as part of a complete suspension and tire package.

Control Arms

You may be tempted to install polyurethane bushings on your C10, specifically around the control arms, but note that these trucks use metal-on-metal threaded bushings for the upper and lower control-arm shafts from the factory.

These metal bushings are known for long life—as long as they are greased regularly. If yours are worn out, you have a few options. You can choose to upgrade to later 1973–1987 parts via a crossmember swap, which use traditional rubber bushings like the ones found in a Camaro or Chevelle. The other option is to use modern tubular pieces that often feature updated geometry and greater strength with rubber or polyurethane bushings for easy serviceability.

Polyurethane bushings are available for other places on your truck, including the rear control arms, leaf-spring eyes, sway-bar mounts and end links, and more. They are an improvement over rubber because they don't deflect as much and tend to be just as long lived as an OEM set. The only downside is possible noise because they tend to squeak.

Delrin bushings offer a significant improvement in ride and handling. These are designed to replace the original bushing on a factory-style control arm. Delrin is known for being long lasting, quiet, and firm. (Photo Courtesy RideTech)

44   CHEVY/GMC TRUCKS 1967–1972: HOW TO BUILD & MODIFY

SUSPENSION

Stock Sway Bars

If you're looking for a cheap sway-bar upgrade for your C10, go to your local wrecking yard and look for a mid-1970s C20 truck. The 1973–1987 3/4-ton GM trucks had 1.25-inch sway bars when they were new that will swap over to your 1967–1972 C10 and offer more control than the stock 1-inch sway bar that was optional on the 1967–1972. If you can't find a 3/4-ton, the 1/2-ton trucks from the squarebody era tend to have 1.125-inch sway bars that will bolt right into your 1967–1972 truck.

Take a 1¼-inch open-end wrench with you to help you hunt for the bigger bar. Sliding the open end over the bar will tell you if you're looking at the biggest available factory bar or not.

This is the most inexpensive upgrade that you can make to your front suspension. You'll feel a difference almost right away when you drive the truck after installation. Just be sure to get all the mounting hardware with the bar, including all the original bushings. You can later swap them for polyurethane to tighten up the suspension even more.

Out back, look for a third-gen Camaro IROC-Z sway bar, as it is large (15/16 inch) and can be adapted to trailing-arm trucks with a few basic hand tools. This bar mounts up and out of the way of other aftermarket pieces, such as rear-mount fuel tanks, which makes it a good option if you're looking to upgrade without spending a lot of cash. If you find one, get all the associated brackets with it.

Keep an eye out for GM trucks from the 1970s. The sway bars used on the front of these trucks (if optioned) will bolt up to the earlier 1967–1972 GM trucks, assuming that you have all of the proper hardware. If you look closely at the edge of this front bumper, you can see that the larger factory sway bar is still intact.

Lowering the Truck

Getting low is key to a great look, and there are a number of ways to get there depending on your budget and goals. Keep in mind that not every method of getting low is created equal.

Dropped trucks have the potential to handle much better than those at stock height, simply because they have a lower center of gravity. The key word is "potential" because there is a right way and a wrong way to go about this. To do this right, consider buying the proper parts because anything else will likely produce mixed results.

Heated Coil Springs (Bad)

The cheapest and worst way to lower a truck is to heat up the front coil springs until they sag. This is usually done with the truck on the ground and the owner or builder using an oxy/acetylene torch setup to heat each coil spring until it starts to lose its tension and lower the truck. This isn't an exact science, and one side will often end up sagging more than the other. There is little the owner can do to correct this issue aside from installing new springs.

The real problem is that a coil spring has a set spring rate from the factory. Heating a coil spring changes that rate and removes the temper of the spring steel. This causes the spring to be less effective at its job and makes it prone to breaking and/or further sagging.

At best, the truck will wallow in the curves, bottom out on bumps, and generally handle poorly. It will also react unpredictably when pushed into a corner. At worst, a spring will break. If you were thinking about

CHEVY/GMC TRUCKS 1967–1972: HOW TO BUILD & MODIFY

this method, think again. If you buy a truck that had this done, consider redoing it.

Shorten Coil Springs (Good)

A better method that is just as inexpensive is to remove each coil and cut it with a chop saw or a cut-off wheel. Doing this required breaking the tapers of the ball joints loose and dealing with the compressed coil spring that has a lot of stored energy within it. Cutting the spring obviously makes it shorter, which, in turn, drops the ride height. The general consensus here is that for every one full coil removed from the spring, the truck will drop approximately 2 inches in ride height.

You can lower a truck by cutting a quarter of a coil or a half a coil from the coil springs using a metal chop saw or cutoff wheel, but doing so will change the front suspension geometry and the spring rate, which can cause unpredictable results. Some have done it with no issues, but there are better options available to achieve improved ride and handling.

Drop Springs (Better)

The better method for getting low is to source and install a set of dropped coil springs in the front and rear (for coil-spring axle applications). These springs typically have a shorter overall height from stock and an increased spring rate, but you can spec out that rate when you choose them, which gives you some control over how the truck will ride. The lower installed height allows the truck to have a lowered stance and lower center of gravity without the bad tradeoff of an unknown rate or tendency of breakage.

The downside here is cost,

Lowering springs are available in a variety of heights and spring rates, which can allow for fairly considerable drops over stock with minimal other changes needed. These work best when paired with drop spindles and a matching, shorter, performance shock absorber. (Photo Courtesy Carolina Kustoms)

although drop springs tend to be relatively affordable.

That said, the benefits are real. There's a choice between linear coils and progressive coils. Linear coils have a constant rate: for example, 800 pounds per inch. For every 800 pounds of force, the spring will compress 1 inch. Progressive springs tighten up their rate more as the spring is compressed, which is typically beneficial in performance situations. With a

Lowering blocks are a good option for coil-spring rear trucks because they raise the axle relative to the suspension so that the factory spring rate isn't changed. The main consideration with something like this is to verify that the axle doesn't hit the frame under compression. If it does, install a proper C-notch to maintain clearance. (Photo Courtesy Kevin Whipps)

SUSPENSION

Pinion Shims

If you intend to drop the rear trailing arm of your truck more than 2 inches, you'll likely need to use pinion shims to correct the driveshaft geometry.

Long trailing-arm suspensions were designed for proper driveline angles at the stock ride height. Dropping the rear of the truck lower tends to aim the pinion down at the ground a few degrees, which can cause a vibration and destroy U-joints.

This can be solved with a set of proper pinion shims that install between the rear axle housing and the trailing arms. They pinch in place and tilt the axle back up to compensate for the dropped suspension. Typically, 1 degree of shim is needed per 1 inch of drop.

If you don't want to use shims, another solution is to remove the front trailing-arm mounts from the crossmember, flip them over, and swap them from left to right. This raises the front of the trailing arms slightly, which offsets the modified angles at the rear. Remove each mount's rivets from the crossmember and then bolt them back in place using Grade 8 hardware.

Doing this swap typically works to bring the pinion back into alignment for up to a 4-inch drop from stock. Note that it's often much easier to shim the axle if the bed is still installed on the truck.

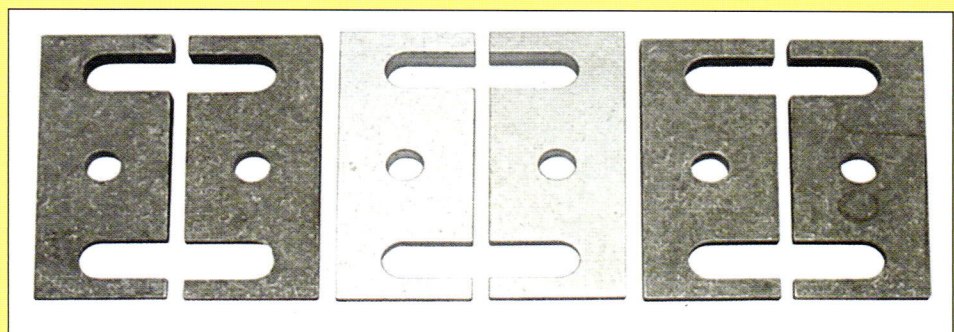

These pinion shims compensate for dropped suspension by installing between the axle housing and trailing arms and rotating the pinion angle back to spec. Start by measuring the angle of both the tailshaft and the yoke with the truck at ride height, and then shoot for equal opposites. If your truck has a driveline vibration under power, shim the axle down slightly. If it vibrates under compression, shim it up. (Photo Courtesy Summit Racing)

progressive coil, the spring rate will increase as it's pushed into a corner but will allow for a looser, more comfortable ride when cruising around town.

This is important information to consider before choosing coils for your application. Before recommending a set of springs, most spring manufacturers ask about your truck's weight and the type of driving you intend on doing with it.

For coil-spring rear axles, the theory is the same. Lowering springs lower the truck, and you can also apply lowering blocks between the control arms and the axle housing to get even lower. You have to be careful that the control arms don't end up lower than the steel rim of the truck, which is considered the scrub line, as a flat tire can prove to be dangerous in that situation. Two inches of lowering block is usually the max you can consider without getting into scrub-line issues.

Lowering trucks with long trailing-arm rear suspension systems (specifically those with stock arms) can cause some issues with the pinion angle, so keep that in mind. If you end up with a vibration, it's likely due to an incorrect pinion angle caused by lowering the truck's ride height.

Getting Low with Leafs

For leaf-sprung rear axle trucks, several options are available. The first is to install an axle-flip kit. This consists of a special bracket and longer U-bolts, which, when installed, places the rear axle above the spring rather than below it, thereby lowering the rear of the truck about 5 inches. These are cheap and effective, and they allow you to run lowering blocks as well, which aren't possible with the axle mounted under the spring.

Another option is to run longer spring shackles, which lowers the effective ride height of the truck without making the ride worse than stock.

Finally, special lowering leaf springs are also available that install in the place of the originals and lower the truck anywhere from 1 to 3 inches from stock.

Many builders select one of those methods, but they also work together. Lowering springs and a flip kit will help get the rear of your C10 as low as possible without major frame modifications.

CHEVY/GMC TRUCKS 1967–1972: HOW TO BUILD & MODIFY

CHAPTER 4

Turning a 3/4-Ton into a 1/2-Ton

Why not take a comparatively cheap 3/4-ton and make it into a 1/2-ton? You can tackle this if you know which parts to use.

Here's what you need to know. First, rear suspension notwithstanding, the frames are generally the same with a few notable differences. The 3/4-ton frames are made of slightly thicker steel than their 1/2-ton counterparts. The heavier-duty trucks take different, taller cab mounts and have increased bracing around the crossmembers. The thickness difference is only a concern when considering the install of C-notches or frame-shortening plates, but in my experience, parts designed for 1/2-ton trucks fit regardless.

Three-quarter ton coil-spring trucks have much larger frame doubler plates that run inside the frame rails over the rear suspension. The long trailing arms are reinforced and the Panhard rod mounts in a different type of bracket, but the systems are otherwise the same.

Up front, the upper control arm uses a heavier-duty, larger-diameter cross-shaft that uses 9/16-inch-diameter studs rather than the 1/2-ton's 1/2-inch-diameter studs. The upper control arms are otherwise the same on the two trucks, so you can swap in 1/2-ton ball joints and use the heavier-duty cross-shaft when swapping over to a 1/2-ton spindle. The lower control arms are specific to 3/4-ton. However, the lower control-arm cross-shaft that bolts to the frame is the same diameter on the 1/2-ton and the 3/4-ton, so a 1/2-ton arm can be installed in the 3/4-ton frame using the 3/4-ton's U-bolts.

Obviously, the spindles, springs, brakes, steering, and rear axles are different on the two trucks. But you can mix and match parts to achieve the truck you want versus the truck you have. ■

The 3/4-ton frame is not exactly identical to a 1/2-ton unit, but aside from being made of thicker steel and having beefier reinforcements and some different brackets, it can be swapped over to 1/2-ton configuration fairly easily.

C-Notches

Regardless of arms or leafs, you can only go so low before the axle housing makes contact with the frame rail. Typically, this is about 5 inches from stock. Anything more than that allows contact between the housing and the frame rails, especially if you intend on hauling any weight in the bed.

The solution here is to install a C-notch, which requires cutting a section of frame away and removing it to make space for the axle to tuck up inside the frame rail under full

A good C-notch is a must if you plan on dropping your truck more than a couple of inches, especially if you intend to haul any weight in the truck after it's been dropped. These can be installed with the bed in place (depending on the design used), but it is almost always easier to do this work with the bed removed for access.

SUSPENSION

suspension compression.

Several companies make C-notches. It's best to find a set that fits the frame tightly, as cutting the frame creates a weak spot just over the rear axle. The C-notch is supposed to reintroduce strength into that area, so the thicker and better that it is made, the better you'll be.

You can pretty much bet on needing a C-notch if you intend on running an axle flip with leafs or if you pass 4 inches of drop with a trailing-arm truck.

Drop Spindles

The best solution for lowering the front of a C10 or C20 is to use drop spindles. These are simple and effective because they simply raise the wheel in relation to the rest of the suspension, which results in a lower ride height without the need to further modify the suspension. Therefore, you can achieve stock ride quality while also having a lower-than-stock ride height. Two-inch drop spindles are common and available for 1967–1970 and 1971–1972 models. Note that ball joints and tie-rod ends changed between those two eras, so you'll need to source the proper spindles for the rest of your suspension.

Pairing a set of drop spindles with a set of drop springs is a great way to achieve up to 5 inches of drop up front, and they're typically cost-effective at doing it. The truck will need an alignment after installing these parts because drop springs tend to introduce negative camber into your front wheels. This can be solved with aftermarket tubular control arms. These are generally engineered to solve that camber problem and return the wheel alignment to its proper general position with the truck at a much lower ride height than stock.

Classic Performance Products (CPP) drop spindles aren't the only choice for C10 use, but they are well liked because they allow the use of either factory or aftermarket brakes without much trouble. They also drop the nose of your truck 2 inches without any other modifications.

Complete Suspension Kits

Piecing together your truck's suspension is certainly one way to get into the weeds. It tends to be a cost-effective way of doing things, especially if you reuse some of the stock components in the process. With that being said, running a complete, engineered suspension system has some major benefits in how your truck can both ride and handle, and a variety of complete kits are available that remove a lot of the guesswork.

The key here is in how the truck rides after the work is complete. It's hard to beat some of what the aftermarket has assembled, especially when it's been engineered to work together as a complete system.

The engineering work is important, as companies such as QA1 and RideTech designed their control arms to provide the proper alignment specifications at lower-than-stock

RideTech's StreetGrip system is a great way to get your C10 to sit lower than stock and improve its ride and handling. These kits are easy to install and come with all the components needed, including new A-arm cross-shafts, drop springs, and drop spindles. It's hard to go wrong for the price and quality here. (Photo Courtesy RideTech)

CHEVY/GMC TRUCKS 1967–1972: HOW TO BUILD & MODIFY

ride heights both in the front and in the back. They also offer more adjustment than the original components while being both lighter and stronger than what the factory produced. The result is significantly improved handling and an improved ride, which is worth the price of the parts.

A variety of companies have kits already sorted out for C10s and C20s, with options ranging from basic springs to coilover systems, air systems, and full-on custom frames that are capable of providing a great ride while also setting the frame rails down on the ground. The kit that you select depends on your goals and budget. It's hard to find a truck owner who regrets installing these parts—provided that he or she really considered the entire build before getting started.

You might find that a complete system is overkill for how you'll really use your truck. Perhaps something as simple as a drop spindle/drop spring and axle flip kit (leaf rear) or shim kit (coil rear) is all you really need. With that being said, you tend to get your money's worth out of a complete, engineered system.

Coilover Conversions

If you're serious about handling, a coilover system is key. A coilover shock works just like a standard shock, but it comes with a threaded body that is surrounded by a coil spring that's captured between an adjustable collar at the bottom and a fixed collar at the top. The lower collar can be threaded up or down the shock body, effectively raising and lowering the installed height of the coilover. With the spring cranked up, the truck sits higher. With the spring cranked down, the truck sits lower.

These units offer great height and ride quality adjustability, compact performance, and light weight, especially compared to stock coils and springs. The higher-end versions offer compression and rebound setting adjustments that provide complete control over how each corner of your truck will react under hard cornering and when cruising down the road.

Coilover kits tend to require specific modifications to work in C10s, namely different upper and lower control arms up front and a revised crossmember and control-arm setup out back.

The benefits here are many (from simplicity of maintenance and adjustability to increased performance) for trucks that see track time or are only street driven. They're modular with the spring contained by the shock's body, so removal is much easier than it is for a dropped coil spring or factory coil spring.

Spring selection still applies here, as the coilover is only as good as the springs that are used. They need to be the proper rate for the weight of your truck. If in doubt, the manufacturer of the coils you have in mind can help, but you need to provide the company with as much information about your truck as possible so that you select the proper spring rate for your rig.

Overall, there isn't much of a downside to a coilover kit other than cost. Complete coilover kits can be expensive, and prices can vary widely depending on the parts you use. You can build your own setup with universal parts, or you can go with one of the several well-engineered systems available for 1967–1972 C10s. Whatever you choose, this is a great option for someone in the market for the best handling C10 they can build.

Air Suspension

If you want the ultimate in adjustability, an air system is what you need for your C10. For years, these systems were mostly great at providing adjustable ride height while lacking performance in the handling department. As they grew in popularity into the 2000s, the technology improved considerably. A good air system, if set up properly today, can rival a coilover system in terms of ride and handling with the added benefit of push-button ride-height adjustment. The days of having mushy, loose handling from the air suspension of the 1990s are over.

An air suspension system uses pressurized rubber airbags in place of steel coil or leaf springs. The truck can be raised or lowered by altering the air pressure in the airbags, which is handled via an onboard air compressor and a few electronic valves. As with any suspension system, the shock is the heart of it all, and the evolution of that technology is what has made air suspension as good as it is today.

Additionally, an air spring is a progressive spring by nature. It increases its spring rate when compressed, which gives it great potential for handling, especially when paired with a properly matched adjustable shock.

The other piece of the puzzle is a solid air management system, such as those offered by AccuAir, Air Lift, and RideTech, along with the proper air line, fittings, air tank, and dual compressors for quick recovery. Today's systems are digital and often

SUSPENSION

If you've ever fought with coil spring removal or installation, a coilover setup is a breath of fresh air. These systems are light, compact, and self-contained. There's no need for spring compressors here. They also allow for more adjustability than stock coils. (Photo Courtesy RideTech)

Scan this QR code with your smartphone to buy *How to Install Air Ride Suspension Systems* (SA500) by Kevin Whipps.

use both height sensors and pressure sensors to help achieve the proper ride height in any situation, which is great for a truck that may continue to see work duties from time to time. It also helps eliminate the possibility of different air pressures in different corners of the truck, which can happen easily when measuring only height.

You can buy a complete air kit for your C10 or you can build your own. The choice is yours. If you're interested in building an air suspension system, check out CarTech's *How to Install Air Ride Suspension Systems* by Kevin Whipps. The book features everything you need to know on the topic, including how to put together a system that's both safe and reliable.

Be prepared to pay at least four figures for a basic turn-key kit, and something specialized will likely be more expensive. For many owners, the positives outweigh the price, as does the ability to roll into a car show, hit a switch, and get lower than the next vehicle.

Air-spring systems have come a long way over the past 20 years. Today, with the right shocks, an air system can just about keep up with a coilover system in performance with the added benefit of on-the-fly height adjustability. This is a great option for builders who want complete control over height as well as a smooth ride.

CHEVY/GMC TRUCKS 1967–1972: HOW TO BUILD & MODIFY

CHAPTER 4

Building and plumbing an air suspension system doesn't have to be a challenge. Complete kits are available, and some are even preassembled, such as this AirPod unit from RideTech. These aren't cheap, but they take all the guesswork and a lot of time out of the process.

Installing RideTech's Coilover Kit on a C20

For this project, I elected to start with a C20 and turn it into a C10. One of the best ways to do that is to use an aftermarket suspension kit. For this build, I chose RideTech's coilover kit for 1967–1970 C10s, which, with a 12-bolt rear axle, can convert a C20 into a C10 without guesswork. This is an easy process for a DIYer with a few weekends on his or her hands. Here's how it works.

Installing a Coilover Front Suspension

1 RideTech's full coilover system includes StrongArm upper and lower control arms, new drop spindles, a MuscleBar sway bar, replacement upper crossmember brackets, the coilovers themselves, and all of the required hardware.

2 First, tear all the factory suspension out of the truck, including the control arms. Use caution when removing the factory coil springs because they store a significant amount of potential energy and can be dangerous if not handled properly.

52   CHEVY/GMC TRUCKS 1967–1972: HOW TO BUILD & MODIFY

SUSPENSION

Installing a Coilover Front Suspension continued

3 With the original suspension out of the way, remove this upper bracket. There are four rivets that need to be center punched and drilled out, and several bolts that need to be removed.

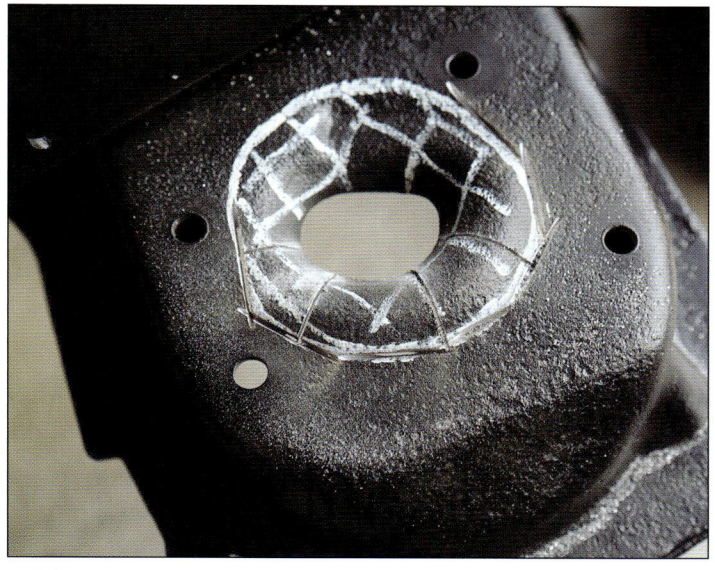

4 RideTech's kit comes with templates that index off the original bracket's four mounting holes, which then shows you a section of crossmember that needs to be removed. I found this is best handled with both a cutting wheel and reciprocating saw.

5 After cleaning up the hole, the bracket can be installed, but you have to make sure it sits flat on the crossmember, and you have to install the two 3-inch-long Grade-8 bolts that come in the kit. These tap in place from the rear and serve as mounting studs for the upper control arm. The bracket can then be bolted in place using the supplied hardware. Torque to 50 ft-lbs.

6 The StrongArm upper control arm comes without an installed ball joint, so it needs to be bolted in place with the supplied hardware. Torque to 29 ft-lbs.

CHEVY/GMC TRUCKS 1967–1972: HOW TO BUILD & MODIFY

CHAPTER 4

Installing a Coilover Front Suspension *continued*

7 The upper control arm comes with two machined caster slugs that slide into place and set the front suspension's caster angle. Several versions of these slugs are available to adjust to the truck's caster 1/8 inch forward or back, which can help with things such as directional stability and steering effort. The control-arm cross-shaft also allows adjustment. Installing it with the logo out, as here, is for a street alignment. If you want a track or autocross setup, installing it with the logo toward the frame will provide more negative camber.

8 Replacing the control arm shims, located here between the control arm and the frame bracket, is a good way to maintain the truck's original alignment specs. You'll need a new alignment regardless once all the suspension is installed. From there, washers and nyloc nuts round out the upper control-arm install alongside the large washers and nuts that retain the upper bushings.

9 RideTech supplies this bracket and bump stop to eliminate tire clearance issues with the inner fender. To install it, position it on the crossmember (as shown here) and then mark and drill two 3/8-inch holes for the supplied hardware.

10 The StrongArm lower control arms install in the original control arm's brackets using the peg at the front to center up on the relief in the control-arm shaft, just like a stock truck. Be careful. There are two different sets of holes in the control arms. For this application, use the holes that are 8.706 inches center to center.

54 CHEVY/GMC TRUCKS 1967–1972: HOW TO BUILD & MODIFY

SUSPENSION

11 Next, the lower control arms get washers and locknuts. There's no need to go ultra-tight on these fasteners because you're just trying to be sure the bushing has the proper preload and can't move out of its bore.

12 The coilover shock and spring assembly can be installed using the machined spacers that come with the kit. They install on either side, both top and bottom. The shock goes with the adjuster knob up and out toward the wheel. Then, the bolt can slide through from the front.

13 It's the same story with the lower mount. There's a spacer on both sides followed by the retaining bolt. Once you have both the upper and the lower in place, torque both the upper and lower bolt to 75 ft-lbs. For now, adjust the springs with a slight amount of preload, which will set the suspension about as low as it will go.

14 The drop spindle installs on the upper and lower ball joints and is torqued down tight using the supplied lower grease boot and upper and lower castle nuts. The kit comes with new cotter keys to ensure the ball-joint castle nuts don't come loose once you've cinched them down. This is also a good time to snug up the grease zerk fittings, which are 8 mm.

15 To install the MuscleBar, remove the factory sway-bar bracket (if equipped) by cutting off the heads of the rivets and driving the remainder out of the way with a punch and hammer. If your truck had no sway bar, you'll still need to remove the lower front crossmember rivet, as this bracket will bolt in its place. Install the bracket but leave it loose.

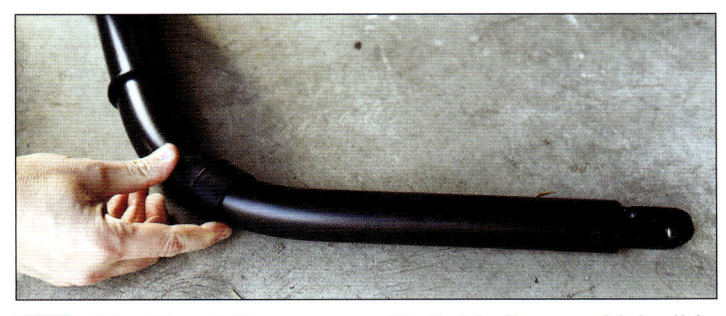

16 The MuscleBar comes with Delrin liners, which slide into place without any lubrication needed. After they're in place, the polyurethane bushings are next, followed by the metal retainers. From there, it can be lifted into the truck and bolted in place using the supplied hardware.

CHEVY/GMC TRUCKS 1967–1972: HOW TO BUILD & MODIFY

CHAPTER 4

Installing a Coilover Front Suspension continued

17 RideTech's PosiLinks allow for some extreme movement without compromising the functionality of the massive MuscleBar sway bar. These use four washers per side (one on either side of the MuscleBar and one on either side of the StrongArm), and then they're torqued to 50 ft-lbs.

18 Once the rest of the MuscleBar hardware is tight, it's wise to run the truck through its complete range of suspension motion to be sure that the bar doesn't contact anything. Once you've done that and double-checked that all of your suspension bolts are tight and your cotter keys are in place and bent, the front suspension is complete, pending an alignment.

Installing a Coilover Rear Suspension

1 RideTech's rear StrongArm kit comes with new trailing arms, crossmembers, C-notches, an adjustable Panhard rod, brackets, and coilovers. This kit is comprehensive and includes all of the required hardware. Installation is not too challenging. This is a great weekend project.

2 Tear all of this suspension out of the truck. The goal is to remove the axle and lower control arms, factory Panhard-rod mount, axle bump stops, and springs. This can be a chore, especially if your truck has spent time somewhere salty, so be ready with penetrating oil, an impact, and a cutting wheel if needed.

3 If you have a 3/4-ton truck, remove these inner frame doubler plates that were used on your heavier-duty rig. Note that my frame here is inverted, as it was completely stripped and easy to flop over. Doing so makes getting to the doubler plate rivets easier. Removing the rivets is as simple as cutting or drilling the heads and driving them through the frame with a punch.

56 CHEVY/GMC TRUCKS 1967–1972: HOW TO BUILD & MODIFY

SUSPENSION

Installing a Coilover Rear Suspension continued

5 Note the space between this crossmember and the frame rail with the doubler plate removed. The easiest solution is to use a cutting wheel to cut a panel out of the doubler plate for reinstallation. If you have a 1/2-ton truck, all this can be skipped, but you will still need to remove the plate where the factory coil spring bolts to the frame rail.

4 These 3/4-ton plates are L-shaped, riveted to the side and rear of the frame, and run under the rear two crossmembers alongside the curve of the frame rail. They're a pain to get out, but they will come out with some work, and they do need to come out for the installation of this kit. Otherwise, they'll interfere with the C-notch installation.

6 With the frame flipped back over, move forward to the trailing-arm crossmember, which needs to be removed for this installation. With the rivets drilled out, it can be slid out from between the frame rails.

7 The new tubular crossmember can go into place next by using the upper bolt holes in the frame rails to locate it. The tabs point to the rear and downward. In this case, the front and rear lower bolt holes were not already present in the frame, so they had to be drilled using a 7/16-inch bit.

8 Next to go is the rear crossmember, which is held in place with several rivets on top and below. If you've already removed 3/4-ton doubler plates, you already have removed the lower part of this crossmember, which makes this an easy six-rivet removal. For 1/2-ton trucks, you'll have rivets on top and below to remove here.

CHEVY/GMC TRUCKS 1967–1972: HOW TO BUILD & MODIFY

CHAPTER 4

Installing a Coilover Rear Suspension *continued*

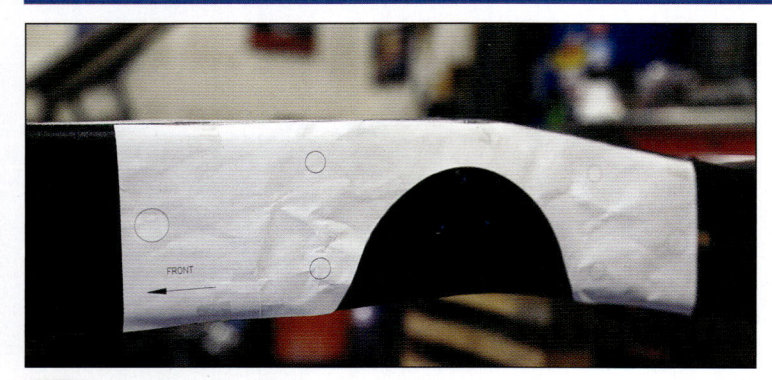

9 The RideTech kit comes with a template that helps locate the cuts that you'll need to make for the C-notch installation, all of which indexes off several holes in the face of the frame. Note that correct placement will have the cut just about centered over the uppermost factory bump-stop hole. A cutting wheel makes quick work of the section to be removed. Next, use a grinder to clean up the edges and make everything smooth.

10 You don't want any angled cuts here, as they can lead to stress cracks. Once you have the cut finished, paint any bare metal to prevent rust.

11 RideTech's C-notches fit the frame nice and tight. A dead-blow hammer will help seat them in place. Then, it's just a matter of installing the hardware, starting with the two 5/8-inch bolts (some trucks only use one), and drilling out and installing all the bolts and nyloc nuts (minus the three in the upper front top section).

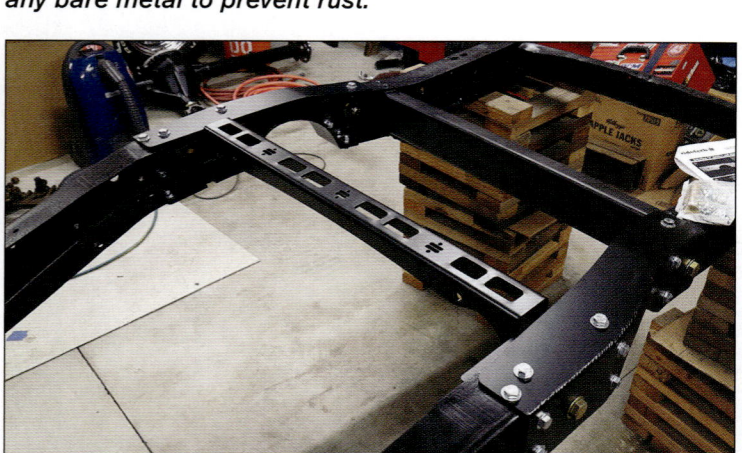

12 The upper-shock bridge is next, and it bolts in place from below the upper frame rail using the original bolt holes from the factory crossmember and the holes in the upper section of the C-notch. This installs with the bridge offset to the rear of the truck.

13 The C-notches come with bump stops that keep the axle from contacting the frame rail, and now's the time to install them.

SUSPENSION

14 The frame bracket for the Panhard rod mounts to the driver's side of the factory rear crossmember and the lower section of the C-notch and frame. This is a slick setup that uses stacked plates to fit the different frame heights in this area. The RideTech logo faces aft.

15 The lower control arms are next. One of the things that makes RideTech unique is its special R-joints, which are seen here at the front of one of the lower control arms. These joints feature a great range of motion and eliminate slop that you might otherwise find with rubber or polyurethane bushings.

16 Each control arm gets two spacers, a bolt, two washers, and a locking nut. There is a difference between driver-side and passenger-side control arms; both are clearly marked. If in doubt, the arm with the Panhard bar mount goes on the passenger's side.

17 The next challenge is to wrestle the rear axle into place over the new lower control arms and fix it in place using the new U-bolts supplied in the kit. A floor jack makes this easier, as an axle is both heavy and awkward to move around.

18 The rear coilovers are installed next. As with the front, these mount with the knobs facing up, but this time they should point in and toward the center of the truck. These use machined spacers to locate them within the shock bridge.

19 Using a floor jack to raise the axle, install the coilover-mount bolts along with the machined shims that fit on either side of the shock eye.

CHEVY/GMC TRUCKS 1967–1972: HOW TO BUILD & MODIFY

CHAPTER 4

Installing a Coilover Rear Suspension *continued*

20 The final piece of the puzzle is to install the Panhard rod with the adjustable side toward the axle housing. There are three different height settings for the rod. RideTech recommends using whichever one will place the rod generally level at ride height. To start, it's best to use the center setting and adjust from there.

21 The final step out back is to tighten up all the coilover mounting bolts and adjust both coilover springs just a little past zero preload, which you can move up as needed. Before reinstalling the bed, double-check all of the fasteners to be sure nothing has been left loose.

How Low Can You Go?

If your goal is to set your truck's frame rails on the ground, you will need to make serious frame and suspension changes from stock, or you can source a partial or complete frame from Choppin' Block, Porterbuilt, The Roadster Shop, Rydman Ranch, TCI Engineering, GSI, or Art Morrison.

Many of those companies offer both custom front and rear frame sections, which achieve the look and can be grafted onto your original frame rails. These allow for a much lower ride height than a truck with a stock frame, but they also require some significant body modifications—from custom inner fenders up front to complete raised bed floors out back. They'll give your truck the ride height of a modern Ferrari or Lamborghini, which is to say, very low.

Generally speaking, setting the rails on the ground requires a link-style rear end and a frame bridge at the rear axle, which is like a C-notch but even more exaggerated, along with a modified front crossmember and custom front and rear control arms. Another option is to Z-cut the frame ahead of the cab and weld it back in place (higher relative to the cab), which achieves the same type of result to level the front crossmember with the lower end of the frame rails under the cab.

However, note that Z-cutting the frame moves the engine and transmission up. While these trucks have plenty of hood clearance as stock vehicles, they don't have much transmission-tunnel clearance, so doing this job means you'll be cutting up and modifying your cab floor as well.

If you're going to go that far, a body drop will help to get even lower. The idea is to lower the body down over the frame, which is typically done by either raising the floor up or lowering the cab mounts down, depending on how much fabrication you intend to do for that lowered look.

Porterbuilt Fab has a 3/4-inch bolt-in body-drop kit that sets the rocker panel pinch welds even with the bottom of the frame, which allows the rockers to sit on the ground when the frame sits on the ground. This is a good option because traditional body drops move the floor pan up, reducing interior space and comfort.

Rydman Ranch makes complete custom suspension systems for C10s that are destined to go as low as possible. These systems move everything up significantly from stock, thereby lowering the truck. These components are well designed and handmade in central Oregon. (Photo Courtesy Spencer Rydman)

60   CHEVY/GMC TRUCKS 1967–1972: HOW TO BUILD & MODIFY

CHAPTER 5

BRAKES AND STEERING

How your truck handles is one thing, but just as important is how it turns and stops. The key with any project today is to build something that's both fun and safe to drive. For a C10 or C20, that means having great dynamics at the wheel and at the brake pedal. There's really no way around that, especially if you intend on driving your truck in modern traffic, and that's kind of the point, right?

Getting better performance out of the steering and brakes is pretty simple, either from using stock upgraded parts or aftermarket performance parts. This is up to you, but after you consider that even the most basic commuter car can both stop shorter and outturn your originally equipped C10, you'll probably end up in the same place most of us do and decide that good enough isn't really good anymore. There are many choices available for upgrades, and all of them will make your truck a better driver.

Brakes

When GM's trucks were redesigned in 1967, they were fitted with the best front and rear drum-brake system that GM could build for a reasonable cost per unit. All GM trucks had drums on all four wheels until 1971, when front disc brakes became standard on all C-series GM trucks.

In general, drum brakes aren't bad, but they've been completely overshadowed by disc brakes, especially in front wheel applications, because discs are more efficient and reliable.

Part of the reasoning is that drum brakes get hot and fade more quickly than discs. They build and retain heat, which then degrades brake performance considerably. Drums don't perform as well as discs do when wet. Drums can also move out of adjustment, whereas discs don't.

In 1971, GM was proud enough of the disc-brake revolution to place a one-year-only decal on every disc-brake-equipped truck to call out the upgraded technology.

If your pre-1971 truck is still stock, chances are good that this is what you're going to see behind the front wheel. For their time and place, drum brakes did their job just fine, but today's technology is much better.

CHAPTER 5

Stock-style discs, which were offered on 1971-and-newer trucks and are easily found in today's aftermarket conversion kits, are just under 12-inches in diameter and use a D52-style basic single-piston brake caliper. This system is tried and true. It's a great upgrade for a street-driven rig. (Photo Courtesy Kevin Whipps)

Stock-Style Front Brake Upgrades

The updated 1971 and 1972 parts can be swapped over to an earlier C10 with some ease if you can find a donor truck, but you also have to consider that GM switched from 6-lug wheels to 5-lug wheels at that same time. If you choose to use later-model parts on an early C10, you'll be shopping for wheels as well. For some of us, that's actually a desirable thing, as there are more 5-lug wheel options—or at least there used to be. The booming truck market has started to change that with more 6-lug wheels available by the year.

When GM swapped to discs for 1971, it also changed the steering's tie-rod diameter from 5/8 inch to 11/16 inch, as well as the adjuster's thread-pitch direction and the taper where the tie-rod meets the spindle. If you choose to swap a 1967–1970 truck over to the 1971 and 1972 parts, you'll need all the matching steering components as well. Later trucks used a different brake-line location at the front of the crossmember versus at the back on drum-brake trucks, so some brake-line fabrication will be required as well. You'll need a fresh brake master cylinder as well as the proper brake proportioning valve for a disc/drum setup.

It's easier to swap to 1973–1987 brake components than to the 1971–1972 pieces. However, this is only in the sense that parts are easier to source and are cheaper, especially if you find a complete crossmember to bolt into place fitted with A-arms and the complete steering linkage. If you go this route, be sure you know which disc brake front end you've found. GM used both a 1¼-inch HD rotor and a 1-inch standard rotor in front applications throughout the square years, and they don't interchange. Look for the wider HD rotor because it's the better of the two options.

Many of the stock-style swap rules are moot these days thanks to the aftermarket. It used to be slightly more challenging to swap an earlier C10 to front disc brakes, as it required using a later spindle and all the later associated parts, such as ball joints, tie-rod ends, etc. However, these days you can buy disc spindles (both standard height and dropped) that are designed for the earlier trucks, which makes this conversion a basic bolt-on job. There are options available for both 5- and 6-lug wheels too.

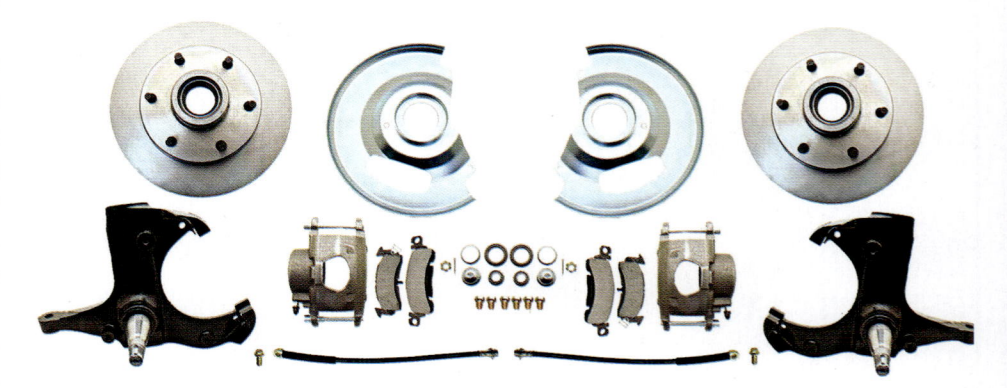

This disc-brake conversion kit is perfect for truck owners who wish to retain 6-lug wheels when upgrading to disc brakes. This kit (Classic Industries part number PB1093) comes with new spindles, rotors, dust shields, lines, bearings, calipers, and pads. (Photo Courtesy Classic Industries)

BRAKES AND STEERING

Beyond stock parts, many companies make aftermarket performance brake options for C10 pickups, and those options range from mild to wild.

Disc Brake Upgrades

If your rig came with front discs from the factory, or if you've swapped factory drums out for factory discs, there is still plenty of room for improvement over stock performance. The world has come a long way from the factory-grade brake pad materials and the solid-faced rotors offered from 1971. Getting a hold of that performance is quick and easy.

The first step to stopping better is inspecting what you have and correcting any issues that might cause uneven or less-than-optimal stopping performance. Be sure that your brakes are in good, serviceable shape with no leaks from the calipers and that there is even pad wear on both the inside and outside pad. If one pad is worn more than the other, you have either bound-up caliper sliders or a sticking caliper piston. Also make sure there are tight wheel bearings. If it all checks out, it's time to upgrade. If not, fix those issues first or plan on how you will eliminate them using upgraded parts.

Brake Pads

If you're looking for the best bang for your buck, the answer is to install a set of modern performance brake pads in place of the old D52s that your disc-brake truck had from the factory. An aggressive set of pads (such as those offered by Hawk Performance, Power Stop, EBC Brakes, etc.) shortens stopping distances considerably, depending on the grade of brake pads you choose. They're available in a variety of compounds

Wilwood offers a dual-piston D52-style caliper that bolts to the standard GM truck's brake system. The benefit here is increased clamping force, forged billet aluminum construction, stainless-steel pistons (to resist rust), and no need for aftermarket rotors. The part number is 140-11290-R. (Photo Courtesy Classic Industries)

geared for everything from towing performance to all-out track use.

The only tradeoff here is regarding noise and dust, which both traditionally increase with more-aggressive pad materials. At the same time, rotor life decreases with harsher brake pads, so that's something to consider as well. It's a good reason to spring for new brake rotors when you're upgrading your front brakes.

With all of that being said, modern pads are better than ever at offering low noise, low dust, and great overall performance. If in doubt, source a set of new performance pads and install them. It's a cheap upgrade that you will be able to feel—whether you're hitting the autocross circuit or just tooling down to the ice-cream stand with your kids.

If you're going to swap brake pads, either resurface or replace the brake rotors. This is important for pad life and for brake feel, as a new set of pads must be broken in and mated to the surface of the rotor. That can't happen if the rotor is already worn-in and smooth, so a brake lathe resurface is very important here. It roughs up the surface of the rotor enough to allow a good bedding in with the new pad, and it removes any imperfections to leave a true, flat surface behind.

Brake Rotors

Modern performance rotors are often cross-drilled, slotted, or both to offer another level of performance. The idea is that brake pads create gas, heat, and dust when pushed hard, which impacts their ability to mate

---

TECH TIP: The Quick Way to Remove Inner-Wheel-Bearing Seals

If you have a stock-style C10 front brake rotor that you want to resurface, you'll first have to remove the inner wheel bearing and seal. Here's a tip that old-school GM mechanics have used for decades.

The outer wheel bearing needs to be removed first to get the rotor off the truck. It's held in place with a cotter pin and a retaining nut under the dust cap. Once that is removed, the trick is to reinstall the nut a few turns but without the outer bearing in place behind it.

With one fluid pull, yank the rotor toward you. The nut will catch the inner wheel bearing, which will push on the seal and pop it out of the rotor. You'll be left with the rotor in your hands with the inner bearing and seal still sitting on the bare spindle behind the mounting nut. The best part is that most of the time, you'll be able to reuse the seal if you don't have a new one in hand.

CHEVY/GMC TRUCKS 1967–1972: HOW TO BUILD & MODIFY

CHAPTER 5

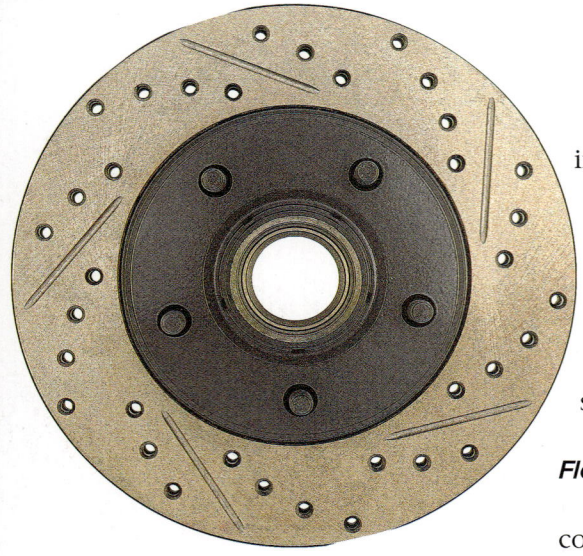

A cross-drilled and slotted rotor offers several benefits over stock, including better gas and dust evacuation and better resistance to brake-killing heat soak. When paired with a good set of modern performance pads and Wilwood's dual-piston D52, you have a winning combination that fits behind a stock rim. (Photo Courtesy Classic Industries)

to the rotor well in extreme conditions, such as when raced or used in stop-and-go traffic.

The slots and drilled sections help vent the gas and dust out and away from the rotor's surface, thereby reducing heat and increasing the brake pad's effectiveness in slowing the rotor.

This isn't measured so much in shorter stopping distances but rather in less fade over time thanks to better control of the factors that impact braking performance. Consistent stops are the result, usually well past when stock rotors would have started to fade. These also look a lot sportier than the stock, solid rotors, which is a bonus.

Flexible Brake Lines

The flexible rubber lines that connect the calipers to the truck's hard lines are commonly overlooked. These can and will crack and leak over time, which is an obvious failure point. It is not so obvious when they start to come apart internally, which can cause calipers or drums to grab and not release. If you have a brake that's sticking, either on one of the front wheels or both sides in the rear, this could be the culprit.

Stock replacement lines are good, but braided steel lines are even better. They don't have the same tendency to flex under pressure as a factory rubber line does, which means that all the braking pressure inside the brake lines is making it to the caliper's piston rather than expanding the hose that leads to the caliper. The result is better, firmer pedal feel and better braking performance.

From the factory, there are three rubber brake lines to consider: front right, front left, and the rear axle line. Replacing all three with braided steel is a wise move for better braking performance and safety.

Steel Brake Lines

While we're talking about hydraulics, plan to (at the very least) make a visual inspection of your factory steel brake lines. These are both 3/16-inch and 1/4-inch lines that run from the master cylinder down under the engine (along the rear of the front crossmember on most 1967–1972 rigs) and out to the flexible lines that connect to each front wheel and to the axle in the rear.

These lines can rust over time, which is an unsafe condition that should not be overlooked. Consider that the highest pressures your truck produces are inside these steel lines. Blowing a hole in one results in a loss of brake hydraulics and, therefore, stopping ability.

As far as replacement goes, you can source a complete brake-line kit bent to stock specifications from just about any restoration parts house, or you can get creative and build your own system. I prefer to make my own, especially when using modern aftermarket parts that take one size of a line over the dual sizes that the factory used on these trucks.

Making Brake Lines

1 *You have many options (from prefabricated stock units to stainless that you can polish to a mirror finish) when it comes to brake lines. I prefer standard steel lines for ease of use over stainless. This is a 25-foot roll of 3/16-inch tube from the Stop Shop. It also comes with an assortment of ends to fit the line diameter.*

BRAKES AND STEERING

Making Brake Lines continued

2 After you have rough measurements in place, start to plan out where you want your brake lines. They need to be clear of heat and anything that's in motion, and they need to route around any bump stops that might contact them when the suspension is in full compression.

3 These are the tools of the trade. Eastwood's brake-line flaring tool (part number 25304-30005), tubing cutter, tubing bender, deburring tool, and forming tool. Getting the proper equipment in place is vital to success with brake lines, especially when it comes to making good flares on which you can rely. This flaring tool uses a bench vise as its base, but Eastwood also offers on-car options if you're modifying a line that's still in your truck.

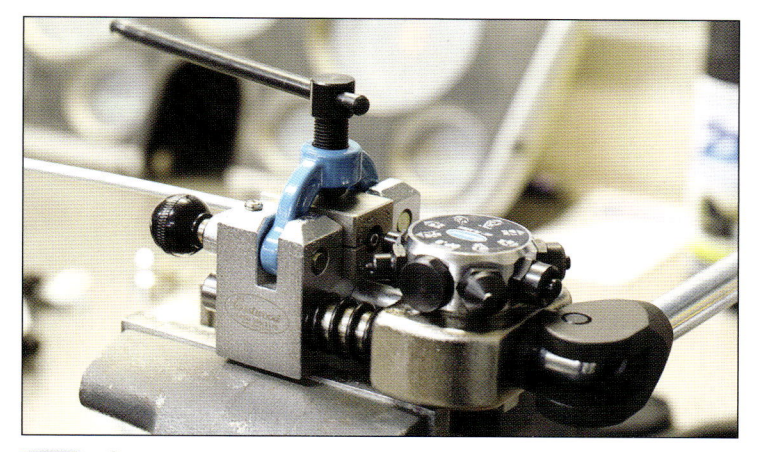

4 Once you have your brake line straightened out, cut to length, and deburred, that's when the flaring tool shines. This is a two-step process. With the line mounted in the dies and clamped down, select Option 1 for the tubing size needed, and pull the handle. Then, select Option 2 and pull the handle. Do this right, and you'll get a perfect result every time.

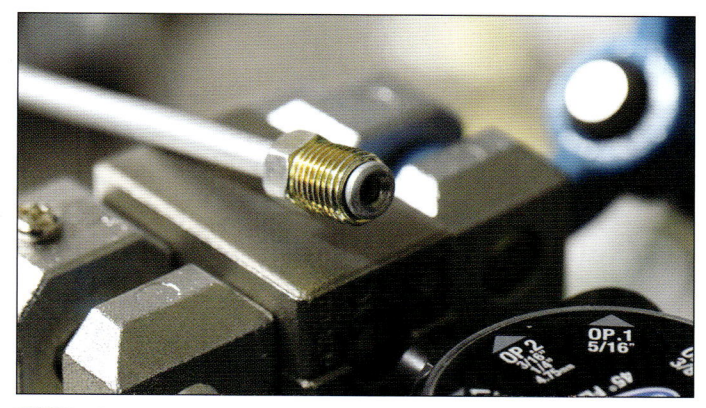

5 This is the final result ready for installation on the truck. Note that this tool also can be outfitted with 37-degree dies, which is perfect for AN tubing work.

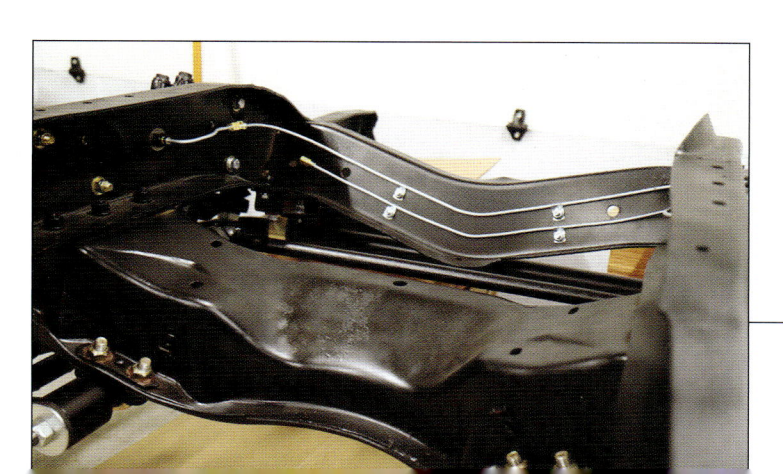

6 The earlier trucks from this generation had brake lines that ran behind the engine crossmember. I elected to run mine as GM did in its squarebody trucks (1973–1987) because it helps keep the lines away from engine heat. The 3/16-inch line is easy to bend by hand to fit wherever you want it to go, and steel clips (available from the Stop Shop) work well to keep it fixed in place.

65

CHAPTER 5

Making Brake Lines *continued*

7 *The final result is what you make of it, but keep in mind that while buying the tools may be more expensive than buying prefabricated lines, you'll have more options available if you make your own setup.*

TECH TIP: Check Your Wheel Cylinders

Leaky cylinders are a common problem in C10s, as they're mounted low in the brake system and close to moisture from the surface of the road. Standard DOT3 brake fluid is hydroscopic, which means it draws moisture into it. The wheel cylinders are usually the first place that this happens, which leads to failure.

Check the drum-brake cylinders from time to time. It's as simple as pulling the drum off the truck and pulling each rubber boot back slightly to look for seeping fluid at both the front and the rear of the cylinder. If you find one leaking, replace it as well as the one on the other side too. ∎

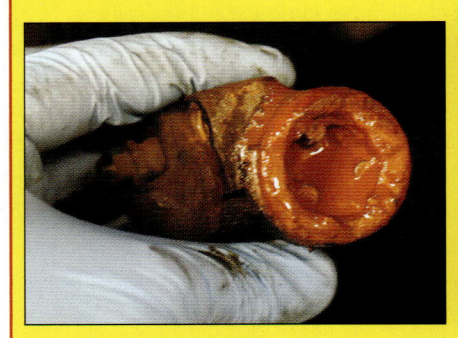

How bad can your wheel cylinders get? This one came out of a car that had relatively low miles but hadn't seen brake fluid service in some time. Brake fluid will draw in moisture, moisture leads to rust, and rust leads to pitting, which is death for a hydraulic system.

Power Brakes or Manual Brakes?

Your C10 could have come from the factory with either a manual brake setup or with power brakes run from engine vacuum via a power booster mounted to a bracket on the firewall. So, which is best? Either one works well. Manual brakes have a firmer pedal by design but use a different pivot point on the pedal assembly to give your foot more leverage to operate, which makes them work just as well as their power counterparts.

Power brakes are a nice upgrade over stock and require much less stopping effort thanks to the vacuum assist taken off the engine. The only time this becomes an issue is when using a radical camshaft that fails to make good engine vacuum at idle. In that case, your truck will feel like it has ineffective brakes at slow speeds, but they'll work better once the engine speed and engine vacuum signal increases. For most of us, that won't be an issue. Electric vacuum pumps can solve the problem, as can hydro-boost setups that run off the power-steering pump. Either of those allow you to have power brake feel with that massive overlap cam you dream of running in your V-8.

Rear Drum-Brake Upgrades

Drums aren't as efficient as disc brakes, but if swapping the factory rear drums isn't part of your plan, the best thing to do is to make sure all the rear drum-brake components are functioning to the best of their ability. That means sourcing new shoes, a new brake hardware kit with new springs and clips, and installing new wheel cylinders and brake shoes.

Some companies sell upgraded friction materials for drum-brake applications, but a good set of metallic shoes will help shorten stopping distances over the old shoes that your truck is likely still wearing, so I'd start there. Begin with searching for restoration parts houses and performance parts suppliers.

Beyond that, it's smart to keep an eye on your drum brakes and keep them clean. A good hose-out with

66   CHEVY/GMC TRUCKS 1967–1972: HOW TO BUILD & MODIFY

BRAKES AND STEERING

Source a Drum-Brake Toolkit

If you intend to do drum-brake work, your best bet is to source a good set of drum-brake tools to help ease you along your way. A drum-brake system isn't particularly complex, but it does offer up some challenges of assembly and disassembly that can be fixed with the proper leverage in the proper places, which is what drum-brake tools are designed to do.

Don't try to cut corners here and use generic tools. You'll use up all the swear words and probably end up inventing new ones if you try to use a screwdriver and a pair of Vise-Grips in place of the proper tools. Your time and sanity are worth something, so get the right tools and save both.

Find a good toolset, learn how to use it, and do one side of the truck at a time for the best results. The other side is your map for when you forget which brake-shoe spring went where. ∎

Snap-on's drum-brake spring plier kit (part number 131A) is my favorite brake line tool kit because it's designed well and comes with all of the bits and pieces that you need to remove and reinstall brake shoes without much effort.

brake parts cleaner is a smart periodic thing to do, as is pulling back the wheel cylinder rubber boots to be sure that the wheel cylinders aren't rusty and leaking.

Drums don't require much constant maintenance. GM engineered them to self-adjust every time you back up your truck and roll to a stop, which (when it's working) keeps the shoes cinched up to the drums as they wear down over time. It's a smart design, even if it's not as efficient as a disc setup.

Big Brake Kits

Braking is all about controlling heat and applying pressure. As you can imagine, the bigger the setup used, the better performance you'll see in return.

Factory brakes top out at just under 12 inches in diameter, but the aftermarket offers solutions that range up to and beyond 14 inches. On top of that, you can add in multi-piston calipers to increase the clamping force on the disc and, therefore, work better than the stock single-piston designs.

Larger, multi-piston calipers also work well over stockers in dissipating heat. Along with rotors, they help eliminate fade while dramatically improving stopping distances. In short, bigger is always better when it comes to brakes. You want these to really work when you need them, especially if you intend on driving your C10 in the midst of commuters. The bigger your brakes, the better performance you'll get out of them.

Should You Swap out the Rear Drums for Discs?

There's no denying that disc brakes are the best bet up front. But what about out back? That's a different story.

Consider that the front brakes in any vehicle do most of the actual braking. Something like 70 percent of the work of stopping typically falls to the front brakes. While the rears are an important part of the system, they're not worked as hard in daily use.

With that being said, the benefits of disc brakes up front are just as noticeable out back, mostly in consistently shorter stopping distances, greater reliability, less noise, less heat, and better wet-weather performance, especially in performance situations or when hauling heavy loads. They're also a lot easier to work on, which is enough of a bonus in itself for many owners.

Don't assume that you must have discs out back to have a good-driving rig. A set of stock-style drums under the bed will do a decent job of bringing your truck to a halt in most situations, especially if they've been revitalized with new shoes, hardware, and hydraulics, and if they're supplemented by a set of discs up front.

If you have room in your budget, a disc setup on all four corners will pay off in better overall performance. ∎

CHAPTER 5

Companies such as Baer, Wilwood, CPP, SSBC, etc. make larger-than-stock systems for C10 applications. All of them offer vast improvements over the stock brakes in a C10.

Selecting a Brake System

Consider the following two things before going all-in on big brakes. First, what size of wheels do you intend to use? Chances are good that if you want 14-inch brakes, you can get away with an 18- or 19-inch wheel, but 20s are preferred. If you don't want to go that big on your wheel diameter, stick with something smaller. Second, what parts are used within the system? Are things like wheel bearings and brake pads off-the-shelf units? Using easy-to-source components will make your life easier in the future, so consider that as well.

Pro Performance offers a custom big-brake kit for 1964–1987 C10 trucks that comes with up to a 15-inch-diameter front brake rotor. This kit works with either a stock-style disc-brake spindle or the popular aftermarket CPP modular unit. Up front, it uses C5 Corvette calipers, while out back, it uses Mustang calipers on 13-inch rotors. This is nice because it allows for big brakes while using off-the-shelf parts and components that are already on your stock C10. (Photo Courtesy Pro Performance)

Installing the Baer Pro+ Front Brake System

1 *This is Baer's 14-inch Pro+ front brake system that was designed for use with CPP's modular 2-inch drop spindles. It features Baer's six-piston caliper, two-piece drilled and slotted brake rotor, billet aluminum hubs, premium bearings, billet dust caps, and all of the hardware required to mount them to the truck. The massive calipers use D0731 brake pads from C5 and C6 Corvettes, which makes later replacement a cinch.*

2 *The caliper mounting bracket fixes in place to the rear of the CPP spindle using 5/8-inch hardware from the kit. This will need to be shimmed for caliper clearance later on, so it's best to only snug these for now.*

BRAKES AND STEERING

Installing the Baer Pro+ Front Brake System *continued*

3 The hub assembly is next, which comes pre-fitted with greased bearings and a rear seal. It snugs in place using a large castle nut and washer that tightens up to set the bearing preload. The key is to snug up the bearing while rotating the hub and then back it off and tighten it up again. Baer recommends using 5 to 10 ft-lbs of torque at first, backing off, and then snugging it up again to remove all play. From there, add another 1/16 turn of preload, and install the cotter key and dust cap.

4 The huge drilled-and-slotted rotor comes next. These are marked "L" for left (driver's side) and "R" for right (passenger's side). They slide in place onto the new hub assembly and fix in place with a few washers and lug nuts. That last part is important because the rotor needs to be completely flush and tight to the hub to properly fit the caliper.

5 The caliper simply bolts into place (after the installed brake pads are removed) on the bracket using two Allen-head bolts. With these snugged up (and after verifying that the caliper bracket is tight to the spindle), it's time to measure for shims. This is done in four locations: top inner, top outer, bottom inner, and bottom outer.

6 Selecting the proper shims is easy. Subtract the top inside measurement from the top outside measurement, and then divide that number by two to determine the amount of shims needed. For example, I had 0.690 inch on the top outside and 0.589 on the top inside, resulting in a 0.101-inch difference. Half of that was 0.050, so that was the amount of shims needed.

CHEVY/GMC TRUCKS 1967–1972: HOW TO BUILD & MODIFY

Installing the Baer Pro+ Front Brake System continued

7 With those measurements in hand, the caliper comes back off, as does the bracket. The shims install between the bracket and caliper mount, and the bolts can be reinstalled, along with the caliper itself to recheck your measurements. Baer suggests getting the gaps to within 0.005 inch to keep brake noise to a minimum.

8 With the pads reinstalled in the caliper, both the bracket and caliper can be torqued in place. The bracket bolts get some thread-lock compound and 110 ft-lbs of torque. The caliper itself should be torqued to 75 ft-lbs.

9 Baer's braided-steel lines are next and install to the caliper using a pair of copper washers and a banjo bolt. From there, they should be installed in such a way to avoid being pinched by wheel travel, suspension travel, etc.

10 Baer's kit comes with nice bulkhead connectors (right), which are just right for C10 frames. My thicker C20 frame required a different style of bulkhead connector for the brake line. My solution was a pair of Allstar Performance (part number 50104) frame fittings that adapt -3 AN to 3/16-inch brake lines and are threaded with enough meat to pass through the thicker C20 frame rail.

11 With the line fixed to where it won't rub, the front brake is complete. With increased size over stock and immense clamping power from 6-piston calipers, these brakes offer super-car performance and everyday reliability.

BRAKES AND STEERING

Installing the Baer Pro+ Rear Brake System

1 Baer's Pro+ 14-inch brake setup for 12-bolt Chevrolets includes a 14-inch two-piece drilled-and-slotted rotor, 6-piston caliper, and a special bracket that includes an integral parking brake assembly. It also comes with all the hardware and hoses required for setup.

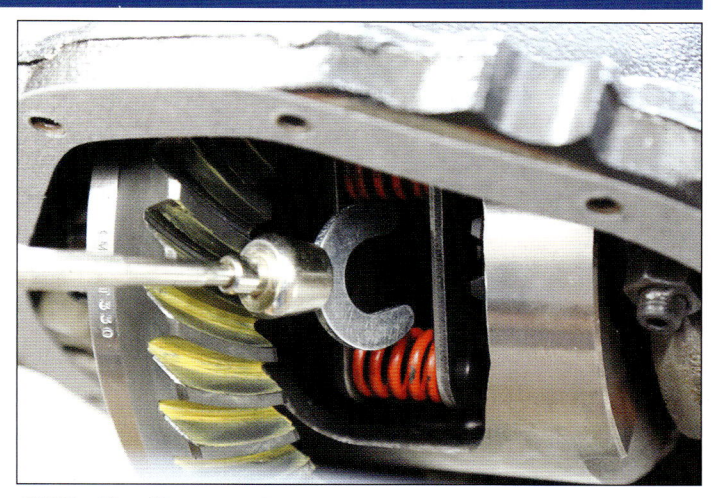

2 The first step is to remove the rear axle housing cover, which gives access to the cross-shaft that holds the C-clips in place. Be ready with a drain pan, as there's no drain plug in a 12-bolt Chevy, and all of your gear oil will ooze out at once.

3 The factory drum-brake backing plate needs to be removed to make room for the new Baer system. The only way to get the backing plate off is to get the axles out of the way first. Once they're out, four fine-thread bolts hold the backing plate to the axle flange. You don't have to pull the original drum-brake system apart to get the backing plate off the flange. You can leave the brakes intact and remove them as one complete system.

4 The Baer backing plate comes with a drum-brake-style parking brake assembly and an integral caliper mount. With the caliper mount positioned to the rear of the truck, this can be installed using your original backing plate hardware or new fine-thread 3/8-inch Grade-8 hardware. Torque to 45 ft-lbs. After that, the axles can be reinstalled.

5 With the backing plates in place, the next step is to reinstall both axles, both C-clips, the center cross-shaft, and the cross-shaft retaining bolt. Then, the rear cover can be reinstalled.

71

CHAPTER 5

Installing the Baer Pro+ Rear Brake System *continued*

6 As with the front, Baer's brake rotors have a left and a right, and they're clearly marked, so you can't get this wrong. Once the rotor is in place, three lug nuts (each snugged up hand-tight) hold it flush.

7 The brake backing plate and caliper mount assemble with room for shims between the backing plate and the mounting bolt (as shown), which is where you adjust the caliper to ride centered over the rotor. This is Baer's Veri-Slide caliper, which Baer developed specifically for C-clip-style axles. These mounts allow the caliper to float with the axle, which makes for quiet, reliable use in this application.

8 With the brake pads removed, the caliper installs next using the Allen-head hardware from the kit. As with the front, it's time to measure, but the Veri-Slide system changes the process slightly. The key is to maintain 0.020-inch clearance between the caliper and the rotor at all times.

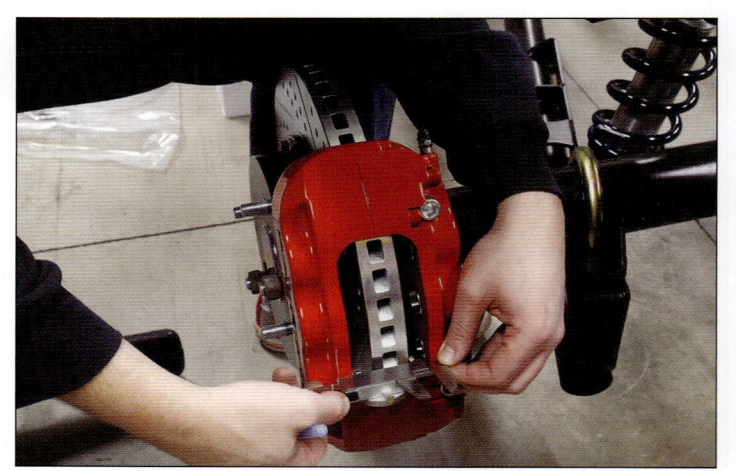

9 Push the axle in all the way and pull the caliper out as far as it will go. Then, measure the upper and lower inboard area between the rotor and the caliper. Pull the axle out and push the caliper in on its sliders, and then measure the outboard upper and lower sections. Subtract the inner upper number from the outer upper number, divide by two, and that's your shim pack for the upper bolt. Do the same math for the lower, and you'll be in the right ballpark to center the caliper on the rotor.

BRAKES AND STEERING

10 After you've installed the shims between the caliper mount and the backing plate and you've verified that the caliper is centered and has at least 0.020 clearance from the rotor at all times, put some thread locker and a final torque (85 ft-lbs) on the caliper-mount bolts.

11 After reinstalling the brake pads inside the caliper, torque the caliper in place on its bracket. In this case, the caliper bolt torque specification is 75 ft-lbs. All that's left is to hook up the supplied brake lines.

Master Cylinder

The final piece of any brake system puzzle is the hydraulic piece. If you're using OEM-style components from your truck or from another GM rig, there's nothing wrong with using a factory-style master cylinder.

If you're planning on any brake parts replacement, that master should be one of the first things on your list because they wear over time and can leak both internally and externally. Be sure to get the proper unit for your rig, as they did change based on the year and on the truck configuration.

Swapping to discs in the rear also means you'll need to ditch the original proportioning valve (the box mounted under the master cylinder) because all the original units are calibrated for increased pressure to the rear to operate drum brakes. Leaving an OEM unit in place with discs in the rear will cause your rear discs to lock up before your fronts, as the original drums that the system was designed for require more pressure to operate. In addition, GM set up its systems to apply rear brake pressure slightly sooner than front brakes for better driving dynamics. An adjustable proportioning valve is an ideal solution, as it allows the driver to dial in the desired amount of braking bias to the front versus the rear regardless of the system used.

While OEM parts work well with OEM brakes, I always recommend

Baer's Remaster is a direct replacement for GM factory units offered in 15/16-inch, 1-inch, and 1 1/8-inch bore for both power and manual applications. This is a machined billet-aluminum piece that's been specifically engineered for a proper balance between pressure and volume. This one is fitted with Baer's optional adjustable proportioning valve, which allows for adjustment of the front/rear braking bias.

CHEVY/GMC TRUCKS 1967–1972: HOW TO BUILD & MODIFY

CHAPTER 5

upgrading hydraulics to match components. Wilwood and Baer both offer their own hydraulic systems to match their brake components. Baer's Remaster is engineered to work with their big brake kits and features billet aluminum construction, three different bore sizes for power and manual applications, and great overall balance for a firm pedal feel and precise action.

Steering

Your truck's steering is the component you'll probably use the most, so it deserves a good look and possibly an upgrade over the stock 4-or-more turns that it had from lock to lock when new.

Every GM truck from this era came with a frame-mounted steering box connected to each spindle via center link, a Pitman arm (steering-box side), and an idler arm (passenger's side) with both inner and outer tie-rod ends. The system worked well, but with so many moving pieces inside the steering box and within the linkage, there's a lot of places that play can sneak in, which will make an old truck drive like an old truck.

GM trucks came with two different styles of steering: power assist and manual. How this was accomplished changed over the years, or more specifically, in 1968, when GM stopped using a complex and leak-prone ram-style power-steering assist and replaced it with an integral power-steering box. That style of steering was the standard for the remainder of the run of this bodystyle.

Otherwise, every C10 and C20 used basically the same style of steering setup. The nice thing about all this is that you can, with some exceptions, swap in a newer steering box with an upgraded ratio, and it will bolt in place of your original steering box with little other modification needed.

Few upgrades bring as much satisfaction as going from a loose 4-plus-turn box to something with a much quicker ratio.

Upgraded Steering Boxes

Many options are available when it comes to steering-box upgrades from remanufactured Saginaw boxes to more modern redesigned units. The key is to know what you're looking for.

Truck steering boxes mount on the outside of the frame rail, which

This original manual steering box on my 1967 C20 was never very tight from the factory, and years of use did it no favors. Even an original power box (offered 1968-and-up) isn't likely in the best of shape, so an upgrade is likely in order.

TECH TIP

Cheap Steering-Box Swaps

What should you look for in a stock-style power box for your C10? Squarebody trucks (1973–1987) used an updated version of the same style of steering box that was used in the earlier trucks. Trucks built from 1973–1978 share the same 3/4-inch input shaft as the 1969–1972 trucks, which make these direct bolt-ins. These boxes have 3.5-turns from lock to lock and feature a variable ratio, which makes them handle better on the highway than some direct-ratio boxes. They're relatively easy to find in wrecking yards or as new or rebuilt units.

Later boxes from the square era (1979 and newer) had a larger input shaft and require a different rag joint for your earlier C10. After 1980, they featured metric O-ring fittings at the power-steering-line connections, so keep that in mind.

If you're looking for a better option than a rebuilt stock box, CPP's 500-series box is worth a look. This is a 14:1 box that bolts into the factory location and is designed to take the slop out of your steering setup. These are available as both new and rebuilt units. (Photo Courtesy Classic Industries)

74　CHEVY/GMC TRUCKS 1967–1972: HOW TO BUILD & MODIFY

BRAKES AND STEERING

is opposite of their car counterparts. The stock-style box with this proper mount casting is known as a Saginaw Type 708, which was used in a variety of models. They're easy to find in wrecking yards and online in remanufactured and new versions. Keep in mind that you get what you pay for, so beware of cheap rebuilds.

Rack and Pinion Upgrades

Several companies make kits that retrofit modern steering racks into the original C10 and C20 frame. This helps sharpen the steering feel and the truck's reaction to input to make your rig feel a lot less like a truck and a lot more like a sports car.

In general, these conversion systems use a heavy steel bracket designed to bolt in place where the original steering's center link and Pitman arm/idler arm were, which then mounts a modern rack and pinion where it can mesh with your factory or aftermarket spindles.

Steering racks are a significant improvement for a few reasons. First, they're lightweight and compact. They also offer reduced friction over a stock box-and-linkage setup, and they have fewer moving parts (so there's less to go wrong).

The only downside is the cost, as well as varied quality in the kits offered today. Ideally, if going this route, you'll want a nice, well-engineered, heavy bracket that will resist motion and wandering. You'll also want a quality rack and not something rebuilt. You also need to verify that the rack you choose will clear all the other under-hood components, including the engine's oil pan and the exhaust system as well as any large sway bars that you may have installed. You'll likely need to change your steering column to match, as most racks use small U-joints and rods with set screws to connect the steering shaft to the rack. All of this will require some custom work, so keep that in mind.

Many of these kits have solved some of these problems for you. Flaming River's system, for example, comes with a steering column and all the required parts for installation, which takes a lot of the guesswork out of the swap. As with a steering box, racks are available in a number of different ratios and your choice of manual or power assist.

Converting a C20 into a Corner Carver

The factory steering box in my C20 might have been good enough for hauling hay bales on a flatbed out in the country, but it wasn't up to snuff for an LS-swapped overdrive-equipped C10 on coilovers with 20s and big brakes. This truck needed something better. Being that it was a C20 with some heavy-duty parts and the aforementioned aftermarket 10-level pieces, I had to get creative to make it all work. Here's what I did.

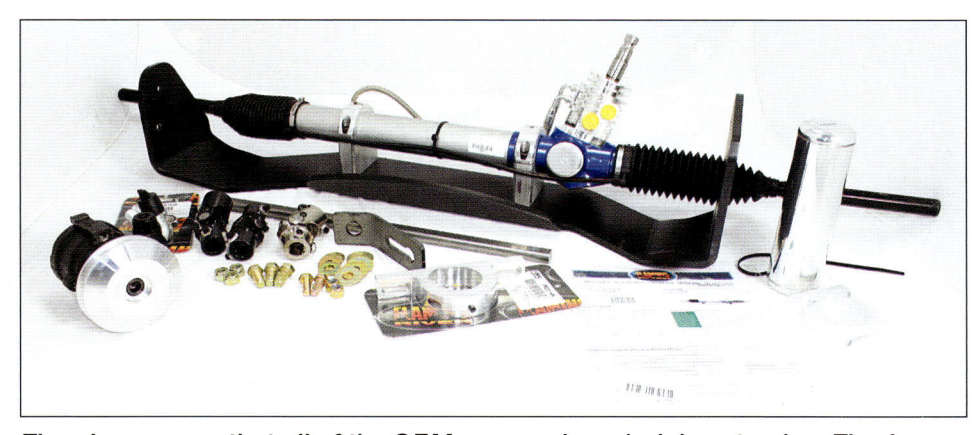

There's a reason that all of the OEMs use rack-and-pinion steering. They're compact and offer sharp response compared to the more complex steering linkage systems. They also save a lot of weight. This system is for C10s (complete with all the parts needed for installation) from Flaming River. (Photo Courtesy Flaming River)

Steering Ratios

If you've been looking at upgraded steering gears for a C10 or C20, you've likely seen them listed by their steering ratio (15:1, 14:1, or 12:1) instead of the 3- or 4-turn nomenclature you'll hear from your friends at your local cruise-in. What does this mean?

It's simple. The first number is the number of degrees needed at the steering wheel to turn the truck's tire 1 degree from center. For example, in a 12:1 ratio system, it takes 12 degrees of steering-wheel motion off center to turn the wheels 1 degree from center.

As you can imagine, the lower the first number, the faster the truck will respond to steering input. ■

Mounting the Steering Box

1 Trucks built in 1967 are unique in a few ways, but one of the more unfortunate is that they don't have the proper frame dimple for integrated power-steering boxes. Upgrading the steering requires making clearance in the frame, which you can do by heating it with a torch and massaging it with a large hammer.

2 With the proper clearance made, Borgeson's (part number 800132) Street & Performance–series steering box can bolt up using new hardware. The original manual box only fastened to the frame with three bolts, while the new box uses four. All of them are already drilled, so this is a bolt-on affair.

3 If you're swapping to power steering, you'll need a power-steering Pitman arm, which is easy to source from just about anywhere. This one is Moog part number K6131. There's one part for 1/2- and 3/4-ton 1968-and-up applications, so this is a no-brainer.

4 My C20 had heavy-duty steering components from the factory. Both the diameter and taper of the tie-rods and idler arm were larger than comparable C10 components, but that doesn't mean the C20 center link/drag link won't work here. Mine was in good shape, so I elected to reuse it.

5 Both C10 and C20 trucks used the same tie-rod adjusting sleeves from 1967–1970 (Moog part number ES350S), so all I had to do was use C20 inner tie-rod ends (Moog part number ES358R), new sleeves, and C10 outer tie-rod ends (Moog part number ES350L) to interface with the 1967–1970-spec CPP modular spindles from the RideTech suspension kit. The other piece of the puzzle is a C20-spec idler arm (AC Delco part number 45C1081).

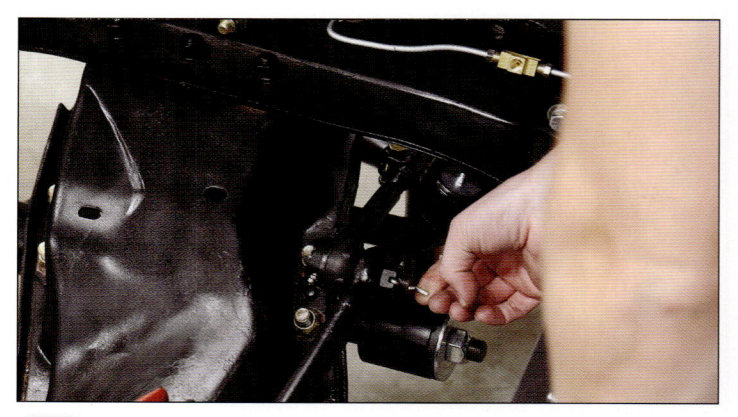

6 All that's left is to tighten the castle nuts, install cotter pins to lock them in place, and roughly set the toe using the new adjuster sleeves. That's all it takes to set up a decent steering system for a C20-turned-C10.

CHAPTER 6

ENGINE BASICS

One of the keys to success for the 1967–1972 GM trucks was a wide range of available engines. Everything from a gas-sipping straight six to a big-block 402 was available at one time or another under the hood of these rigs. That made these trucks flexible and well adapted to a variety of tasks from the factory, and it makes them easy to customize today.

The engine compartment on these rigs is large. It had to fit everything GM offered, which makes installing a wide range of engines possible here. If you have the right mounts, just about any engine from GM's arsenal will slide under the hood and bolt in place.

If you have one of these trucks, you likely have a small-block Chevy under the hood, as they were made in large numbers with both 327s and 350s throughout the era. That's good, but keep in mind that any engine under the hood of a 1967–1972 GMC or Chevrolet has already put in many years of work. You'll likely need to tear into it to make it perform the way that it really should. Still, there aren't many engines that are easier to work on than a small-block, except for maybe an LS, but we'll get to that in a second. The payoff to freshening or hopping up a small-block is worth the time and money spent.

GM truck engine compartments are big enough to fit everything from inline sixes to the biggest GM big-block. In the case of this truck, it's a 6.2L supercharged Mopar Hemi from a Hellcat.

The small-block may be an old design, but that doesn't mean it's not still hot. GM continues to offer ultimate versions as crate engines, complete with roller camshafts and a range of performance options. The best part is that they come with a warranty if you buy from GM.

CHEVY/GMC TRUCKS 1967–1972: HOW TO BUILD & MODIFY

CHAPTER 6

One of the nice things about GM engine architecture is the interchangeability. This late-model 427 shares the same basic dimensions with the 396 or 402, which means it will bolt in place inside any C10 or 20 with the proper big-block mounts.

This 292 may seem about as basic as it gets, but the base-level 250 was even smaller. The 292 is the more desirable of the two inline-six engines thanks to the mountains of torque that it delivered.

While these rigs are considered collectible, they were intended to be trucks and not the muscle rigs that many consider them to be today. Low-speed grunt was favored over the big power seen in contemporary muscle cars. Even the factory big-blocks in these trucks were fitted with small-port heads designed to make low-RPM torque rather than all-out horsepower. Even a minty original with low miles could benefit from a few performance modifications for modern use.

These trucks were built just before the smog era, so you won't find any emissions controls here, except for possibly a smog pump on California rigs. For most of us, the lack of federal or state restrictions means that we can go as wild as we want with traditional engine builds or with modern, cleaner-burning computer-controlled V-8s designed for maximum power and good economy. The sky (and your budget) is really the limit here.

Available Engines

Before we get into what a builder can do, we need to take a quick look at what you might find under the hood of one of these trucks. GM used a variety of engines here, depending on what the customer needed and the year the truck was manufactured.

Inline Six

GM offered two different straight six engines from 1967 to 1972: The 250-ci inline six and the 292-ci inline six. The 250 was the third evolution of GM's 6-cylinder platform. It was introduced in 1966 and used through 1985 in base-level trucks. While these engines aren't spectacularly powerful, they are simple and reliable. They make 155 hp with a single 1-barrel carburetor. The RPO code for this engine is L22.

The 292 featured a slightly taller engine-block deck height and a revised passenger-side engine mount that was shifted ahead of the fuel pump. These engines are known for having a lot of torque on demand and are basically bulletproof. If a six is what you want, a 292 is what you need. However, they tend to use more fuel, considering their longer stroke and larger bore over the 250. They were available throughout 1967–1972 production. The RPO code for the 292 is L25.

V-6

If you run across a strange-looking V-series engine under the hood of a GMC, you've found one of two types of 60-degree V-6s made for truck use in the 1960s. These units came in two different sizes in half-ton and 3/4-ton rigs: 305 ci and 351 ci. In both cases, these engines are known for stump-pulling torque, but they don't offer much in the way of higher-RPM capabilities, and there aren't many parts available for them today. If you have a running example, chances are good that it will continue running with basic periodic maintenance.

78 CHEVY/GMC TRUCKS 1967–1972: How to Build & Modify

ENGINE BASICS

These are true truck engines in just about every sense. They are designed to work and pull heavy things. They can be hopped up slightly, but it will be cheaper to swap in a small-block that makes more power.

The 305 was GMC's standard truck engine up until 1970 and made 170 hp and 277 ft-lbs of torque. The larger 351 was only available in 1967 and 1968 and was rated at 220 hp and 320 ft-lbs of torque. Both were only found in GMCs.

V-8

V-8s came in several forms in these trucks, starting with a 283-ci V-8 offered in 1967 only as RPO L32. It featured a 2-barrel carburetor and made 175 hp, which was decent enough for the time, even if it seems yawn-worthy today. For 1968, it was dropped in favor of a 200-hp 307. In both of those years, a 327 was also available and offered as RPO L30. It made 220 hp in 1967 and 240 hp in 1968. That was the hot ticket to get, aside from the big-block 396 that also launched in 1968.

In 1969, GM added the 350 to the lineup as RPO LS9. This engine made 250 hp from the factory and was fitted with a Quadrajet 4-barrel carburetor. It became the go-to small-block almost immediately thanks to a great combination of light weight, reliability, and good power and torque delivery. The LS9 continued on beyond this era of truck, well into the square years. If you have one of these, you have a good basis for a build.

As for that 396, it was offered as RPO code L47 starting in 1968 and made 325 hp with a 4-barrel carb and cast-iron manifolds. These engines are tough and make fantastic torque, which is why they were well suited for truck use. They were only available from the factory in two-wheel-drive trucks. They're known gas hogs, but most owners don't care. Drive one and you probably won't care, either.

In 1970, GM changed its marketing slightly and called the L47 a "400" in both printed materials and truck badging. This engine is actually a 402, which is basically a 396-spec engine with a 0.030-inch overbore. Some enthusiasts swear that in 1970, GM still delivered 396 engines and called them "400s." Confused yet?

GM also offered a 400 small-block in 1970, which caused even more engine confusion among enthusiasts who aren't clear on the differences between big-blocks and small-blocks. Nonetheless, for big power, a big-block is a great starting point.

Common Power Upgrades

Before diving into power upgrades, consider which engine you have and its overall health. It doesn't make sense to try and fit modern aluminum heads on a tired 307 with low compression in a cylinder or two. The same thing is true for any 283 (healthy or not).

Generally speaking, it's always smarter to plan on an engine swap these days versus building one of the smaller V-8s. If you have a 283, 307, or 327, you'll get more bang for your buck by dropping in a 350, 383, or 406 than you would in rebuilding the original unit. Aftermarket parts for stroker small-blocks (built using the 400's longer stroke crank in a 350 block) have never been more affordable than they are today. Those engines can make a lot more power than the small-blocks that came from GM's factories from 1967–1972.

Summit Racing sells a variety of brand-new small-block 350s from

GM's ZZ6 Turn-Key is the ultimate development of a GM-built small-block, complete with aluminum 62-cc Fast Burn heads, LS-style beehive valve springs, hydraulic roller cam, forged rods and crank, 770-cfm Holley carburetor, and 9.72:1 compression. It's rated at 405 hp and 406 ft-lbs of torque direct from GM, and it comes with a warranty.

GM and other aftermarket sources with prices starting around $3,000. If you do the math on a legit engine build that includes all the proper steps and machine work, you'll find that price hard to beat. It also is a great basis for additional power upgrades.

Small- and big-block builders have more options for power today than ever before thanks to a variety of stroker kits, aftermarket blocks, high-lift cams, and great-flowing cylinder heads. The sky is the limit in terms of power production and the associated budget required. As they say, speed costs money. How fast do you want to go?

GM offered a number of engine options in these trucks, but for the sake of argument, I'll use the LS9 350 (introduced in 1969) as an upgrade example. Just about every upgrade I'm about to mention would work for any of GM's original V-8s.

Cylinder Heads

Torque may be king when it comes to hauling a load of firewood, but engines made to build a lot of off-idle torque don't like to rev and make a lot of horsepower, which limits tire-smoking high-revving fun.

Engines with smaller port designs tend to be more efficient at providing the kind of power and economy that trucks require, so that's what GM used most of the time in its trucks. A set of good, modern cylinder heads can really wake up the small-block in a C10 and make it drive more like the hot rod you want it to be.

GM's cast-iron Vortec heads are a great upgrade option, as are any of the aftermarket aluminum heads offered today. Companies such as AFR, Trick Flow, Dart, Edelbrock, GM Performance, and others have aluminum heads available with all types of runner sizes and port volumes to suit everything from towing to drag racing.

It's important to understand what the current compression ratio is when looking at a set of heads to install because the head's combustion-chamber volume has a lot to do with that number. In the case of an LS9, the factory rated it at 9.0:1 compression in 1969, complete with open-chamber 76-cc heads that used volume to keep the compression relatively low for truck use.

Lowering the combustion-chamber volume raises the compression, which helps an engine build power. Ditching the 76-cc heads for something with 64 cc's brings an LS9's compression to about 10.2:1, which helps add power. Compression is only part of the equation. Builders also need to consider the truck's intended use from street driver to all-out racer, and match the other parts accordingly.

Aluminum heads offer a range of benefits over cast-iron from weight savings to better heat dissipation. As modern castings, they tend to offer much improved flow characteristics. These heads are Edelbrock's basic E-210 heads for flat-tappet cams that feature large runners, revised exhaust ports, and bigger springs for high-lift cams. (Photo Courtesy Edelbrock)

Camshafts

A cam is the heart of an engine. If your C10 still has its original unit, I'm willing to bet it has a flat lobe or two.

Unfortunately, while the design GM used in its V-8s has been a solid setup for years, the EPA has eliminated many of the compounds within modern oils that allowed flat-tappet cams to survive. The basic design of a flat-tappet cam requires the proper oil. Without it, lifters will begin to wear into the camshaft lobe surface, which sends metal shavings through the engine and eventually kills lift at the valve.

Considering the low lift that an original truck V-8 cam had from the factory and the oiling problems created in the modern era, it's wise to consider a cam upgrade in a modern performance C10. The best plan is to upgrade to a roller-style camshaft, as that design solves the problem inherent in flat-tappet cams used with modern oils. Rollers allow for steeper ramp rates than flat-tappet cams and tend to last a lot longer. The only downside is cost, which is higher thanks to more complex pieces and other required parts, such as shorter pushrods, a cam button or retainer plate, bronze distributor gear, and fuel-pump pushrod.

Whatever design you choose, thousands of camshaft profiles are

ENGINE BASICS

Bang for the Buck: Vortec Heads

If you're using a 350 engine in a 1969-or-later C10, consider a Vortec head swap. In terms of power per dollar, there isn't much that can touch a set of Vortecs on an otherwise-stock or stock-ish engine.

These castings represented revolution in small-block head design when they were launched for the 1996 model year in GM trucks and vans. They were based on the LT1 heads used on the Impala SS but with a revised design for standard water flow engines. What really made them special was a tumble designed into the port. This helped swirl the mixture as it entered the combustion chamber to boost power numbers over just about all the GM heads that came before while using less timing and fuel.

The Vortec head is a fantastic bolt-on solution for otherwise stock small-block engines because it offers a smaller chamber design that helps bump up compression while featuring an improved port design for better flow. Since these were stock from the factory on GM trucks starting in 1996, they're still easy to find. (Photo Courtesy Classic Industries)

All of that sounds good, but the key for truck folks is chamber volume. Most 1960s and 1970s trucks featured large 76-cc chambers, which kept compression low with stock pistons. Vortecs have smaller chambers (typically around 64 cc), which will boost compression significantly over a set of stockers and offer better flow and an efficient chamber design.

The downsides are few. Vortec heads don't take a lot of cam lift in stock form, so lifts of 0.500 inch and below are recommended. High spring pressures will pull out the stock pressed-in rocker-arm studs. They also require a different intake manifold with 8 mounting bolts versus the original small-block's 12.

Vortec heads were used on small-block truck and van engines from 1996 to 2000, which means they're still easy to find in junkyards and are usually cheap. Look for casting numbers 906 and 062.

If you'd rather source a brand-new set, Summit Racing and Classic Industries both sell ready-to-run versions of the Vortec head for under $400 as of this writing. That's dirt cheap for a head that will just need to be bolted into place with no machine work or setup required.

Add in a decent cam with a modern profile, a new set of lifters, new rocker arms, and a new intake and carburetor, and you'll have a significant boost in power over stock for less than the cost of a new crate engine. ■

---

available for a variety of uses that range from towing performance to drag-strip glory. As with any internal engine component, camshafts are part of a package that must work together, so consider the other parts that you intend to use as well as how you plan to use the truck before selecting a camshaft. In fact, most custom cam grinders will ask for everything from your engine's static compression ratio to the rear tire diameter before making a recommendation on what to run. This isn't overkill. It's vital information needed to achieve the best possible result.

For those who are picking an off-the-shelf design for street-driven performance, it's wise to keep duration relatively conservative so that off-idle performance isn't adversely affected. Unless you have a high compression ratio, a loose converter, and a massive carburetor, you won't need the biggest grind on the list with the highest lift and longest duration. Running that massive cam will require other modifications such as rocker arms, valve springs, and more for it to live.

Cam selection for street use is usually a case of "less being more" with a cam well matched to the flow characteristics of the heads that are used as well as the compression ratio of the engine and its intended RPM

CHAPTER 6

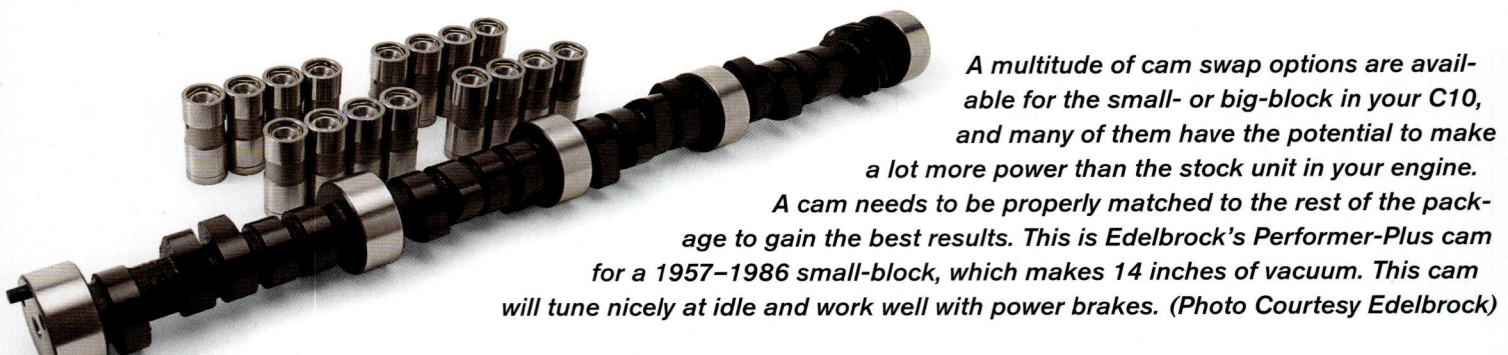

A multitude of cam swap options are available for the small- or big-block in your C10, and many of them have the potential to make a lot more power than the stock unit in your engine. A cam needs to be properly matched to the rest of the package to gain the best results. This is Edelbrock's Performer-Plus cam for a 1957–1986 small-block, which makes 14 inches of vacuum. This cam will tune nicely at idle and work well with power brakes. (Photo Courtesy Edelbrock)

range. If in doubt, contact Comp Cams, Crane, Lunati, Edelbrock, or Crower Cams and ask for advice before you buy.

Electronic Ignition

All trucks built from 1967 to 1972 came stock with breaker points ignition systems, which was perfectly suitable for the time. Of course, the world has moved on. Now, better options are available for an otherwise stock small-block or big-block from GM or elsewhere.

GM launched the high-energy ignition (HEI) system in 1975, which offered better performance over the older points systems. The HEI used a pickup coil and electronic ignition control module to create and control spark, and the system has been the go-to swap for years. An HEI system makes a truck that starts easier, burns less fuel, and requires less periodic maintenance over the original points systems.

HEI is probably the simplest and cheapest solution available for electronic ignition conversion, but be sure to find a decent OEM unit. Stay away from offshore pieces if you can, as they tend to have reliability issues.

Regardless of which HEI you source for your 350 or 396, keep in mind that HEIs were primarily used in the smog era, so they have wheezy advance curves from the factory that are controlled via a set of springs

If you want the benefits of electronic ignition without the looks of a modern distributor, a PerTronix Ignitor (part number 1181) is just the ticket. These use a Hall-effect integrated circuit to replace the old breaker points in the factory Delco distributor, so there's nothing to wear out, and the conversion is a quick and easy process that blends in under the hood. (Photo Courtesy PerTronix)

and centrifugal weights that advance as the RPM increases. Recurving an HEI to match other performance upgrades is key, and it generally only requires a spring swap to get all of the distributor's available advance in by 3,000 rpm or less.

Cammed Chevrolet V-8s tend to want somewhere in the range of 36 degrees of total timing as a starting point. The more lift and duration of the cam, the more timing it may need at idle to behave, especially with a carburetor. This can cause some trouble with stock-style HEIs that are set for 36 degrees of total advance. For builders who want to run more base timing for better idle characteristics with large cams (sometimes up to 20 or 22 degrees at idle), MSD offers its own version of an HEI that includes stop bushings to help keep total advance where it needs to be, even with increased base timing.

For those who plan to install an HEI, note that it requires 12-volt keyed ignition to run, and the stock coil wire in a C10 is a resistor wire that only provides 9 volts. Running a new keyed 12-volt wire is required for this upgrade to work. Most builders run a wire to the 12-volt keyed unfused source on the fuse block.

MSD, Accel, Mallory, PerTronix, FAST, and others offer a variety of ignition solutions for V-8 performance. The best route really depends on the other upgrades working as part of a package. For a generally stock LS9, a good GM-style HEI is a great place to start for a street driver, but anything with higher compression and more performance potential can benefit from an MSD capacitive-discharge system designed for multiple spark events.

CHEVY/GMC TRUCKS 1967–1972: HOW TO BUILD & MODIFY

ENGINE BASICS

Carburetors

If the cam is the heart of an engine, the carburetor is its brain. A carburetor has a tough job. It has to meter the proper amount of fuel for the engine in all conditions (from idle to full throttle), and it must control the engine's speed.

Many carburetor options are available, but the one you choose and its condition can really make or break the performance and drivability of your rig.

Quadrajet

From the factory, the go-to carburetor used in GM trucks of this era is the Rochester Quadrajet. These 4-barrel carburetors are fantastic street carburetors in factory applications. They feature small primaries and large secondaries that promote fuel economy and crisp power delivery when properly set up. In stock applications, a good, tuned low-mile Quadrajet is probably the best all-around carburetor for street use, even after decades on the job. In fact, I think they're the closest you can get to fuel injection in terms of drivability.

These carburetors use metering rods that can be swapped for different fuel-delivery characteristics, similar to what you'll find inside an Edelbrock or Carter aluminum 4-barrel (AFB) carburetor. While tuning one may not be as easy as an Edelbrock or Holley, they tend to stay in tune after they are set up. If you know which part numbers to look for, getting one properly calibrated isn't too tough, even on an engine with other aftermarket performance modifications. GM used Quadrajets on everything from 350s to LS5 454s, so they're suited for a wide range of different applications.

While the Quadrajet is known as a great all-around carburetor, it also has a bad reputation that is well-earned thanks to its basic construction. A Quadrajet isn't the easiest carburetor to disassemble and reassemble. These units are made of somewhat-soft material that can warp at the baseplate due to overtightening, which generally manifests as a vacuum leak after a rebuild. Fifty years after your C10 was built, you can bet your carburetor has been rebuilt at least once already.

In addition, these carburetors don't feature bushings where the primary and secondary throttle shafts run through the carburetor body. This means that over time, they'll wallow out and develop vacuum leaks that are hard to track down. This can lead to drivability issues that will have owners chasing their tails, which is why you'll often find an original Quadrajet rig fitted with an aftermarket carburetor instead of its original unit.

If you have a good-functioning Quadrajet, there's no reason to think you need to swap it for something else in terms of a performance boost. For most street-driven rigs with mild modifications, a Quadrajet will do the job and it will do it well. If you're in the market for one, be sure to look for a low-mileage example. NOS versions are available too, but they're usually expensive. You'd likely be able to buy a modern fuel-injection conversion setup for the price of a true NOS Quadrajet, so keep that in mind.

If you're determined to run a Quadrajet, be sure to use a copy of Cliff Ruggles's *How to Rebuild and Modify Rochester Quadrajet Carburetors*, which covers all the ins and outs of making a Quadrajet perform its best.

If you find yourself with a Quadrajet under the hood, never fear. When these carburetors are working the way they should, they're fantastic performers for daily use. Any bad experiences tend to come from adjustment issues or worn baseplates that allow unmetered air past the carburetor. Small primaries help with both response and fuel economy, which makes for great drivability.

Scan this QR code with your smartphone to buy *How to Rebuild & Modify Rochester Quadrajet Carburetors* (SA113) by Cliff Ruggles.

CHEVY/GMC TRUCKS 1967–1972: HOW TO BUILD & MODIFY

CHAPTER 6

Edelbrock AFB

It's a good bet that if your truck once had a Quadrajet with issues, it's now fitted with an Edelbrock 4-barrel AFB. These are great street carburetors that are designed after the Carter AFBs of the 1960s. The benefits here are numerous—from swappable rods and jets for dialing in a tune to gaskets that generally sit above the fuel level, which means fewer leaks. These carburetors are easy to set up and tune, and they generally stay in tune once they're set up. They may not make the same levels of power as a 4150-style Holley, but they make up for that with all-around usability and reliable performance. They're fantastic for use in dual-carburetor setups.

Edelbrock offers these carburetors in 600 cfm all the way up to 800 cfm, so regardless of the engine in your C10, there's an AFB that will fit. I like these for their ease of tuning. A rod and jet kit will provide a wide range of different tuning options for your engine, and the owner's manual comes with an easy-to-read chart that helps determine what changes you might need to make to come up with a better-running engine. For a stock 350, a 650 Edelbrock AFB is a fantastic choice for a no-nonsense all-around driver that needs to perform in a range of conditions.

For any aftermarket carburetor that's going on an engine that had a Quadrajet from the factory, going from a spread-bore carb (Quadrajet) to a square-bore carb (Edelbrock, Holley 4150/4160) requires an adapter plate or a new intake manifold to fit properly, so keep that in your budget. CarTech has you covered again with the book *How to Rebuild and Modify Carter/Edelbrock Carburetors* (SA130P) by Dave Emanuel.

Edelbrock's AFB carb is another common go-to for daily use, and they're great all-around carburetors for power and economy. These are easy to set up, service, and rebuild when the time comes. They also won't fuel stain your intake thanks to most of their gaskets being above the fuel level.

Scan this QR code with your smartphone to buy How to Rebuild and Modify Carter/Edelbrock Carburetors (SA130P) by Dave Emanuel.

Holley

If total performance is your goal, Holley is likely the answer. Holley has been building both OEM and aftermarket carburetors for decades. Its aftermarket performance carburetors are second to none in terms of adaptability and horsepower delivery.

Holley offers a carburetor for every engine from drag machines to daily drivers. The key, as with other engine components noted above, is to be realistic with your goals and to pick a proper carburetor to deliver the best performance possible. While the Holley 4150 design has more tuning options than a Quadrajet or Edelbrock, you can only do so much to tune a carburetor that's either too big or too small for the application or one that's not properly configured.

For a typical small-block, a 650-cfm carburetor from the Avenger series is a great choice. These are great street carburetors with available vacuum secondaries and electric chokes. For an all-out drag machine, bigger may be better. The HP series with swappable air bleeds is a better

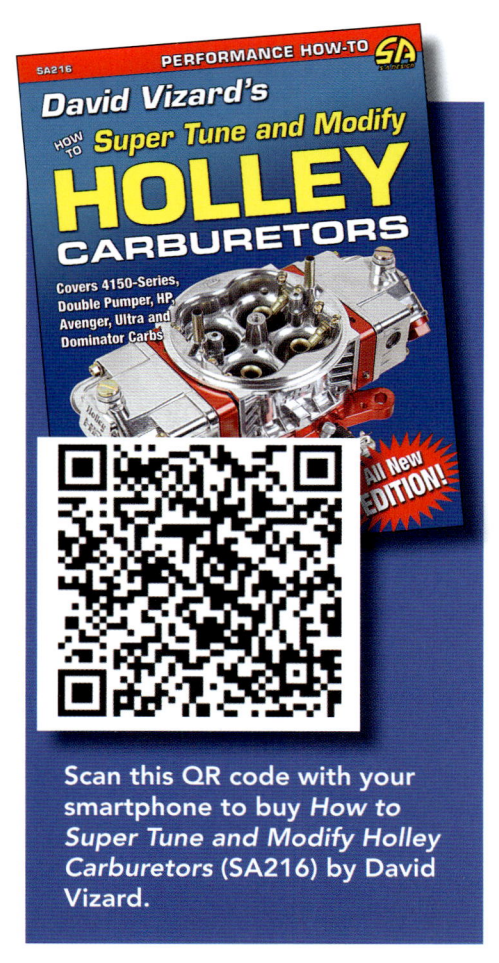

ENGINE BASICS

David Vizard's Super Tune and Modify Holley Carburetors

Scan this QR code with your smartphone to buy *How to Super Tune and Modify Holley Carburetors* (SA216) by David Vizard.

choice with even more tuning flexibility. If in doubt, contact Holley or one of its many vendors directly to ask for assistance. Be ready with all your engine's specs before you call.

In general, carburetors with mechanical secondaries are best suited for lighter vehicles with higher stall converters and more aggressive rear-end gearing. Carburetors with vacuum secondaries, which will come in more gradually and not create a bog under acceleration, are better suited for trucks and for cars that are heavier and geared for street applications. This is, however, just a guideline. There's a lot to love about a good old Double Pumper Holley—everything but the fuel bill, that is.

David Vizard wrote the bible when it comes to rebuilding a Holley carburetor.

Fuel Injection

If the best in drivability and performance is your goal, a modern injection system is the tool you need. Over the past five years, the aftermarket has delivered some truly fantastic self-tuning systems that deliver all the drivability of OEM modern injection in a bolt-on package. There's a lot to like here as well as several options to consider.

Holley is the dominant force in modern injection systems for old cars and trucks. The company even offers a spread-bore Quadrajet-style electronic fuel injection (EFI) system that bolts to the factory intake of any 4-barrel-equipped 1967–1972 GM truck. If you want stock looks and modern convenience in your truck, this is a good place to start.

The Sniper range of electronic fuel-injection (EFI) units, both for spread-bore and square-bore applications, are more expensive than just about any carburetor setup, but they make up for that price by transforming the drivability of your classic rig into something more akin to a new Silverado pickup. This is done by including a range of other OEM-spec sensors and controllers that keep your engine running within a certain set of adjustable parameters. If you want your engine to start and settle into a stable, constant idle speed regardless of the situation, this is the direction for you.

If a modern engine swap isn't in the cards, an aftermarket injection system is a fantastic option, depending on how you want things to look under your hood.

Engine Swaps

Swapping the engine in a C10 may seem like a big job, but it's not nearly as challenging as you may think—provided that you come equipped with the proper components. For those of you eyeing a big-block in place of the stock 307 or 350 in your truck, note that you'll need to source the proper big-block engine-mount perches to be sure that the engine will fit properly.

The same is true for an LS or LT swap, but in those cases, you'll either build your own motor-mount solution or source something from one of the many aftermarket companies that specialize in fitting modern engines into vintage vehicles.

LS and LT Swaps

There's no denying the overall benefits of GM's modern pushrod V-8s. Both the LS and LT engines are

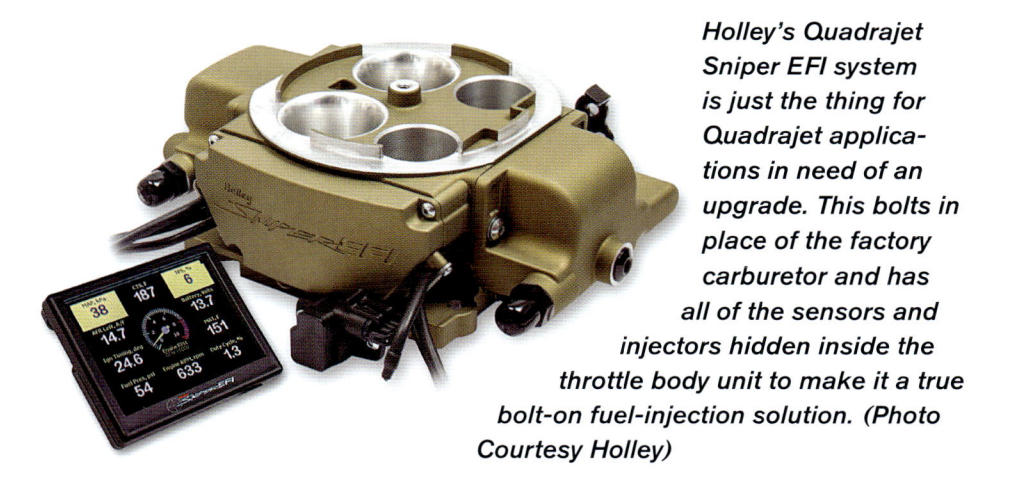

Holley's Quadrajet Sniper EFI system is just the thing for Quadrajet applications in need of an upgrade. This bolts in place of the factory carburetor and has all of the sensors and injectors hidden inside the throttle body unit to make it a true bolt-on fuel-injection solution. (Photo Courtesy Holley)

CHAPTER 6

Big-Block Swaps

Everyone loves a big-block in a C10, right? Swapping one into your truck requires a few special items that you should know about before you get started.

The main item, which is often overlooked until mid-swap, is the style of engine perches used. GM's small-block perches don't play nicely with a big-block two-wheel-drive application because the shape of the small-block mount was designed for Ram's Horn manifolds, which don't drop down below the cylinder head ahead of the motor mount. Big-blocks, on the other hand, have manifolds that do hang down and hit the small-block perches. Headers do too, so you'll need a set of big-block-style perches to fit the big-block engine. Note that they use the front holes in the frame versus the small-block perches that use the rear holes.

Big-block motor mounts are different than small-block motor mounts, but either will work in a big-block application.

Beyond that, a big-block will need a completely new accessory drive system because the small-block parts, including the brackets for the alternator and the power-steering system (if equipped) are different for big-blocks. The key here is to find a complete system, perhaps in a donor truck, as individual brackets can be hard to source from the aftermarket. There's no reason not to use parts from a later rig if you can find them, but it's a better option to go with a modern serpentine setup if it's in your budget.

Big-block engine perches are different than small-block units thanks to the way GM chose to run its exhaust systems. The days of scouring junkyards looking for a set for your two-wheel-drive big-block swap are over, as several aftermarket companies now sell reproductions. These (part number T82245) are available at Classic Industries. (Photo Courtesy Classic Industries)

Big-block trucks use a different fan shroud than small-block trucks with three-core and smaller radiators, so factor that into your plan if you plan on running a mechanical cooling fan. The radiator itself should be upgraded, as a big-block requires additional capacity.

If you're using the original transmission, verify that the big-block flexplate is drilled properly for the small-block torque converter (in automatic applications). Don't wait until your engine is installed to check. ■

fundamentally better in every way to the V-8s that came before. You can't beat the reliability, performance, and economy that they bring to the table. There's a good reason most of the custom C10s you see today are fitted with a 5.3, 6.0, or 6.2 LS- or LQ-style engine from the 2000s and beyond. They make a lot of power and are incredibly durable.

GM built millions of LS-based engines starting in the late 1990s, which means that they're easy to find in salvage yards today and relatively cheap. There's huge power potential here thanks to a booming aftermarket that's feeding the engine-swap craze. Everything from cams to heads and intakes are easily available for these engines, and all

If you're looking for both reliable power and great economy, there's nothing better than an LS or LT swap. They may seem like a dime a dozen these days, but there's a good reason for that. This is a complete 5.3L LS V-8 engine as offered by GM Performance. This one has the truck-style intake manifold that will clear a 1967–1972 GM hood with room to spare.

ENGINE BASICS

the typical power adders apply here. In fact, they work better than they do on your average small- or big-block.

In 2014, GM launched an all-new Gen V V-8 known as the LT, which was based on the LS platform but featured more improvements in cylinder head design, a stronger bottom end, variable valve timing, cylinder deactivation, and direct injection that all provide better power delivery than what's possible in an LS. All these upgrades provide a boost in power over a comparable LS engine but with added complexity in setting up a fuel system to support direct injection.

Regardless of which engine you like more (LS or LT), this is all good news for a truck builder today because it means there are many options available for reliable, modern power to fit under the hood of a truck project.

Junkyard LS and LT Engine Spotter's Guide

LS ENGINES

4.8L Engines

Name	Years	Horsepower	Vehicles	Other Details
LR4	1999–2007	255 hp in 1999, 270–285 hp thereafter	Chevrolet/GMC vans, 1500 trucks, and Tahoe/Yukon	VIN code "V," cast-iron block, and aluminum heads
LY2	2007–2009	260–295 hp (the only Gen IV truck engine without variable valve timing)	Chevrolet/GMC vans, Chevrolet/GMC trucks, and Suburban/Yukon	VIN code "C," cast-iron block, and aluminum heads
L20	2010–2017	260–302 hp	Chevrolet/GMC trucks and vans	VIN code "A," cast-iron block, and aluminum heads

5.3L Engines

Name	Years	Horsepower	Vehicles	Other Details
LM7/L59	1999–2007	270–295 hp	Chevrolet/GMC 1500 trucks, Chevrolet Avalanche, Tahoe/Yukon, and Suburban	VIN code "T," cast-iron block, and aluminum heads
LM4	2003–2005	290 hp	Chevrolet Trailblazer, Isuzu Ascender, Buick Envoy XL, Chevrolet SSR, and Buick Rainier	VIN code "P," aluminum block and heads
L33	2005–2007	310 hp	Chevrolet/GMC 1500 trucks	VIN code "B," aluminum block and heads
LMF	2010–2014	301 hp	Chevrolet/GMC vans with AWD and the 4-speed transmission	VIN code "4," cast-iron block and aluminum heads, no active fuel management
LH6	2005–2009	302–315 hp	Chevrolet Trailblazer and Trailblazer EXT, GMC Envoy XL, Isuzu Ascender, Buick Rainier, GMC Envoy Denali, Saab 9-7X 5.3i, and Chevrolet/GMC trucks	VIN code "M" and aluminum block and heads
LY5	2007–2009	315–320 hp (LMG is a Flex Fuel–capable version, VIN code "0")	Chevrolet Avalanche, Chevrolet/GMC Trucks, Chevrolet Suburban, and GMC Tahoe	VIN code "J," cast-iron block, and aluminum heads
LC9	2007–2014	302–315 hp	Chevrolet Avalanche, Chevrolet/GMC trucks, and Chevrolet Suburban/GMC Yukon	VIN code "3" (2007–2011), VIN code "7" (2012–2014), aluminum block and heads
LH8	2008–2010	300 hp (LH9 is a variant with variable valve timing, VIN code "P")	Hummer H3 Alpha and Chevrolet Colorado/GMC Canyon	VIN code "L," aluminum block and heads

CHAPTER 6

5.7L Engines

Name	Years	Horsepower	Vehicles	Other Details
LS1	1997–2005	305–325 hp	Chevrolet Corvette, Chevrolet Camaro, Pontiac Firebird, and Pontiac GTO	VIN code "G," aluminum block and heads
LS6	1999–2004	385–405 hp	Chevrolet Corvette Z06	VIN code "S," aluminum block and heads

6.0L Engines

Name	Years	Horsepower	Vehicles	Other Details
LQ4	1999–2007	300–330 hp	Chevrolet Suburban, Chevrolet/GMC 2500 trucks, Chevrolet/GMC 3500 trucks, Chevrolet Express van, GMC Yukon, and Hummer H2	VIN code "U," cast-iron block and cast-iron heads (1999–2000) with long-style crank, aluminum heads (2001–2007)
LQ9	2002–2007	345 hp	Cadillac Escalade, Chevrolet Silverado SS, Silverado HO, and VortecMAX trucks	VIN code "N," cast-iron block, and aluminum heads
LS2	2005–2009	400 hp	Chevrolet Corvette, Chevrolet Trailblazer SS, Pontiac GTO, and Saab 9-7X Aero	VIN code "U," aluminum block and heads
L76	2006–2009	376 hp (Car versions feature more compression and a smaller cam but only make 370 hp due to the truck versions featuring a long-runner intake. L77 is a Flex Fuel version offered in Holden-sourced Chevrolet Caprice police cars, VIN code "2")	Pontiac G8 GXP and Chevrolet/GMC trucks	VIN code "Y," aluminum block and heads
LY6	2007–2013	361 hp (Similar to LQ4 spec with variable valve timing, rectangle-port heads. L96 is identical other than Flex Fuel capability)	Chevrolet and GMC HD trucks and 3/4-ton Suburban/Yukon XL	VIN code "K," cast-iron block, and aluminum heads
LFA	2008–2009	332 hp (LZ1 is an upgraded version with Active Fuel Management and variable valve timing, VIN code "J")	Chevrolet and GMC pickup/Suburban hybrid	VIN code "5," aluminum block and heads

6.2L Engines

Name	Years	Horsepower	Vehicles	Other Details
L92	2007–2008	403 hp (L9H is Flex Fuel capable, VIN code "2")	GMC 1500 Sierra Denali, Yukon Denali, Cadillac Escalade, and Chevrolet Tahoe LTZ	VIN code "8," aluminum block, and rectangle-port heads
LS3	2008–2017	426–436 hp	Chevrolet Corvette, Pontiac G8 GXP, Chevrolet Camaro SS (manual), and Chevrolet SS	VIN code "W," aluminum block, and rectangle-port heads
L99	2010–2015	400 hp	Chevrolet Camaro SS (automatic)	VIN code "J," aluminum block, and rectangle-port heads
LS9	2009–2013	638 hp	Chevrolet Corvette ZR1	VIN code "T," aluminum block, rectangle-port heads, and supercharged
LSA	2009–2015	556–580 hp	Chevrolet Camaro ZL1 and Cadillac CTS-V	VIN code "P," aluminum block, rectangle-port heads, and supercharged

ENGINE BASICS

7.0L Engines				
Name	Years	Horsepower	Vehicles	Other Details
LS7	2006–2015	505 hp	Chevrolet Corvette Z06	VIN code "E," aluminum block and heads, and dry-sump oiling

LT ENGINES

5.3L Engines				
Name	Years	Horsepower	Vehicles	Other Details
L83/L84	2014–present	355 hp	Chevrolet Silverado/GMC Sierra and Tahoe/Yukon	VIN code "C," cast-iron block, aluminum heads, and direct injection

6.2L Engines				
Name	Years	Horsepower	Vehicles	Other Details
LT1	2014–present	455 hp	C7 Corvette and Camaro SS	Aluminum block and heads, 11.5:1 compression
LT2	2020–present	490 hp	C8 Corvette	Similar to the LT1 but revised for mid-engine applications
L86/L87	2014–present	420 hp	Chevrolet Silverado/GMC Sierra and Tahoe/Yukon	VIN code "J," a revised LT1 with lower compression for truck use
LT4	2015–present	650 hp	Corvette Z06, Cadillac CTS-V, and Camaro ZL1	An updated version of the LS9 with direct injection, cylinder deactivation, and variable valve timing, fitted with an Eaton TVS Supercharger
LT5	2019	755 hp	Corvette ZR1	Utilizes both direct injection and port injection coupled with a 2.6L Eaton TVS supercharger

6.6L Engines				
Name	Years	Horsepower	Vehicles	Other Details
L8T	2020-present	401 hp	HD-series Chevrolet and GMC trucks and vans	Iron block, same bore as the L86 but with longer stroke for reliable torque

You can source an LS or LT in a variety of places from your local wrecking yard to Craigslist or Facebook Marketplace. It's wise to only purchase an engine you've heard and seen run. Unless there's a written guarantee, know that you may run into an issue with your new engine. It's no fun to have to tear into an engine you thought was turn-key to repair unexpected damage.

Selecting an LS or LT

What's the right engine for you? In general, bigger is better when it comes to LS power, but with more cubic inches comes a higher cost of entry. Once you figure in all the other components you'll need to buy (engine mounts, an oil pan, headers or manifolds, accessories, an engine control unit [ECU], fueling, etc.), you might price yourself into a corner by going bigger out of the gate.

All LS engines feature the same external dimensions from the 4.8 to the 7.0, which makes installing them relatively easy and swapping from one to another even easier.

The most common LS engine is the 5.3. These are available in pretty much any wrecking yard in the US. There are many variants of the engine, including all-aluminum versions. These are popular for forced-induction applications because they're usually relatively low compression and cheap enough that they can be replaced without too much cost after a boost-related boom.

For naturally aspirated applications, the cast-iron 6.0 LQ4 and LQ9 are fantastic options for performance builds for relatively little money compared to an aluminum LS3 or LT1.

The all-aluminum LS1 might be tempting to consider, but they're getting more expensive and have relatively thin cylinder sleeves that don't allow much more than a hone. GM considered these blocks one-time-use items, so keep that in mind before paying good money for a bare LS1 block that needs to be cleaned up.

If a cast-iron version of an LS is your goal, expect to pay anywhere

GM's LS1, the engine that started the LS craze, is a great performer, but it has some limitations, including a very low tolerance for any sort of overbore. While there are benefits to some of the cast-iron truck engines, the LS1 is lightweight and just as durable as the other LS/LQ engines.

Build Theory: A Stout LS

An LS engine is only as good as the components that make it function. To that end, I put together a streetable combination of add-on parts for my LS 364/450 crate engine that will provide great power and long life with room for future improvement.

For LS power, the key is airflow. I elected to run Holley's Hi-Ram intake (part number 300-117) along with a 102-mm Holley Sniper throttle body (part number 860002-1). Handling the fueling is a set of 42-pound EV1-style injectors (part number 522-428) that provide enough fuel for future growth. On the exhaust side, long-tube headers scavenge the fumes (Hooker part number BH13243), while a Terminator X ECU for the 24x reluctor and EV1-style injectors handle all the computing (part number 550-903).

These are basic, proven components that are available in different configurations and sizes, which makes them great for any LS swap from a 4.8 to a 6.2. ■

---

from $1,000 to $2,500 for a used, running example with no issues and good oil pressure. Prices have been climbing on LS engines, so if you find a good one for a reasonable price, you might want to grab it, even if a swap isn't something you intend on doing right away.

All the normal checks apply here. Look at the engine's oil, check the coolant, and pull the plugs to look for visible indications of oil consumption that might suggest worn rings or valve guides.

Intake Manifolds

LS power is all about airflow, and to make the most of what the engine can provide, it's important to have an intake manifold that's matched to the kind of performance you're looking to build.

There are generally two types of intake manifolds: long runner and short runner. In basic terms, the longer the intake runner, the more torque an engine will make and peak power will come in earlier. Short-runner engines tend to build less torque but more overall horsepower with a higher peak-power RPM potential.

If you ever wondered why the stock GM truck intake was so tall, now you know. The longer runners provide more torque for towing and hauling performance, which was more important to GM for trucks than peak horsepower.

Scan this QR code with your smartphone to buy How to Build Big-Inch GM LS-Series Engines (SA203P) by Stephen Kim.

Scan this QR code with your smartphone to buy How to Rebuild GM LS-Series Engines (SA147) by Chris Werner.

ENGINE BASICS

In terms of stock GM manifolds, most will swear by the plastic LS6 manifold, which is still available in the aftermarket as a stock-style replacement part. There are plenty of dyno operators who say that the long-runner truck intake is just as effective at building horsepower and torque, and for the money, it's the key for decent power. In car applications, fitting one under the hood can be a challenge, but C10 owners don't have that problem. There's plenty of room for the taller intake under the hood of these trucks.

Beyond that, Holley is known for its Ram-style intakes offered in everything from low to high configurations with several stops in between. It even offers a dual-plenum intake that offers the best of both worlds: long runners and divorced plenums for good distribution and off-idle power that carries all the way to redline.

It's hard to go wrong with any of these options, but you'll get the best bang for the buck by sticking with an intake that's tuned to deliver power in concert with the selected cam.

The Hi-Ram has become a performance staple in the LS world thanks to its long runners and modular design. Holley offers the same basic design in several heights and several top configurations to suit a variety of needs from carburetor-style throttle bodies to side-entry units.

Going Big on LS Power

When it comes to building big LS power, more options are available today than ever before. So, should you leave your LS swap stock or not?

LS engines are fantastic performers even in stock trim, but there is a lot of performance left on the table when running stock-style manifolds and relatively small lift/duration stock camshafts. You can do better.

The first step to upgrade any LS engine should be a cam swap, as that's easily the best place to pick up gains over a stock engine. The LS cylinder head, even in stock form, is a great flowing head out of the box. A good cam will help make use of the flow characteristics that GM designed. For the most basic stock-style upgrade, look to an LS6- or LS9-style cam and matching valve springs, but even those are easily outdone by a custom grind that's designed to work with your combination. If you have room for only one upgrade in your LS, that's where you should direct your attention.

Summit Racing has complete stroker kits available for LS engines that include everything you need (other than the machine work) to turn your 5.3, 5.7, or 6.0 into a more potent powerhouse than it was from the factory. Another option is to boost your LS with a supercharger or turbo. Both are very common in the LS world, and both will net a significant amount of power over stock.

If you're in the market for LS performance, it pays to get your hands on a copy of Chris Werner's *How to Rebuild GM LS-Series Engines* and Stephen Kim's *How to Build Big-Inch GM LS-Series Engines*. Both provide great detail on the options available for big power from your LS engine and the methods to do the job right the first time. ■

Looking to go big? Stroker kits are available for most LS engines. If you're already planning a rebuild, you might find that the benefits they provide outweigh the added cost of adding in a longer stroke and more cubic inches of displacement. These pistons boost a standard 3.903-inch-bore LS1 block to a 383-ci monster. (Photo Courtesy Summit Racing)

CHEVY/GMC TRUCKS 1967–1972: HOW TO BUILD & MODIFY

CHAPTER 7

INSTALLING AN *LS* IN A *C10*

So, you've decided that LS or LT power is the way to go with your C10 project. That's a great decision. While the LS or LT is a compact, versatile performer, a few steps are required to get one to fit down between the frame rails of a 1967 to 1972 C10 or C20.

People have been swapping LS-based engines into just about everything since the engine was introduced in 1997. Thanks to those two-plus decades of engineering know-how from the aftermarket, everything you need to complete this task already exists. The days of needing to make your own motor mounts or transmission mount are over. That is, unless you like the challenge and have the materials and fabrication skills to make up your own set of mounts for less than the cost of buying a decent prefabricated setup.

As a C10 builder, you have more space than just about any other LS-swap project. These trucks have cavernous engine compartments, which means you'll have plenty of room to work and fit aftermarket components to your LS engine. The stock tall-style truck intakes fit fine under the C10 hood from this era, and so do turbochargers and superchargers. Pretty much anything is possible here thanks to the space available.

The overall popularity of LS power in classic trucks means there are many mount options available for C10s. Some of them are universal and adjustable, and some of them are application-specific. All of them will work, but you need to think carefully about the direction of your project before you buy. If possible, try to get all the mounts and associated parts from the same vendor.

Why? It's simple. While getting the engine bolted between the frame rails is vital, it's only the first step in the process. There are other things to consider from cooling to exhaust routing to transmission linkage and driveshaft length. All of these will change based on the placement of your engine and transmission. A kit that's been engineered to function

For my project, I elected to go with a crate engine direct from GM via Summit Racing. This is an all-new 6.0L LQ4-based engine with LS3-style square-port heads and an LS6 cam. The engine is sold as part number NAL-19370163 and is rated at 452 hp. It comes just as you see here without an intake or water pump. This is a fantastic base to start from and one of many options for crate LS power.

INSTALLING AN LS IN A C10

together in a C10 will help make sure that all of the components will clear the body and each other. That may not seem like a big deal when the truck's apart, but it will when that set of stainless headers you bought hit the crossmember because the engine isn't placed quite right. Various companies have been engineering solutions to these problems for a few years now, and it pays to use their knowledge.

Be smart about this on the front-end and you'll save a lot of time, and it will make your swap both cleaner and less complicated.

Engine Mounts

The LS and LT engine don't have much in common with the original small-block (other than some fundamentals of design), but they have similar overall dimensions. A small-block Chevrolet is 26 inches wide, 28 inches long, and 27 inches tall. The LS and LT have a similar size but they're 2 inches shorter at 25 inches (not including the intake). That's good because it means that the LS and LT will fit where a stock small-block would have sat.

However, the LS engine has revised engine-mount locations over the small-block Chevy, and the LT is revised yet again. This means that all three require different mounts that may or may not interface with the truck's engine perches bolted to the front crossmember.

On the LS engine, the mounts are placed farther back than they were on the small-block, which requires a set of conversion mounts to be fitted. Holley, Summit Racing, Dirty Dingo, Trans-Dapt, ICT Billet, and Speedway are just some of the companies that make conversion mounts to solve this problem as well as helping to fit LS-style transmissions into C10s.

Adjustable or Fixed Mounts?

Many options are available for C10 LS engine mounts. Adjustable mounts that are designed to allow an LS engine to slide forward and back on the frame rails are nice because they can help solve some clearance issues, but this is similar to plugging a hole in a boat. Sliding an engine back to solve a clearance problem with an oil pan and the crossmember can create issues with the transmission and the cab, so it's a fine balance. If you already have a driveshaft that you intend on retaining, a slider-style mount may be the better option because it allows for some adjustment to keep everything where it

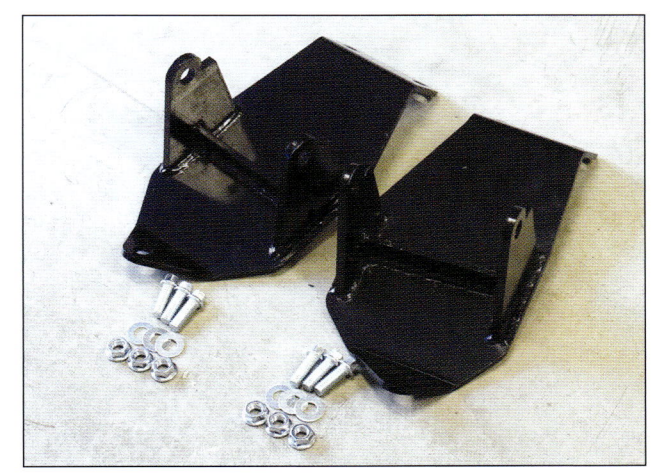

Hooker offers two different mount solutions for LS engines in 1967–1972 GM trucks, as there were two different frame configurations available over those years. The earlier trucks through early 1968 have a wider upper frame rail and require part number BHS538 engine stands. These (shown) are part number BHS511, which are designed for narrow-frame trucks. The difference? GM had to make clearance for big-blocks starting in 1968, which required a cut-down upper frame rail around the engine.

The nice thing about Hooker's Blackheart line is that they're engineered to work with Holley's line of oil pans and Hooker's exhaust manifolds and tubular headers. That removes a lot of guesswork and makes LS and LT engine installation a breeze. These clamshell mounts are the other piece of the LS engine-mount puzzle and are offered as part number VK090152 for the kit. These (shown) are LS1 Camaro-style mounts.

CHAPTER 7

Here's a good look at BHS511 installed on a 1967 frame. Note the clearance that I created on the upper frame rail as you'd see on a 1968-and-newer frame. Why not use the wider mounts? They provide less room for long-tube headers, but that is also an option. I elected to make the space here, as I already had the cab off the frame, so access was easy.

needs to be. They also make it easy to use the factory engine perches with conversion-style LS motor-mount plates and a set of OEM-style motor mounts.

Hooker's Blackheart line of engine mounts and exhaust accessories is a fantastic option for C10 builders, as everything is designed to work together—from the engine mounts to the exhaust manifolds or headers, oil pan, transmission crossmember, and more. These take the guesswork out of the job of getting an LS fitted between the frame rails.

How to Clearance a 1967 Frame for LS and Big-Block Power

If you read the original engine section in Chapter 6 closely, you may have noticed there were no big-block trucks in 1967. Those trucks have wider upper frame rails in the engine compartment than those that came starting in 1968 because GM had to make clearance for the bigger 396 engine that year. As such, you may run into clearance issues with engine swaps in your 1967 truck. These photos show one way to solve that. ■

Here's what it looks like when it's all said and done. Basically, it's just like a 1968-and-newer frame. This will allow for big-block swaps later on, as well as better clearance for exhaust systems with any LS or small-block V-8.

Here's a good look at how wide a 1967 upper frame rail is. You don't need to cut this for LS installation, but doing so provides more options when it comes to exhaust. Factory 1968-and-newer trucks measure 1 7/8-inches wide, compared to the 1967's 2 7/8 inches. A tape line will help mark the area to be cut.

94 CHEVY/GMC TRUCKS 1967–1972: HOW TO BUILD & MODIFY

INSTALLING AN LS IN A C10

The pan that GM Performance generally supplies with its crate engines is basically the same style of pan that GM uses in truck applications. It measures approximately 8¾ inches tall. These pans fit most GM muscle cars and trucks, but in lowered applications, they tend to be too tall for comfort.

Holley part number 302-2 is a great solution for lowered trucks, as it doesn't hang down lower than the factory crossmember. This is the polished version, sold as part number VK090001, with a fresh gasket, mounting bolts, RTV sealant, and the proper pickup tube and baffle.

Oil Pans

Getting your engine to fit between the frame rails is one thing, but what about ground clearance?

The LS engine truck pan, which was used on most 4.8s, 5.3s, and 6.0s, is a fairly deep unit that measures at about 9 inches at its tallest point. It does fit in 1967–1972 C10s, but if you have a C10 that's lower than stock (or will be lower than stock in the future), consider swapping the pan for something with a lower overall profile.

Remember that LS engine oil pans are generally (at least from stock) cast aluminum and are a structural member of the engine itself (unlike other GM V-8s). This means they're rigid and robust but also susceptible to impact damage. They crack rather than dent, so hitting the ground isn't a good option. There are, however, many solutions to solve this problem.

One solution is the Cadillac CTS-V pan (part number 12631828), which measures about 5½ inches tall compared to the truck pan's nearly 9-inch height. It does clear the front crossmember of a 1967–1972 C10. Another is the Hummer H2 pan (part number 12614821), which is 7¾ inches at its tallest point. This one is sold as the "GM Muscle Hot Rod Oil Pan" and works with C10 applications, depending on the engine mounts used. Some builders have had luck using the F-body Camaro pan, but it may require you to modify the crossmember for clearance, depending on the engine mounts you use.

An even better solution for C10 owners is the Holley line of retrofit oil pans, which are among the lowest-profile options. They're available in several configurations, but for 1967–1972 truck owners, the pan to look for is the 302-2 or 302-3. Both are designed to offer more clearance under the front of the engine, which makes fitting them into C10 chassis much easier. The 302-1 is another option, but you may need to space your engine mounts up for clearance between the front of the pan and the crossmember.

The 302-3 comes with turbo drains plumbed into it as well as increased clearance around the sump compared to the 302-2 for longer-stroke applications, such as the 7.0L LS7. While these pans are shallower than the stockers, particularly over the crossmember, both retain approximately 5.5 quarts of oil capacity, which is plenty for most LS applications.

Fitting the Engine in the Truck

The most important part of any engine swap is a spare set of eyes and hands. It's a lot easier to do with someone else there to help wiggle, shake, jostle, and kick things into place when needed.

Beyond that, all you really need for the task of installing an LS is a good set of metric hand tools, a trustworthy engine hoist, and a way to get your truck's frame high enough up off the ground for said engine hoist to slide underneath. Jack stands do the trick, but it's usually better to use either wheel ramps or fabricated wood blocks under the tires because jack stands can get in the way of the legs of an engine hoist as you slide it into place.

CHEVY/GMC TRUCKS 1967–1972: HOW TO BUILD & MODIFY

CHAPTER 7

Installing an LS in a C10

1 This 6.0 may look ready to drop in your C10, but there are a few things to add that will make the install go a lot smoother and give you a better finished product. The first step is to clean the engine well using solvent and remove the oil pan.

2 With the pan out of the way, you can see the factory windage tray and the factory oil-pump pickup tube. Both need to be removed before proceeding.

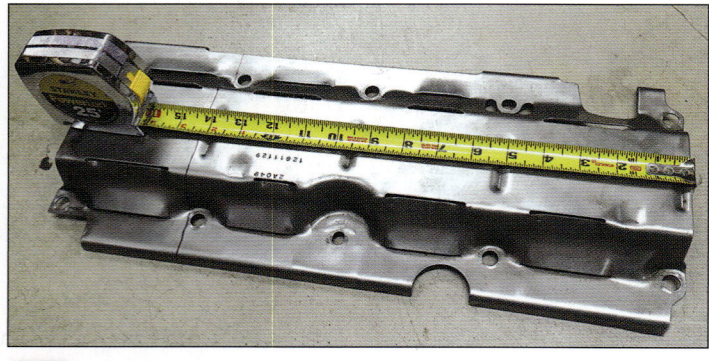

3 Holley's 302-2 pan requires trimming the original windage tray for clearance before the pan can go on. Measuring from the back, it needs to be 14¼ inches long. A cutting wheel makes quick work of it.

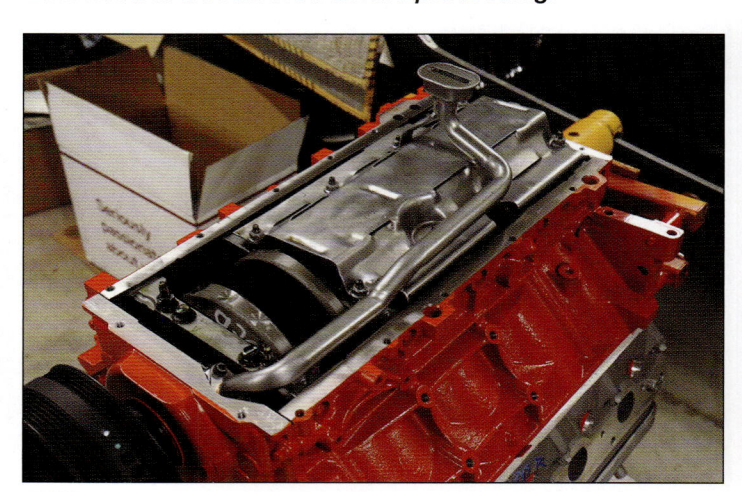

4 Holley's 302-2 pan comes with a new, slightly different oil-pump pickup tube that requires further clearance of the front corner of the windage tray (as shown here). Painting the engine is easiest to do with the pan off. Be sure to install and liberally lubricate the oil pickup tube's O-ring.

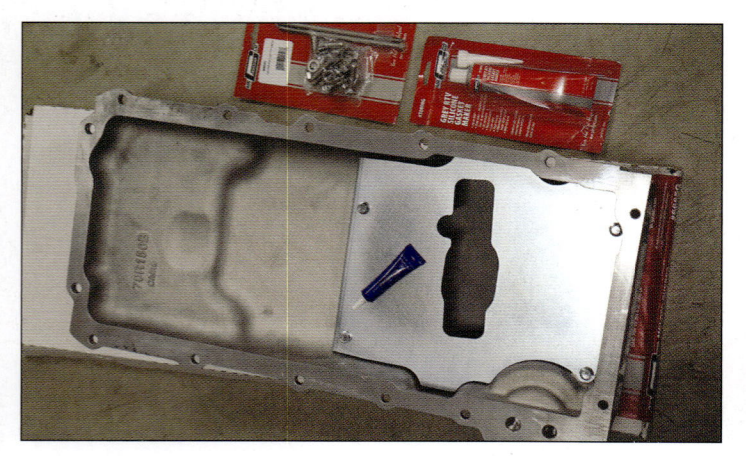

5 Install the pan baffle, which simply bolts in place. Thread-lock here is a must.

96 CHEVY/GMC TRUCKS 1967–1972: HOW TO BUILD & MODIFY

INSTALLING AN LS IN A C10

6 LS engine oil pans feature a robust steel-core O-ring-style pan gasket, but they require some RTV sealant at the corners where the timing cover and the rear cover meet the engine block. A quick dab in each corner is all that's needed.

7 The pan can drop into place and be snugged up using the supplied hardware, but it must fit flush to the back of the block, as the transmission mounts both to the block and to the pan. The torque specifications are important because the pan is a structural part of the engine. Tighten the pan to the front cover and block bolts to 18 ft-lbs, with 106 in-lbs on the rear cover bolts.

8 Hooker's Blackheart engine swap LS/LT brackets take the place of the factory engine pedestals and are set up to work with Holley's oil pans and exhaust solutions. The brackets are part number BHS511 and are designed for 2WD trucks with the 1968–1972 narrow frame rails. Installation hardware comes with the kit.

9 With the engine mated to the transmission and the mounts in place on the engine block, slowly lower the engine into place. Placing a floor jack under the transmission tailhousing makes this process much easier, as you can tilt the engine to get it to slide into place.

CHEVY/GMC TRUCKS 1967–1972: HOW TO BUILD & MODIFY

CHAPTER 7

Installing an LS in a C10 continued

10 *The other piece of the puzzle for LS fitment is a set of clamshell-style engine mounts, as found on LS1 engines. This is Hooker Blackheart part number VK090152, which was designed to mount to LS engines using the matching Blackheart engine-swap brackets. These bolt in place on the engine side and slide into the brackets upon engine installation. Together, these parts locate an LS engine where a factory small-block would sit in regard to the bellhousing mount.*

Engine Accessories

The engine is only part of the puzzle. You also need to consider everything from the alternator to the starter. As with the engine itself, many options are available from GM and from the aftermarket.

The most basic drive kit may be the best solution for you. GM truck accessories came on every 4.8, 5.3, and 6.0 that GM delivered in its LS-powered truck lines, and many builders use them because of convenience. Depending on the engine mounts used, the low-mount A/C compressor can interfere with the frame rail and require some frame clearance either for the compressor itself or for the A/C lines.

This is Holley's low-mount LS accessory drive system (part number 20-162) that tucks in the accessories tightly for increased clearance. This kit comes complete with a Sanden SD7 A/C compressor, a CS-style 105-amp alternator, and a Corvette-style Type II power-steering pump with reservoir and hardline kit. This kit fits middle (Camaro) or long (truck) setups with the proper spacing kit (part number 21-4 for truck setups), and it fits GM truck chassis without any modification needed. It's a bolt-on affair for C10s and is a lot cleaner than a stock GM truck setup.

LS engines came in everything from Corvettes to panel vans. Assuming you bought a complete engine from a donor vehicle, you likely also sourced a complete front drive kit with a water pump, alternator, power steering, and A/C compressor. The good news is that GM's drive components will make parts swaps a breeze, but the downside is that not every setup will fit between the 1967–1972 truck's relatively narrow frame rails without some modification.

GM offered three different LS drive kits based on harmonic-balancer depth. Corvettes were the shortest, measuring in at about 1½ inches from the face of the balancer pulley to the crank-bolt surface.

Fourth-generation Camaros featured a slightly longer balancer, measuring 2¼ inches, and trucks were the longest, measuring 3 inches. Some mixing and matching is possible, as there are available water pump spacers that allow the use of shorter Camaro or Corvette pumps with truck accessories.

Fifth-generation Camaros share the long truck spacing, which is a bonus for those who wish to run a Camaro-style water pump with its front-facing driver-side hose location in place of the standard truck water pump. Only one custom bracket for the idler is required along with some clearance of the water pump in that location.

If you're looking for the simplest overall solution, the stock GM truck system is what most builders use. While it's considered to be pretty bulky, it's easy to find and doesn't require much in the way of modification to work. Every 4.8, 5.3, and 6.0 delivered in a truck had this system. It's a basic bolt-in, except for the A/C pump, which will likely need to be swapped out for a more modern fixed-displacement Sanden-style compressor on a custom bracket, particularly if you intend on using either a Vintage Air system or the rest of your original A/C system.

Aftermarket drive kits tend to be a lot cleaner looking than factory GM components, and they often tuck up their components tighter to the engine, which solves many clearance issues. Many options are available from a variety of sources, including Holley, Chevrolet Performance, March, Eddie Motorsports, LSSimple.net, ICT Billet, and others. Most provide measurements on their websites to help you determine if the kit in question will fit before you buy.

Some builders have gone the route of making their own kits, which you can do if you have a lot of time and some solid fabrication skills. However, this is the kind of thing where time is money, especially when the majority of the GM and aftermarket kits were computer designed.

Exhaust

How your engine breathes is directly correlated to how much power it will make. As with just about every other component under the hood, many options are available when it comes to a system for your C10.

LS engines came from the factory with cast-iron manifolds. Many different versions are available for various OEM applications from trucks to Corvettes.

Cast-iron manifolds are durable and quiet, and if you source a set from a wrecking yard, they can be cheap too. Note that one of the best OEM swap options is a set of LS3 Camaro manifolds, as the manifolds will clear the frame rails, unlike stock GM truck manifolds that flare out and hit the frame rails on C10s. The LS3 manifolds have a 2.5-inch outlet and are plenty capable of supporting the LS3's 430 hp. In terms of stock solutions, they're good for truck builds.

Beyond the LS3 setup, Hooker makes an industry-standard set of cast-iron manifolds in a variety of sizes and finishes that have proven to be great flowing units that last as long as stockers and flow even better. In addition, Hooker makes a great set of turbo manifolds for those looking to add boost to your LS equation. In terms of easy power, there's no better way than turbocharging. The LS engine, with its durable construction and good flow characteristics, loves boost, even in otherwise-stock form.

When the LS engine began gaining traction in the late 1990s, one of the first things that Camaro and Corvette builders learned was that a set of long-tube headers with a matching tune could provide massive power gains over standard manifolds. In the following years, both head design and intake design has gotten even better. Wherever air enters, it needs to leave as well, so long-tube headers have become even more effective than they were back then.

As such, if you're looking for the best possible solution for a naturally aspirated LS or LT, the only answer is a set of tube headers. A variety of companies make them in both mild steel and stainless-steel construction.

Regardless of what you choose, it's important to build an exhaust system that fits the profile you want. It needs to be loud enough to be fun but quiet enough to keep your brain from rattling around in your skull on

CHAPTER 7

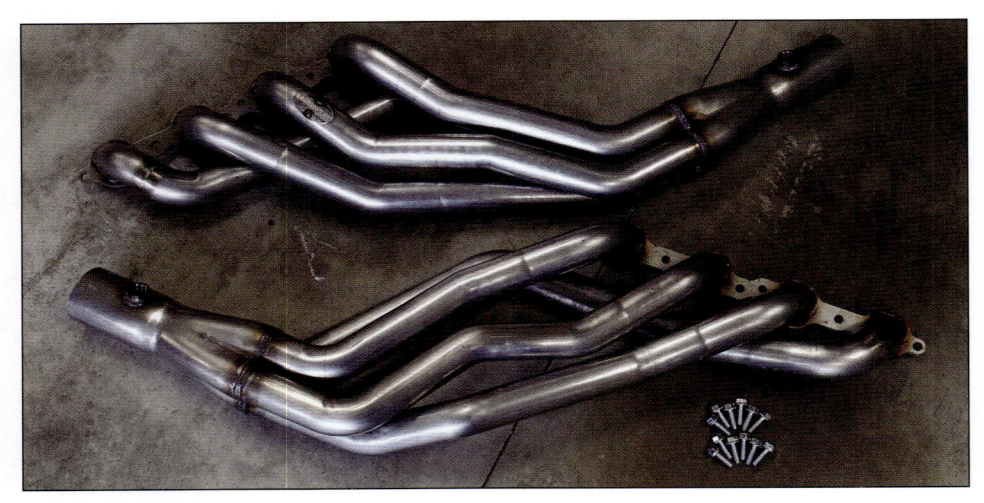

Hooker Blackheart offers several 304 stainless headers for C10 applications, depending on the motor mounts used. This set (part number BH13243) is set up to work with narrow-frame trucks and can accommodate stock straight-end spark-plug wires. For wide-frame trucks through 1967, part number BH13231 tucks in tighter to the block but requires special angled-boot plug wires. Both have $1^7/_8$-inch primaries and 3-inch collectors, and $1^3/_4$-inch tubes are also available.

long road trips.

Louder may be more fun at first, but if drivability is the goal, a setup that's too loud will have you parking the truck after any kind of extended driving, which is counterproductive.

Bigger-diameter pipe, such as 3-inch, will make more power than 2- or 2.5-inch, but at the cost of increased noise and the potential for clearance issues, particularly on lowered rigs that have the long-trailing-arm suspension.

Power delivery is one thing, but I'd argue that sound quality (not volume) is just as important for a truck you're planning to drive regularly. Before you choose a direction for your C10, get out and listen to as many systems and configurations as you can—from full out-the-back systems with glasspacks to shorter systems that feature chambered mufflers and turndowns. Every system sounds different due to its construction and routing, and the best bet is to get an idea of what you like by hearing what others have done before spending any money. Going to the exhaust shop and asking for it to sound "good" when done isn't going to get you anywhere because your idea and the person's idea at the shop are likely two different things.

Keep in mind that noise is directly related to pipe size and length. Generally speaking, the longer the system, the quieter it will be. The smaller pipe will help limit volume compared to a larger pipe too.

C10s are popular rigs, and that means there are a number of ready-made exhaust systems you can buy in a box and install in your truck without too much hassle. That's a good option, but if you have a little time and some key tools on-hand, such as a MIG welder, a bandsaw or PortaBand, and a grinder, there's nothing to stop you from building a complete exhaust system by hand out of U-bends and straight sections of aluminized steel pipe. Depending on your welding skills, it may or may not end up as pretty as something mandrel bent and machine welded or TIG welded, but there's a lot to like about making your own system that routes exactly where you want it to be.

H-Pipe or X-Pipe: What's Better?

Selecting the right exhaust is an exercise in balance: great sound and great flow combined with the realities of use. You can't talk about balance and exhaust without talking about H-pipes and X-pipes.

Both are crossover tubes designed to link the two banks of a dual-exhaust system together for better performance. Both the H-pipe and the X-pipe solve the same problem. Evening out exhaust pulses helps scavenge each bank and promote better flow and, therefore, power. They also have a pretty big impact on sound delivery, and for most of us, that's probably just as important.

A system with an H-pipe installed just aft of the header collector will have a deeper tone than a system without the H. An X pushes out a higher-pitched tone, but as it physically crosses over each pipe, it does a better job at scavenging and tends to make more power.

Each has its place depending on your goals and setup. If you want the best performance from your exhaust system, it's smart to choose one of them versus running duals that aren't linked together. ■

INSTALLING AN LS IN A C10

Making Your Own Exhaust

1 I elected to build my own exhaust system using aluminized 2½-inch steel pipe because it's generally inexpensive and easy to work with. Summit Racing sells a good ready-to-run H-pipe assembly that I used as the basis of this setup, alongside several U-bends.

2 The headers sat wider than the reliefs in my Silver Sport Transmissions crossmember, which meant that I needed to jog my pipes inboard slightly, which required a few fabricated bends. The key is to always cut perpendicular to the pipe, even in a corner, so that the cross-section remains round and easy to weld to another section of pipe.

3 Once you've cut a few pieces and deburred them, start to piece together your bends. The beauty of this is that you don't end up with kinks like you would from a typical exhaust-shop pipe bender. A permanent marker can help with alignment prior to welding.

4 Many methods can be used to weld pipe together, but I like the high-heat tack method, which is similar to how you can stitch sheet metal back together. The idea is to turn up the welder and stack the tacks all around the pipe. If done correctly, you'll have good penetration and a clean result.

5 This quick-and-dirty setup required some trial and error, but it fits well and is tight to the floor when installed. Once here, you can clean up your welds with a grinder to make it look seamless, but you'll need to paint anywhere you welded and ground away the aluminized coating. I prefer white or black header paint, and I like to paint the whole system (minus the headers) to keep rust away.

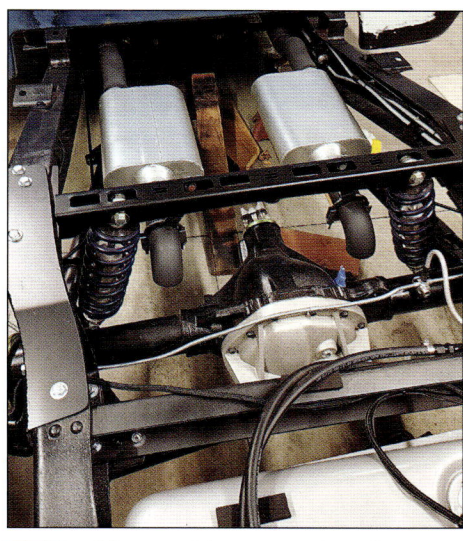

6 After making sure that the rear control arms don't hit the pipes, the final step is to fit the mufflers and weld them into place. I elected to run simple chambered mufflers from Summit Racing and turndowns here, but you can easily route pipes all the way out the back for less cab drone. Two clamps and exhaust hangers are all you need to hold the system in place—preferably rubber mounted to the chassis.

CHEVY/GMC TRUCKS 1967–1972: HOW TO BUILD & MODIFY

CHAPTER 8

Fueling, ECU, and Cooling System

Big power is great in any custom car or truck. The real key is feeding that power reliably, controlling the spark and fuel properly, and keeping it cool even on the hottest summer day.

If your C10 is stock, none of that is a big deal. GM's factory systems are basic and fundamentally sound. There aren't any real electronic controls to speak of, except for an electric choke that might have been added if the factory Quadrajet carb on your C10 was swapped at some point.

If you plan on swapping to fuel injection, you'll need a way to control that injection. If you need a way to fuel it beyond what the original mechanical system can do, it requires a reengineered fuel delivery system with new fuel lines. On top of that, bigger power than stock requires upgraded cooling capabilities. Fortunately, none of this is a very big deal thanks to a wide range of aftermarket and late-model OEM solutions.

A fuel tank mounted behind the seat was the industry standard in trucks throughout the 1960s and early 1970s. If you're comfortable with having the tank in the cab, by all means leave it there. However, if you plan to swap to EFI or just want more storage space, changing the tank location is a good idea.

Fueling

From the factory, every single C10 built from 1967 to 1972 was equipped with a mechanical fuel pump that was driven off the camshaft of the engine and fed fuel from either a 5/16-inch steel line or 3/8-inch steel line, depending on years and options. This system is fundamentally the same as just about every muscle car built in the era, and that makes serviceability straightforward.

There's typically only a feed line with no return back to the fuel tank, and most of that line is standard steel connected in several locations with sections of rubber hose. That rubber hose is known to deteriorate over time. Even if you plan on keeping the stock engine and fueling system intact, it pays to swap out the rubber lines used throughout the truck. There are rubber sections at the tank and likely at the pump as well, depending on how your truck was serviced over the years. Swap them all before they become brittle, cracked, and leak-prone.

Something else to factor in is your truck's early evaporative emissions system, which became part of the truck's fuel system on half-ton

FUELING, ECU, AND COOLING SYSTEM

Move the Tank or Leave It?

GM didn't have a problem fitting fuel tanks inside the cabs of their trucks in the 1960s, but the sentiment has changed a little over the years. Granted, if the safest place isn't the inside of your truck's cab, then we're doing something wrong. However, riding shotgun with 21 gallons of gas (or worse yet, 3 gallons of gas and 18 gallons worth of fumes) isn't my idea of a party.

You might think its nice to be able to gauge your fuel level by hearing the gas slosh around when you turn a corner. When it's really low, you'll hear pebbles rolling in the bottom of the tank. However, having the filler neck by the driver's window means that there will be fuel fumes inside the cab. Also, if things go badly and you ever end up with your truck on its lid, the last thing you'll want is fuel running out of the filler and into your interior. That is a real concern.

Fortunately for truck builders, GM's full-size truck construction was modular back in the day, which means that Blazer fuel tanks that mounted behind the rear axle in those rigs are basically swap-in units for trucks. The aftermarket has several fuel-injection-ready fabricated rear-mount tanks from companies such as Tanks Inc. and Boyd's Welding, so you don't have to leave the original tank where it was. Behind the axle may not be a perfect relocation solution, but it's arguably a lot better than having fuel inside the cab, and it's better for fuel-injection swaps.

Whether or not you swap your tank is up to you, but moving the tank out of the cab, if nothing else, provides more room behind the seat.

This is a reproduction fuel tank relocation kit supplied by Classic Industries (part number CX5052) that has a 17-gallon capacity and top-mount filler neck. This tank won't require bed clearance, but it will require cutting a hole in the bed floor for your custom-designed filler solution. Neither this tank nor the larger available 20-gallon unit have internal baffling. (Photo Courtesy Classic Industries)

---

trucks in 1971. This system consisted of a charcoal canister and a group of hoses and check valves that routed fumes from the fuel tank into the engine rather than into the atmosphere. This can be either retained or bypassed depending on your state's laws, but be sure you're within the rules before you route around a factory emissions system, even in an early rig. Again, replace any rubber lines.

Fuel Tanks

Trucks from this era all share a similar basic fuel-tank design, where the tank was mounted behind the seat. Some trucks had added-on sidesaddle tanks as well. Depending on the year of your truck, the cab tank can have one of two different filler neck sizes, but otherwise the tanks are the same.

Sending units read from 0 to 90 ohms to match the factory gauge, and they typically don't give much trouble for stock applications. Unless you plan on running an in-line electric fuel pump, swapping over to a modern high-pressure fuel system for LS or LT use can be a hassle with a cab-mounted tank. Any sort of in-tank pump solution will be noisy if your tank is still in the cab. Electric pumps don't like to pull fuel as much as they push it, so an in-cab tank with an external pump down on the frame rail is not a great option, either.

CHEVY/GMC TRUCKS 1967–1972: HOW TO BUILD & MODIFY

CHAPTER 8

Keep that Gauge Reading Correctly

If you're keeping the original fuel tank, you may run into an issue with your fuel gauge reading empty even when the tank is full. The cause may be a sunken float on the fuel-tank sending unit. This is particularly common among aftermarket reproduction fuel-sending units due to brass floats that develop pinholes and fill with fuel.

There's a good replacement plastic float designed for 1970s Jeeps that swaps directly with the OEM-style brass float. It is part number OMX-1772901, which is originally for a 1970s CJ-5. The float won't dissolve in modern ethanol fuels, which makes it a great swap. ■

Moving a Fuel Tank and Converting to EFI

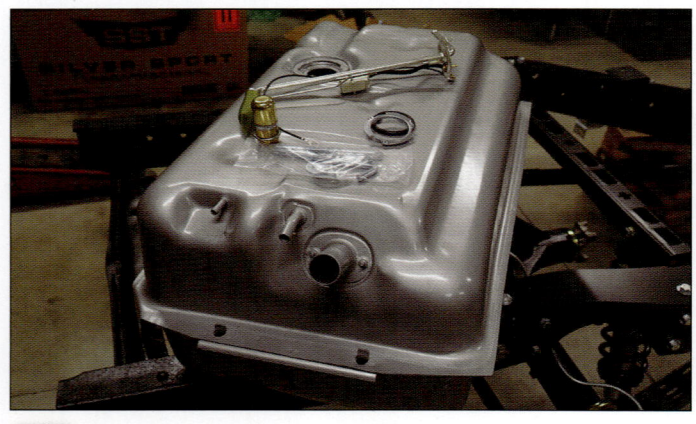

1 The 20-gallon tank from Classic Industries (part number 5024) is a good choice for factory capacity in a rear-mount tank. It comes set up for carbureted applications, but it can be converted to handle an in-tank pump.

2 These tabs, originally used to locate the tank in a Blazer frame, need to be removed before the tank can be fitted. A simple grab and wiggle with a pair of Vise-Grips does the job.

3 If you don't already have the bed out of the way, tackle that before trying to mount the tank. There's a factory spare-tire-mounting crossmember that will have to go, but once that's out of the way, you can see where the tank will fit. Note the location of the bed-mount holes in the frame and the filler neck. The tank needs to be pushed back as far as possible to clear the bed-mount crossmember.

FUELING, ECU, AND COOLING SYSTEM

Moving a Fuel Tank and Converting to EFI *continued*

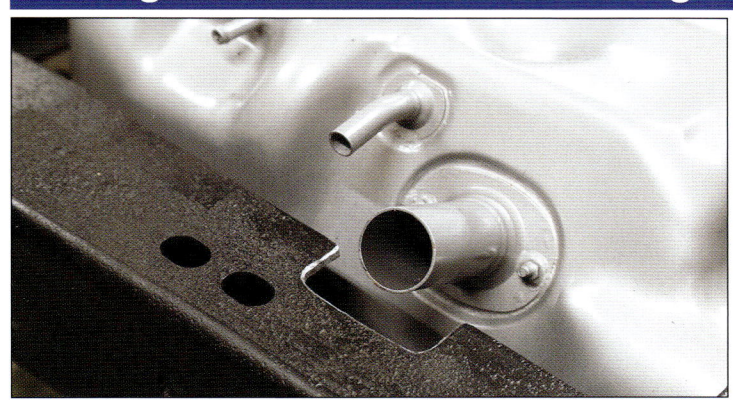

4 To make the tank filler neck access possible (and for future tank removal), a little frame clearance around the filler neck is needed. Mark around where the filler neck will sit, remove the tank, and cut out the section.

5 These two straps are bent up like this from the manufacturer, but the 90-degree bend at the 3/4 mark needs to be flattened prior to installation. After that, mock them up to the tank, mark your holes, and drill.

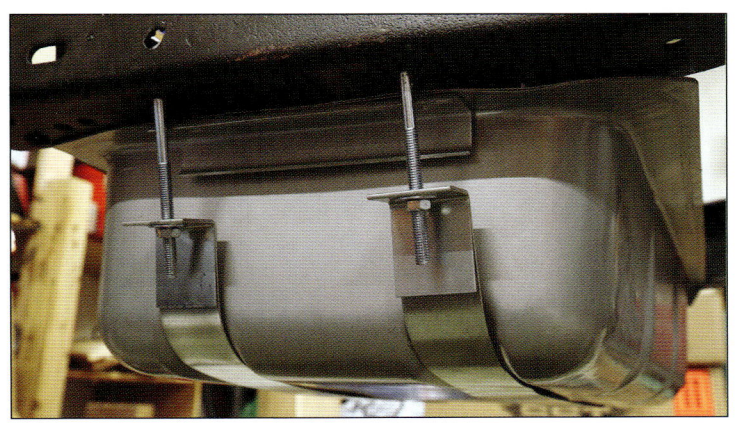

6 The kit comes with two J-bolts that are used to affix the tank to the frame along with standard nuts and bolts on the other side. The J-bolts should sit opposite of the filler neck to allow tank removal for service after installation.

7 Since this truck is LS-powered, I elected to install a diecast Holley Retrofit fuel module (part number 12-136) that features a 255-lph pump that can support up to 550 hp in EFI applications. This unit installs on and in the fuel tank and uses Holley's HydraMat system, which acts as its own baffle and sponge to keep the fuel pickup submerged at all times—no internal tank baffling is required. This is a great solution for longevity, reliability, and simplicity.

8 After marking where the bed crossmember is going to sit on top of the tank, locate a place away from it and the OEM fuel float (generally centered in the tank), drill a pilot hole, and then drill a 3¼-inch hole for the pump. Be sure to vacuum out any metal shavings from the tank when you're done.

CHEVY/GMC TRUCKS 1967–1972: HOW TO BUILD & MODIFY 105

CHAPTER 8

Moving a Fuel Tank and Converting to EFI *continued*

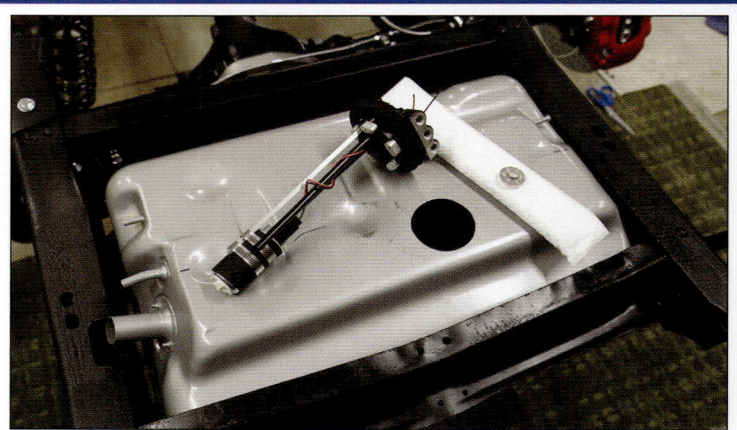

9 The Blazer-style 20-gallon tank is a bit tall, but Holley sells extended pickup tubes for its Retrofit modules. In this case, I used Holley part number 12-161 for tanks that range from 12 to 15 inches deep. The goal is to place the HydraMat on the tank floor with the module sitting flat on the tank top. It only takes a few quick measurements prior to assembly.

10 Next, install the pump assembly and HydraMat. It's a simple process of dropping it in place, double-checking the fit (which can be done with the sending unit removed), and tightening down a few Allen-head mounting screws that turn rotating clamps to pinch the module in place. Don't forget the gasket.

11 The final piece of the tank puzzle (other than running new fuel lines, vent lines, and proper-gauge wiring for the pump) is to install the supplied sending unit, O-ring, and lock ring. If you're careful, you can accomplish this with a flathead screwdriver and a small hammer. This sending unit is calibrated to work with the stock OEM fuel gauge.

12 Since the 20-gallon Blazer tank sits higher than the frame rails, make clearance for it within the rearmost bed crossmember. Mark and cut it out but save the bottom edge. If you trim it down and weld it back in place, you'll retain most of the bed's strength. You'll need to remove about 2½ inches of height between the two rear bed-mount holes.

FUELING, ECU, AND COOLING SYSTEM

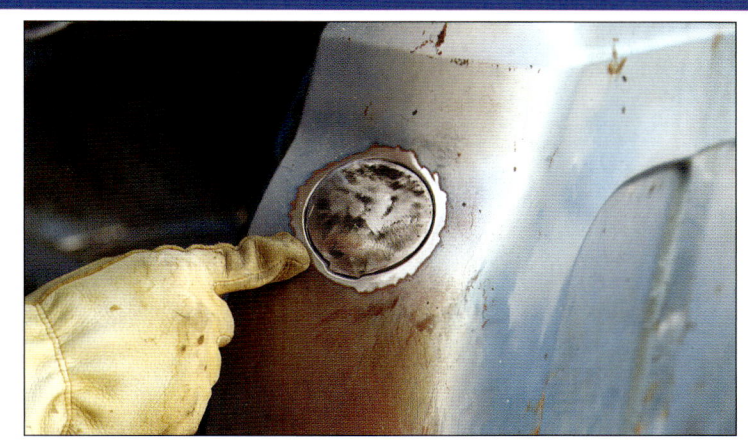

13 With the factory tank removed from the truck, make a patch panel for the cab hole. This is easy to do using a cardboard template and some sheet metal. The key is to match the curve of the body as well as you can to limit the amount of body filler required, weld the new panel in place, and grind the welds down flat.

14 If you're matching patina the way I am, get creative with your paintwork over the neck filler patch. If you're using OEM paint or an OEM color, check with automotivetouchup.com for a spray can of primer, base-coat color, and clear. That's what we used here after some body filler, and the paint was delivered in ready-to-spray cans.

Fuel Lines

When it comes to a stock-style carbureted system, the basic original steel fuel supply line your truck had from the factory is still a viable fueling solution, particularly if the lines aren't rusty and all the rubber sections are replaced. Original fuel systems put out about 7 psi, and that was only from the output of the mechanical fuel pump to the carburetor itself. Aftermarket pumps and carburetors may run anywhere between 8 and 12 psi inside the line. It's nothing a stock-style setup can't handle.

If you've swapped to an LS engine, or anything that runs higher-than-stock fuel pressure, you'll need to make new fuel lines to support your engine. This is especially true for anything fuel injected, as the pressures that EFI requires are much higher than the 7 pounds that these trucks saw when stock. Plus, most fuel-injection systems require a return line to feed fuel back to the tank.

If your truck is still mostly assembled, you'd benefit from running new flexible rubber feed and return lines from your tank. They're easy to install and route around things, which can be a real bonus for cleanliness and ease of installation. The key is to keep them away from heat and any moving components—suspension, driveshaft, etc.—and to use rubber isolated clamps to mount them to the chassis to eliminate the possibility of chafing and leaks.

Earl's Performance offers a variety of flexible fuel-injection hose and matching ends, generally with Teflon liners to extend life and limit fuel odor. You can run these the full length of the truck to make the install simple, but it's not the only solution.

Steel is a lot more robust. It won't break down over time the same way that a rubber-based line will. A steel fuel line will last longer than just about any other type of line, and you can buy spools of steel line that can be bent into any shape. This requires line benders, line cutters, and some way to flare the ends for use with AN-style fittings.

CHEVY/GMC TRUCKS 1967–1972: HOW TO BUILD & MODIFY

CHAPTER 8

Filler-Neck Solutions on Rear-Mount Tanks

If you use a Blazer tank in your C10, you'll have to get creative with regard to the filler neck. OEM-style solutions aren't available to fix this problem, so you'll have to engineer something yourself or find an aftermarket solution.

You can source a fuel-filler door from a later-model truck and install that in your bedside, or you can figure out a way to run a filler neck into the wheel well and fill the truck there. Better yet, some builders have had success putting the filler behind the driver-side taillight, up in the stake pocket, or behind the side marker in 1968–1972 rigs. Of course, this only applies to side-fill-style Blazer tanks. Top-fill tanks need a hole cut into the bed floor for access.

One thing to note is the filler-neck size on your tank. OEM-style tanks use a small 1 3/8-inch junction hose that can be hard to find and difficult to adapt to other sizes. You can get around that by changing your tank's filler neck to a size that's more commonly available these days (2-inch) or by using a matching neck size to that OEM setup.

The last item to consider is the old tank, which you'll need to remove from the cab. The original fuel lines need to be rerouted or replaced to function with the new rear-mount tank, as does the fuel sending unit wire. ■

3 Once you've cut a hole in your bed floor for a filler hose, sourced a 90-degree bend fuel filler hose section, and mocked up the panel, the only thing that's left is to install it. There's plenty of finish work left, but this is a simple leak-free, trouble-free solution that won't be slow to fill.

1 My favorite filler-neck solution for side-mount Blazer tanks comes from Carolina Truck Shop (carolinatruckshop.com). This fabricated steel filler comes with a 2-inch waterproof filler neck, the fabricated housing and all of the proper mounting hardware to mount the filler inside the bed and out of the way.

2 If you're running a Blazer tank with the small 1 3/8-inch outlet, adapting the 2-inch filler may be a challenge. I prefer using a 1947–1955 GM truck fuel filler neck kit, as it comes with the proper grommet, neck, and fuel cap. It's the same diameter as the Blazer inlet, has a vent tube, and easily tucks inside the Carolina Truck Shop filler housing.

4 With the bed complete, here's how the Carolina Truck Shop filler looks installed and functional. The key is usability. Even with the bed loaded, you'll still have access to fill the tank, and no wires are running near the neck like you'd find with a taillight or marker-light mount. It's also removable for service.

FUELING, ECU, AND COOLING SYSTEM

The proper tools make all the difference when making steel lines. The Eastwood part number 25304 tube flare tool is just as handy for AN-style fuel lines as it is for brake lines. The AN dies (part number 30005) come separately but allow you to use 37-degree AN tube sleeves and tube nuts.

Edelmann part number 3600ST is a 25-foot spool of 3/8-inch (or -6) line, which is great for fuel use, but use Summit tube nuts (part number 220633-2B) and matching tube sleeves (part number 220634-2B) to support the 37-degree AN flare and make a leak-proof seal. It's important to map out the fuel system before you start so that you can plan for all the junctions and fittings needed for assembly.

The only downside, other than the need for some special tools, is in the difficulty of working with steel line. It's easy to put a bend in the wrong place or get all the way to the end of your fabbed line, bend it the wrong way, and have to start over from scratch. Room is your friend here. The best time to make fuel lines is when you have the bed and cab off the frame.

Fuel lines come in all kinds of sizes and materials. What should you know before you build your system?

First, don't try to flare your original steel fuel lines for use with AN fittings. Original fuel lines have seams that often leak when flared and mated to the 37-degree AN flange. Buying new, spiral-core steel line in a 25-foot roll is a much better idea. Plus, it allows you to put the lines wherever you want them versus where the factory put them.

Second, avoid aluminum tubing for fuel-injection use. It's an option that does work for carburetor-level pressures, but it tends to crack when

A good fuel system needs a few good filters, particularly when running electric pumps. You need a 100-micron prefilter ahead of the pump and a 10-micron filter between the pump and the injectors. This filter is a reusable 10-micron HP unit from Holley (part number 162-550) installed in the feed line using one of Holley's billet brackets to keep it from vibrating.

submitted to vibration, and it's typically only rated to about 25 psi.

Third, if you choose rubber line, match the hose to the application. EFI hose is rated for higher pressures than standard fuel hose, so match your hose ends to the brand and style of hose used. For example, if you use Earl's Vapor Guard hose, get the matching Earl's ends because they're designed to work with the hose's internal lining. Use the proper recommended fuel injection–style hose clamps as well.

CHEVY/GMC TRUCKS 1967–1972: HOW TO BUILD & MODIFY

CHAPTER 8

A quality adjustable fuel-pressure regulator (Holley part number 12-880 in this case) is vital because set pressures are needed for computer-controlled EFI to function properly. What that pressure needs to be varies by EFI system. In this case, the regulator is installed after the fuel rails, with one of the two inlet ports blocked off and the return line heading out the bottom of the regulator and back to the tank.

Don't overlook a factory PCM as a good controller for your LS or LT swap. Understand that using something like this will require harness customization and special software for you to tune it, such as EFILive.

Regarding steel line, I like Edelmann part number 3600ST, which is a 25-foot spool of -6 (3/8-inch) line. That's plenty of length for most C10 builds, but I always buy two 25-foot spools so that I have enough line (with mistakes) to complete a system before I begin.

Wherever fuel comes anywhere close to exhaust, protect the lines with insulating heat wrap. Heat in the fuel is always detrimental to performance, so insulation is important.

Finally, draw out your entire fuel system on a piece of paper before you buy any parts. Mark out what types of fittings you'll need and where you'll need them. This will help you to be sure you have everything you need before you get started.

Holley made a big name for itself thanks to its easy-to-use EFI systems, such as this Terminator X system for LS1 and LS6 V-8s. Holley has a variety of LS and LT EFI kits on the market today, with both drive-by-wire and transmission controls available as well as many options from traction control through boost control, nitrous, transbrake control, and more. These systems are plug and play and self-learning, and most feature touchscreen control. Holley also offers free tuning software to help you dial in every last detail of your tune.

ECU

If you've swapped to a modern engine in your C10, there are a lot of options when it comes to ECUs, ranging from factory-style powertrain control modules (PCMs) to aftermarket computers with a range of functions.

The least expensive solution is to use a factory PCM that comes with the LS or LT engine you've likely sourced from a wrecked GM truck

110 CHEVY/GMC TRUCKS 1967–1972: HOW TO BUILD & MODIFY

FUELING, ECU, AND COOLING SYSTEM

or car. Using a stock PCM means also using a factory wiring harness, which likely includes components that you won't need. If you go this route, either make or buy a modified harness to suit your needs. That's not as hard as it might sound. PSI Conversion (psiconversion.com) specializes in custom harnesses designed for factory PCMs, and GM has a line of Connect and Cruise PCMs with universal harnesses that are ready to go and stripped of everything but the basics of engine and transmission control.

There's a lot to like about today's aftermarket ECU solutions from Holley, Edelbrock, FAST, and others. Most of these are plug-and-play, come with their own wiring harnesses, and they tend to be self-tuning, which is an important point, as it's a real plus to get out and drive while the system adjusts its fueling at different loads and RPMs. Installation tends to be simplified compared to using a stock take-off PCM. These ECUs tend to be smaller than stock units, which means they're easily hidden.

Additionally, aftermarket ECUs often offer more flexibility and ease of control than stock PCMs, especially when adding a range of speed parts to your LS or LT. In Holley's case, they also can support handheld displays or complete digital dash solutions. They also data log with great software that makes tuning easy.

Installing Holley EFI

1 The first step after installing an LS engine and plumbing it is to figure out where to mount your ECU. In this case, I'm using a Terminator X system, which is relatively compact and easy to tuck inside the glove box. It's best to isolate the ECU from heat and moisture if possible, and there are diagnostic LEDs on the top that should be mounted in a visible location.

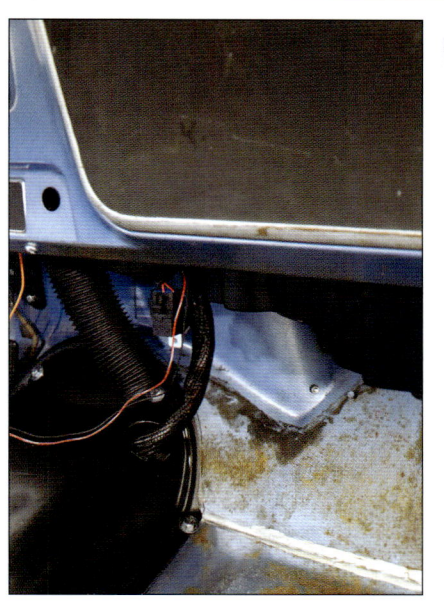

2 Holley's wiring harnesses are universal among their ECUs, which means you can install a basic Terminator X now, and if you need more features later, you can upgrade to an HP- or Dominator-series ECU without having to swap the wiring harness. Once the ECU is mounted, drill a hole that is large enough for the harness to pass through to the engine compartment. I prefer to do this in the transmission tunnel. Be sure to use a rubber grommet anywhere wiring passes through sheet metal.

3 Holley's kit comes with only a few wiring connections that need to be made. There's a constant hot wire that goes to the battery, a keyed ignition source that needs to be hot even when cranking, a tachometer signal wire, fuel-pump relay wire, and several wires that trigger cooling-fan relays. The harness also includes an A/C kick input, an A/C wide-open-throttle-shutdown circuit, and additional undefined triggers that can be set up inside the Holley software. The main power and ground wires must go straight to the battery for the best performance.

CHEVY/GMC TRUCKS 1967–1972: HOW TO BUILD & MODIFY 111

Installing Holley EFI *continued*

4 Holley's harnesses are pre-terminated with all the proper GM-style weatherpack connectors for everything from the coolant temp sensor to the idle air control (IAC) motor, throttle-position sensor, oil-pressure sensor, fuel injectors, coil packs, cam and crank sensors, etc. This makes installation a snap. Note the 102-mm Holley Sniper throttle body.

5 The Terminator X system uses a single O_2 sensor that can be run in either the driver-side or passenger-side exhaust collector. Wherever you choose to mount it, it needs to be angled with the tip slightly down to keep moisture from pooling on the sensor.

6 Once everything is wired up and all connections are double-checked, put power to the system and walk through the setup wizard within the Terminator X handheld touchscreen display that should be mounted somewhere where the driver can see it. It will ask some basic questions that will help the system generate a base tune prior to you starting the engine for the first time.

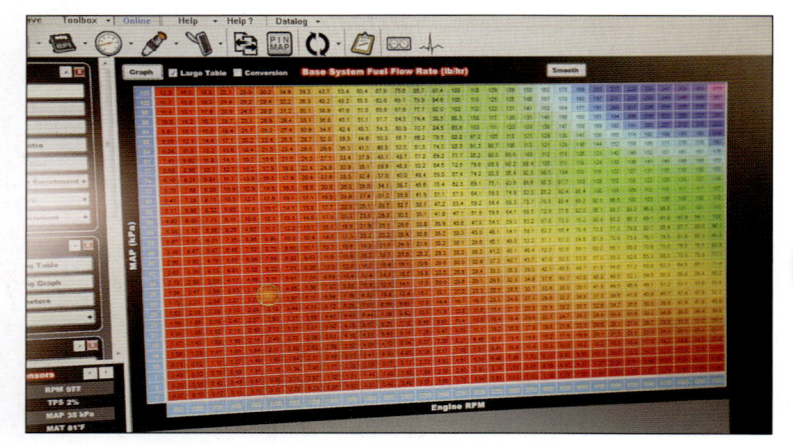

7 With the proper cable, you can connect your ECU directly to a laptop to tune it with Holley's Terminator X laptop software. This software gives you complete control over every aspect of your truck's tune from the timing curve to the fuel map, cold-start settings, power adders, and more.

Cooling System

If usability is key, consider how to maximize your C10 project's cooling system. Once you think about how your truck is going to be used, the importance of the cooling system comes into focus. In reality, classic car and truck owners love to use their vehicles when the weather is nice, which also happens to be when your stock cooling system is pressed to its limits.

Radiators

GM trucks all featured copper/brass cross-flow radiators from new, which are more effective at cooling than the top-tank style that GM used in earlier years. Chevy truck radiators are generally the same size as muscle-car units from the same era, which makes sourcing replacements easy.

Truck radiators were originally offered in four different sizes. The smallest is a $26^3/_8$-inch-wide unit with two rows of fins. It was used in 6-cylinder applications. Most got the $28^3/_8$-inch-wide unit, either in 2-row (non-A/C), 3-row (increased cooling), or 4-row (heavy-duty cooling) configurations. All had 17-inch-tall cores.

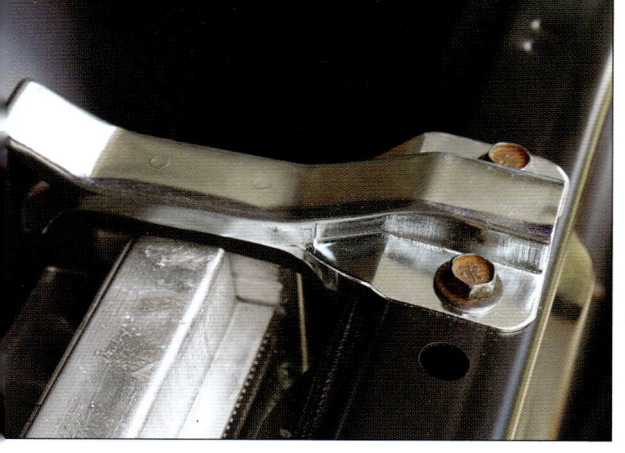

If you're adding a four-row radiator, you'll need to source four-row radiator retainers that Auto Metal Direct sells as a kit under part number 349-4067. It comes complete with upper and lower rubber cushions.

OEM radiators don't cool as well as modern units, especially in LS applications. This is a modern double-pass radiator from Holley Frostbite (note the inlet and outlet on the same side) that passes coolant through the core twice, thereby increasing heat transfer and cooling ability. It also features thread-in hose fittings, which means you can size the outlets to the hose you intend to use.

The 4-row is the best of the OEM-style radiators in terms of cooling capacity, but even a 3-row radiator is usually stout enough for most stock and mild builds. Mounting one of the larger stock-style radiators is as simple as picking up the proper wider mounts that are specific to the wider 4-row radiators.

Regardless, today's aluminum radiators do a much better job of cooling than the original GM Harrison radiators thanks to larger cooling tubes with greater surface area than the original-style radiators. A modern high-quality 2-core radiator will cool better than an original 4-core copper/brass unit thanks to its ability to transfer heat more efficiently because of aluminum construction and due to wider-than-original cooling tubes. If you're looking to upgrade a stock unit to a 4-row, consider applying that cash to a modern aluminum unit instead.

Fans

The key for any radiator is airflow. Without air moving through the radiator, it can't do its job, so fan shrouds are a must with mechanical fans. High-quality, high-capacity electric fans are key with any injected LS or LT swap or any small- or big-block that's pressed into high-stress high-heat situations (stock or not).

Most C10s featured viscous fan clutches from the factory, which are thermostatic in nature and only lock the fan to its driveshaft once the ambient under-hood temperature reaches a certain point. Pluses here are simplicity of design and good cooling in stock applications, but they're noisy and don't work that well in low-RPM, slow-speed situations, especially if there's no shroud.

If max cooling is your goal, use a set of electric cooling fans. These tend to be mounted directly to the radiator, either in pusher or puller configurations. They're generally wired up via a thermostatic switch that will connect to ground and activate a relay to kick the fans on until temperatures drop.

A good-quality wiring harness for electric fans is a requirement with heavy-gauge wiring and fuse-protected power. You'll also need a pair of relays, preferably 40-amp or larger in capacity, to handle the switching of the fans. Most aftermarket kits come with thermostatic switches that connect to ground at a certain temperature. If you're using a computer to control your LS or LT, a trigger wire can be used instead to kick on the fans at whatever temperature you'd like or when things such as A/C systems are activated.

For the best cooling method, twin fans are generally the best bet and the most efficient in puller configuration when mounted to a shroud that pulls all the air through the radiator. This setup (Frostbite part number FB513H) is designed to fit the part number FB301 radiator for a 1967–1972 C10 pickup. Wiring in relays is a must here, and they need to be sized appropriately to account for the draw of the fans. The 40-amp units are generally preferred.

CHEVY/GMC TRUCKS 1967–1972: HOW TO BUILD & MODIFY

CHAPTER 9

TRANSMISSIONS

GM built its trucks with a good range of available transmissions in the 1967–1972 era. Most of them are stout units that can and will provide years of service without much fuss, aside from periodic maintenance. Many great options are available today to modernize your truck's shifting performance over what it could do from the factory in terms of upgrades and complete transmission swaps. Regardless of how you get there, using modern parts in your C10 can improve performance and economy, which are both welcome traits in a custom truck that you intend to drive regularly.

Beyond that, consider this: as a custom truck builder, your goals are very different than what GM's engineers considered when they were designing and engineering the gearboxes in the 1967–1972 truck line. Hauling a lot of weight slowly is one thing, but cruising down the highway at 75 mph is quite another.

The best performing LS swap or big-block isn't going to do anything for you without a great gearbox behind it. Beyond that, the weakest low-compression 6-cylinder or 283 will see a big gain in usable performance with a tight, modern overdrive transmission that offers a steep first gear and one (or more) overdrive gears for low-RPM highway cruising. Today, you can have the best of both worlds behind whatever engine you're running. You just need to select and install the right parts.

Before getting into what's possible under the high- and low-hump C10 floors, let's take a quick look at what was available from GM when these trucks were new.

Manual

Three pedals were standard equipment on just about every truck in the American market in the 1960s, generally in either 3- or 4-speed configurations and with grunt prioritized over shift feel and ease of use. GM offered a few options for buyers, depending on the truck's intended use.

3-Speed Saginaw

The base-level transmission on all GM trucks of this era was the Saginaw 3-speed manual. The Saginaw is a column-shift design, which is great for anti-theft in today's world. It looks like an automatic on the column but still has a clutch pedal.

The Saginaw is a decent enough

Don't be surprised to find a grimy truck transmission behind the small-block or Stovebolt in your C10 project. Units such as this SM465 4-speed were common back in the day. While they aren't great performance transmissions, they are strong units that shouldn't give you much trouble.

TRANSMISSIONS

transmission, but it can't handle a lot of power. The earlier versions didn't have a synchronized first gear, which can make driving in traffic a chore. They're weak and somewhat hard to use depending on your level of skill and patience. In addition, the 3-speed column linkage is known for binding, which can jam and cause the transmission to not go into gear. Because of this, many 3-speed trucks have been converted to floor shift.

The other downside to the Saginaw is the limitation that only three forward gears provides, although there was a rare overdrive-equipped version offered in 1967 and 1968 (only on 10-series rigs). It was RPO M10.

There was a heavy-duty 3-speed offered by BorgWarner mostly on C20 and heavier trucks. It can handle more power, but it's not as common.

Earlier rigs used a transmission mount at the bellhousing versus at the rear of the transmission, so keep that in mind when getting ready to swap. You'll need a different transmission crossmember as well.

4-Speed Muncie

In 1967, the SM420 was available in GM trucks but only for that one year, as it was replaced by the SM465 in 1968. Both these transmissions are granny-gear floor-shift models, but the 420 is slightly smaller overall than the 465.

These transmissions are typically driven as 3-speeds and use second gear to start unless the truck is heavily loaded. First gear in the 420 and the 465 is too steep for daily traffic use.

Both these transmissions are generally bulletproof, and both share similar characteristics: long shift throws and heavy cast-iron cases. In either case, this is about as tough and basic as a truck transmission can get, but you won't ever forget you're driving a truck when rowing one of these things. They were used in dump trucks for a reason. For strength and towing/hauling prowess, look no further. For performance use, look elsewhere.

This is your standard car-style Muncie 4-speed, which came in M20, M21, and M22 variants. This is an M21 wide-ratio transmission that shares its basic mounting configuration with a TH400 automatic. It's easy to swap into a C10 if a row-your-own muscle car transmission is your goal.

A column shift and a clutch pedal are indicative of the base Saginaw 3-speed manual transmission in your C10. This isn't a great performance option, but there's something fun about shifting on the column, especially if you grew up in the era when these were common.

Manual Gear Ratios and Measurements						
Transmission	First	Second	Third	Fourth	Case to Tailshaft	Output Splines
Saginaw 3-speed	2.85:1	1.68:1	1.00:1	N/A	16.25 inches	27
Muncie SM420 (1967 only)	7.05:1	3.58:1	1.71:1	1.00:1	10.7 inches	11
Muncie SM465	6.55:1	3.58:1	1.70:1	1.00:1	12 inches	10, 35, 32

Automatic

Automatic transmissions made their way into more trucks by the time the 1967 C10s and C20s hit the market. Several options were available through the years.

2-Speed Powerglide

GM's Powerglide is probably the most basic automatic transmission available. It's also very durable, lightweight, and has a great reputation among serious drag racers.

CHEVY/GMC TRUCKS 1967–1972: HOW TO BUILD & MODIFY

CHAPTER 9

The TH350 is a great overall 3-speed automatic transmission, but it's not as strong as its TH400 cousin. However, these will run for a long time when properly set up. GM installed many of these in C10s, so parts are easy to come by. These units can be built to do just about anything from drag racing to towing.

GM used the Powerglide from the early 1950s through 1973, which means you can find them in most C10s, at least as an option. They became harder to find toward the end of the production of this generation of trucks thanks to the widespread use of the TH350.

The Powerglide operates with a basic low and high gear range with a standard 1:1 final-drive ratio. As such, trucks with these units tend to be a little slower off the line than other automatic transmissions in stock applications because they only shift once. They don't have the same spread of gear ratios as in a 3-speed auto, such as a TH350 or TH400, and that can impact performance in a generally heavy truck.

However, a Powerglide doesn't use nearly the same amount of power to run as a TH350 or TH400. That, combined with durability, is why racers love them so much. They're also relatively compact. The low-hump floor design used in some C10s and C20s was developed with this transmission in mind.

Here's the easiest, quickest way to spot a TH350 versus the bigger and stronger TH400: the oil-pan shape. The top pan is from a TH350, and the bottom one is from a TH400. These aftermarket pans have the benefit of added drain plugs, which you won't find with a factory pan in most cases.

3-Speed TH350

This is GM's ubiquitous 3-speed automatic that was introduced in trucks in 1969 and designed to be a replacement for the aging 2-speed Powerglide. These units are stout in nature but aren't as strong as their TH400 cousins, although they were the transmission of choice in most half-ton trucks throughout the 1970s.

The 350 is easily identified thanks to its square transmission pan with one angled corner and because of the five or six fluid leaks that they all seem to have. One thing to keep in mind is that 4x4 and two-wheel-drive TH350s are not the same, so be careful when shopping for a replacement.

If you have a TH350 behind a small-block, you have a strong basis for a build that will last a long time, even in big-power situations. As with anything mechanical, your mileage will vary based on the quality of the build work that went into it.

3-Speed TH400

The TH400 is widely considered GM's toughest automatic transmission and was an option in C10 and C20 trucks throughout the 1967–1972 era, particularly in rigs set up for more substantial towing and hauling. It was the transmission that was used behind a big-block in most cases.

The TH400 is a physically larger transmission than both the TH350 and the Powerglide, which meant it sometimes required a slightly larger transmission tunnel in the rigs in which it was installed. GM offered both low- and high-hump-style cabs, which were set up with different floor-pan center sections based on the options ordered. Not every TH400 truck had the high-hump

116   CHEVY/GMC TRUCKS 1967–1972: HOW TO BUILD & MODIFY

TRANSMISSIONS

GM Automatic Gear Ratios and Measurements

Transmission	First	Second	Third	Overall Length	Bellhousing to Transmission Mount	Output Splines
Powerglide	1.82:1 (6-cylinder), 1.76:1 (V-8)	1.00:1	N/A	25 23/64 inches (short), 27 9/16 inches (long)	16 5/16 inches	27
TH350	2.52:1	1.52:1	1.00:1	27 5/8 inches (short), 30 5/8 inches (long)	20 3/8 inches	27
TH400	2.48:1	1.48:1	1.00:1	28 1/4 inches (short), 34 inches (long)	26 3/4 inches (short), 28 inches (long)	27

floor, but many did, particularly those with big-block engines.

For basic brute strength, a TH400 is your friend. GM put these behind everything from heavy-duty trucks to L88 Corvettes, and they were rated from new to be good past 450 ft-lbs of torque. Of course, the aftermarket has made them even stronger, much like with the TH350 and Powerglide. However, don't assume that an original transmission (Powerglide, TH350, or TH400) is ready to live behind your new crate engine. Rebuilds are smart insurance, and they're not particularly expensive, either. Anything in stock form is going to need a once-over before you put real power to it.

If you intend on diving into any automatic GM transmission, be sure you have a large, clean workspace, and get yourself a dedicated rebuild manual and the proper tools for the job. There are a lot of small pieces inside a TH350 or TH400, and they're all vital to your transmission's operation.

Upgrades

Assuming that your original automatic transmission is in good working order, you can do a few things to stiffen up those shifts to match a hotter engine under the hood.

Shift Kits

Just about every GM automatic was a mushy shifter from new, thanks to GM's policy of making things softer and more comfortable for average, everyday drivers. Of course, all that cushy nonsense meant extra heat and diminished performance for the rest of us, but that can be solved with a shift kit.

Generally speaking, a shift kit reprograms the OEM valve body inside an automatic transmission to increase line pressure and direct more fluid flow to the clutches, which firms up and quickens shift performance considerably over stock. In short, you get firmer shifts, less heat, and better performance overall, which is just the thing for a truck that's getting pressed into performance duty. These are available in various stages, ranging from a mild performance boost to an all-out manual-only setup for racing use.

Summit Racing offers shift kits for both the TH350 and TH400. In both cases, some transmission disassembly is required, but both transmissions can be upgraded with the transmission still in the truck. In both cases, the pan and the valve body have to be removed for the install, but it's basically a messy weekend project that has the potential to offer some serious performance benefits.

If you intend to use a TH350 or TH400, consider a shift kit because it's a great upgrade that can improve both shift firmness and transmission longevity. These kits include internal components that essentially reprogram your transmission's shift quality by altering fluid flow through the transmission's valve body. Installation can be handled with the transmission still in the truck. (Photo Courtesy Classic Industries)

CHAPTER 9

If your transmission has a lot of miles on it already, it might be smart to wait on the shift kit until you're in for a complete rebuild. Worn-down clutch packs aren't going to benefit much from increased line pressure and more fluid volume. In that case, it's best to spend the money once and do it right.

Torque Converters

Between the engine and transmission sits a fluid coupling known as a torque converter. Various converters are suited for different tasks from towing strength through drag-strip launches. Whatever your plans are for your truck, a replacement torque converter can be tuned to deliver the best performance possible to achieve your goals.

A converter uses an impeller, stator, and turbine mounted inside a drum-style housing that's filled with transmission fluid. The impeller is coupled directly to the engine's crankshaft, while the turbine is meshed to the transmission's input shaft. The stator helps multiply torque during periods of high slippage, such as when pulling away from a stop. In any case, the fluid is what drives the coupling here.

Converters are generally measured in stall speed. Looser converters with higher stall speeds are typically used in drag-race environments, where a higher-RPM launch is preferred or where other engine modifications require a higher stall speed for optimal performance, such as running a large camshaft and high compression. If you opt for a high stall converter, note that anything more than 3,000 rpm is going to be too loose for most extended street driving as it will feel mushy at low speeds and build a lot of heat.

For most stock street use, GM's factory converters stalled at around 1,300 rpm. Most towing performance converters have similar specifications today.

Upgrading a converter requires pulling the transmission from the truck, which isn't a small job. But when properly matched to the engine and rear gear ratio, a performance-style converter is a key piece of the performance puzzle. Companies such as Hughes, B&M, ATI, and others are more than happy to run your specs to be sure you choose the proper converter for the type of driving you have in mind. Just be sure to have all the specifications in-hand before you call, including tire diameter, rear gear ratio, engine RPM range, cam specs, compression ratio, and weight. All of these things factor into picking the right torque converter for your application.

Transmission Swaps

Any of the original transmissions offered in these trucks serve as a good basis for basic performance, except for the 3-speed manual on the tree. If a cost-effective swap is on your

The torque converter is another component that can deliver a lot of bang for the upgrade buck, especially if you've swapped cam profiles from stock. Success depends on multiple factors from your truck's intended use through its curb weight, final-drive ratio, compression ratio, cam profile, and more. For a mild engine combination, something in the 2,000- to 2,500-rpm stall range provides good street drivability and better power delivery over stock.

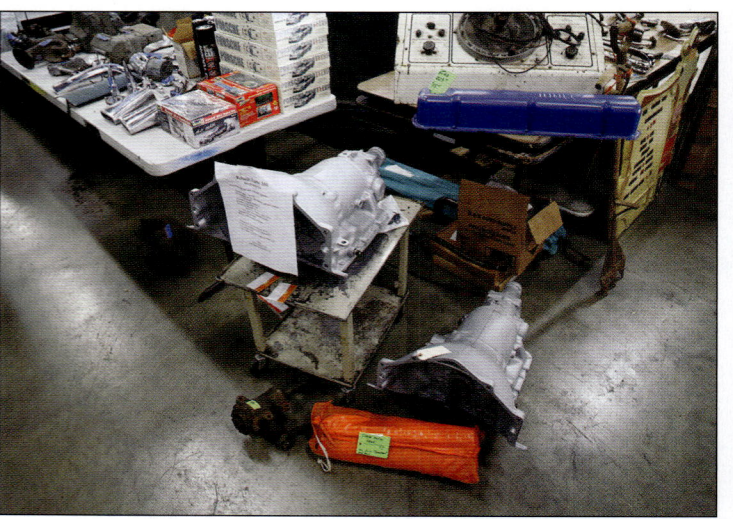

It's common to find rebuilt TH350s at swap meets, and they can be a great deal if you can find a reputable seller. However, this is a case where you have to take the builder's word for the work that's been done, so be careful if you intend on going this route. It might be smarter to find a TH350 core for rebuild by your local aftermarket transmission shop or source a fresh unit from Gearstar, Summit, etc.

TRANSMISSIONS

mind, going with something that would have been stock is likely the best route. A TH400 or TH350 automatic can be made to stand up to just about any power you can throw at it, and it will be a lot easier to live with than the Saginaw 3-gear or SM465 4-speed truck transmission. Even a Muncie or Super T10 4-speed from the muscle-car era is a basic, direct swap behind a small- or big-block Chevrolet, and there won't be any clearance issues. In fact, if you decide to run a Muncie, you'll be able to use the same transmission crossmember that a TH400 truck had from the factory.

GM didn't put car-style Muncies in these trucks, but that doesn't mean that you can't.

There's one thing to consider regarding OEM-style swaps. If you choose to go this route, try to find a complete setup that has everything. For manual transmissions, you'll want everything from the crossmember to the clutch pedal, Z-bar, rod, clutch, clutch fork, throwout bearing, flywheel, and clutch. In terms of automatics, get the kickdown setup, neutral safety switch, slip yoke, cooler lines, and flexplate. Piecing this together later can be expensive and time-consuming, so if you can get it all from the same source, do it. It will save you a lot of trouble later.

If you're going to go to the trouble to swap out a transmission, it's important to consider the difference in cost between a more modern overdrive automatic or manual compared to a 3-speed automatic or 4-speed manual. The difference in price may not be as much as you initially think, and even if it is, that extra overdrive gear is something you'll eventually wish you had, especially if you intend on driving your truck on the open highway. With gas prices

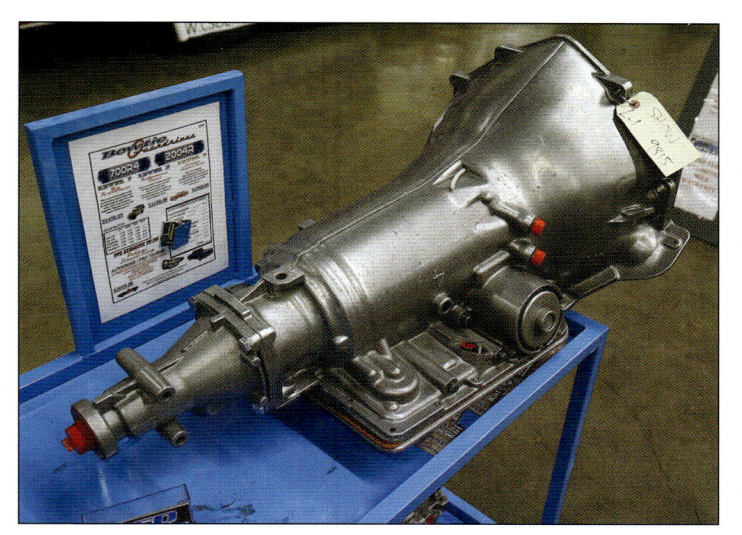

Think of the 700R4 like a TH350 with an extra gear and a lockup converter. Look for units built in 1988 or later because they have some stronger internal parts than the earlier versions. This is the simplest overdrive automatic you can swap into your C10, as it doesn't require special electronics to function properly.

climbing, it's better to have your C10 use less of it. Lower RPM means less noise and less heat, which makes for a better drive.

Overdrive Automatics

GM offered a number of overdrive automatics in the 1980s and beyond, and many have become standard swaps for earlier-generation trucks.

700R4

The 700R4 was intended to be a replacement for the TH350. It was introduced in 1982 and has been used in all sorts of things over the years, so they're easy to find. These transmissions have no electronic controllers, which makes them great for use in traditional carbureted small- and big-block applications. Since they were designed to live where the TH350 used to live, they'll generally bolt in place.

Not every 700R4 was created equal. The earlier versions are weaker, so look for the 1988-and-later versions that had upgraded internal parts for greater longevity. Every 700R4 has the same square oil pan, and trucks with them have an overdrive selector on the column. These units all have a throttle valve (TV) cable that connects to the throttle arm and tells the transmission to firm up shifts based on throttle input.

4L60/4L60E/4L65E/4L70E

The 4L60-series was an evolution of the 700R4 and was launched in 1992. It became the 4L60E in 1997, thanks to the addition of some electronic controls that were used to help increase performance and economy as well as a removable bellhousing that was designed to work with the LS series of engines. These later units require a transmission control module (TCM). If you're using a Holley Terminator X ECU, note that it can be ordered in "Max" configuration to control a 60E or 80E.

In 1998, GM upgraded the 60E with a 300-mm input shaft for LS engine use as well as a bellhousing bolt in the 12 o'clock position. Earlier 60s can be used behind LS engines but only with an additional pilot spacer and special dual-bolt-pattern flexplate. That's not a hard-and-fast rule, as some early LS engines

CHAPTER 9

The 4L60E gets a bad rap in stock form as it's not known for living long behind any kind of power beyond what a stock LS engine produces. Companies such as Gearstar build improved 4L60Es that can survive in high-horsepower situations. This is Gearstar's Level 4 build, which is rated for up to 650 hp and 600 ft-lbs of torque. (Photo Courtesy Gearstar)

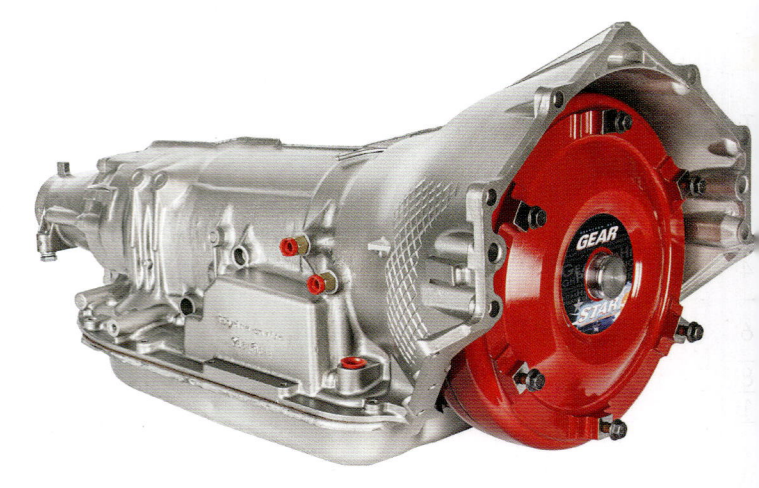

If you're going to use a stock-sourced 4-speed automatic, start with the beefier 4L80E that will fit where a TH400 did from the factory (more or less), as they have similar overall dimensions. There are versions for traditional Gen II small-block and big-block engines as well as LS engines. This is the upgraded Gearstar 4L80E rated for 800 hp and 700 ft-lbs of torque. (Photo Courtesy Gearstar)

featured a longer, small-block-style crankshaft output design. Nonetheless, the later 60E transmissions are beefier internally than their older siblings, so they're the better choice for swaps.

Overall, these units aren't any bigger than the 700R4 they replaced, which makes them good candidates for use here. Note that they don't usually live long in high-power applications without some significant modification.

The 4L65E was launched in 2001 alongside the 6.0 LS engine. It is generally stronger but requires a different torque converter than the 60. Better yet is the 4L70E that shares the 60's external dimensions but has completely revised internals for more reliable power handling.

4L80E/4L85E

What do you get when you add a gear, a locking converter, and some electronics to the legendary TH400? You get the 4L80E range, which is the strongest GM 4-speed automatic out there.

This transmission was launched in 1991 for use in heavy-duty trucks. Its greater torque handling than the 60E has made it the go-to for many LS builders today. Just like the 60E, this range of transmissions requires a TCM to control its shift functions, but there are a number of both stock and aftermarket solutions to that problem.

The nice thing about the 80 is in its brute strength. These transmissions were designed with heavy-duty use in mind, and as such, they'll hold up to a lot of power in even stock configuration. Add some aftermarket components, and you'll have a bulletproof transmission for just about any power level that you're making with your small-block, big-block, or LS engine.

The 4L85E is basically a stronger version of the 80E. It was originally designed for additional towing capacity and features additional clutch packs over the standard 4L80E.

A 4L80E will fit in most places that a TH400 did, but it is both slightly wider and 4 inches longer than a TH400. The transmission mount is pushed back about 1.5 inches from where it was on the TH400. There's plenty of transmission tunnel clearance, especially with the high-hump floor. It is a tight fit with the low-hump floor. Note that you'll have to relocate the stock crossmember to use one.

6L80E/6L90E

If you're in the market for more gears, GM's got you covered with the 6L80E and 6L90E 6-speed automatics. These were launched in 2005 for the 2006 model year and aren't well suited to anything other than LS power. These units were designed to be electronic over hydraulic, which means they require their own internally mounted computer for operation. They feature a clutch-to-clutch gear change operation rather than bands and clutches (as were seen in previous designs).

120   CHEVY/GMC TRUCKS 1967–1972: HOW TO BUILD & MODIFY

TRANSMISSIONS

Gear Ratios and Measurements

Transmission	First	Second	Third	Fourth	Fifth	Sixth	Seventh	Eighth	Ninth	Tenth	Overall Length	Bellhousing to Transmission Mount	Output Splines
4L60-range	3.06:1	1.62:1	1.00:1	0.69:1	N/A	N/A	N/A	N/A	N/A	N/A	27¾ inches	22³⁄₈ inches	27
4L80-range	2.48:1	1.48:1	1.00:1	0.75:1	N/A	N/A	N/A	N/A	N/A	N/A	31½ inches	30³⁄₈ inches	32
6L80-range	4.03:1	2.36:1	1.53:1	1.15:1	0.85:1	0.67:1	N/A	N/A	N/A	N/A	30.85 inches	25.409 inches	32
8L90-range	4.56:1	2.97:1	2.07:1	1.68:1	1.27:1	1.00:1	0.84:1	0.65:1	N/A	N/A	29 inches	25.3 inches	N/A
10L90-range	4.69:1	2.98:1	2.14:1	1.76:1	1.52:1	1.27:1	1.00:1	0.85:1	0.68:1	0.63:1	29 inches	25.3 inches	N/A

While these transmissions have six forward gears compared to the 4L60's and 4L80's four, these units are physically shorter. That said, they are larger in diameter, so a high-hump floor is a must if you intend on installing one in a C10. They are strong units, and the extra gearing allows for both a steep first and a long-legged sixth.

The TCM in the 6L80 is internally located, which means it can't be swapped out with a different unit, as is the case with the 4L series. It's also dependent on other engine controllers to function correctly, namely the body-control module and the engine controller. That complicates swaps, but there are aftermarket solutions that will allow one to use a 6L80 in a swap situation. You can also get a complete controller solution from GM directly alongside a crate engine, such as with its Connect and Cruise line.

8L90E/10L90E

To reduce cruising RPM even more and produce better overall mileage figures, GM released an 8-speed automatic known as the 8L90E in 2015. These units are similar in size to the 6L80E, but they're only compatible with the later LT engines thanks to their later bellhousing designs. Other notable features are an external TCM, adaptive-learning capabilities, and female output shaft.

The 10L90E added even more forward gears into the mix starting in 2017, along with a lot more strength. As of this writing, this is state of the art when it comes to GM-offered automatics (which was designed in conjunction with Ford), but they require complex computer controls to support the self-learning functions, the clutch-to-clutch shifts, and more. GM Performance sells these for use behind Gen V LT engines, so that's an option if you're in the market for the best possible mix of off-the-line performance and low cruise RPM.

Manual Swaps

If your truck came with a third pedal from the factory, there's no reason to swap it out for an automatic to get those extra overdrive gears. In fact, the aftermarket has a number of excellent overdriven manual transmissions that keep the fun of a third pedal while lowering revs on the freeway.

Tremec TKO/TKX 5-speed and Magnum 6-speed

Do you want to keep that third pedal and add some overdrive capabilities to your C10? Tremec has you covered with a range of overdrive manuals, all of which can be easily adapted to whatever engine you're running in your C10.

The TKO is a stronger version of the original Mustang-based T5, built to live well beyond where the T5 would have given up and equipped with multiple shifter locations and mounting configurations. These transmissions are rated for up to 600

Tremec's TKX 5-speed is all the rage in the aftermarket because it features great power-handling abilities and shift quality in a compact package designed for tight transmission tunnels. This fits under a low-hump or high-hump C10 floor section, which makes it ideal for C10 applications.

CHEVY/GMC TRUCKS 1967–1972: HOW TO BUILD & MODIFY

The Tremec Magnum transmission, otherwise known as the T56 in its stock configuration, is another great choice for C10 builders. Its size generally requires floor modifications for C10 use, particularly at the rear of the original high-hump floor. Its aggressive first gear and double overdrives are hard to beat, and it's strong enough to live behind any street motor.

ft-lbs and are a good option for just about any powerplant. In addition, Tremec offers the TKX, which has taken the automotive aftermarket by storm. The TKX is physically about the same size as the TKO, but it has a smoother case for easier clearance in a wide range of transmission tunnels, including under a low-hump C10 floor.

The TKX is rated for 600 ft-lbs of torque, is smooth shifting, and can bang gears up to 7,500 rpm. It also features multiple shifter locations for different applications, including a front-mount shifter location that works with C10 trucks that still have a bench seat.

Finally, there's the Magnum 6-speed manual, which is based on the T56 6-speed found in the fourth-gen Camaro, C5 Corvette (transaxle), Dodge Viper, and Shelby GT500. The Magnum, like the TKX, was designed as an aftermarket transmission with swaps in mind and features multiple shifter locations, a smoother case, and a revised transmission mount located over OEM take-outs. Running a stock-style GTO or Camaro transmission works fine too, but you'll have more fabrication to do. You'll also need to disassemble the transmission if you intend on running a front-mount shifter for bench seat clearance. This is not the case with the aftermarket Magnum.

Despite having a smoother case than a stock take-out, the Magnum is physically a lot larger than the TKO and TKX, which means transmission tunnel and floor modifications are required if you plan on running one in your C10. With that being said, there's a lot to like about the Magnum's two overdrive gears, third pedal, and that 700-ft-lbs torque rating.

All three of these Tremec transmissions are available with multiple gear-ratio options to add flexibility. In any case, if you have a stock freeway-friendly 3.08 rear gear ratio, plan on swapping in something steeper to make use of the overdrive gears along with the more aggressive first-gear ratios offered here.

The key to any of these manual swaps is to source the proper parts for the job, and that's easier than ever thanks to several aftermarket companies that make complete conversion kits for C10 pickups. Modern Driveline, Silver Sport Transmissions, and American Powertrain all offer various solutions engineered to get a modern overdrive manual fitted under the floor of your C10. Depending on the kit you choose, they can have absolutely everything you need included—down to the wiring for the backup light switch and all the fluids required.

Gear Ratios and Measurements

Transmission	First	Second	Third	Fourth	Fifth	Sixth	Overall Length	Input to Transmission Mount	Output Splines
TKO 500	3.27:1	1.98:1	1.34:1	1.00:1	0.68:1	N/A	30.4 inches	22.1 inches	31
TKO 600	2.87:1	1.89:1	1.28:1	1.00:1	0.64:1 (or 0.82:1)	N/A	30.4 inches	22.1 inches	31
TKX	3.27:1 (or 2.87:1)	1.98:1 (or 1.89:1)	1.34:1 (or 1.28:1)	1.00:1	0.72:1 (or 0.81:1 or 0.68:1)	N/A	31.0 inches	22.7 inches	31
T56 Magnum	2.66:1 (or 2.97:1)	1.78:1 (or 2.10:1)	1.30:1 (or 1.46:1)	1.00:1	0.80:1 (or 0.74:1)	0.63:1 (or 0.50:1)	33.5 inches	26.5 inches	31

TRANSMISSIONS

Setting up a TKX from Silver Sport Transmissions in a C10

1 This is Silver Sport Transmission's 1967–1972 C10 TKX conversion kit. It comes with everything you need to complete a 5-speed overdrive swap from the transmission to the bellhousing, clutch, hydraulics, pedal assembly, crossmember, shifter, wiring, and even the transmission fluid and clutch hydraulic fluid.

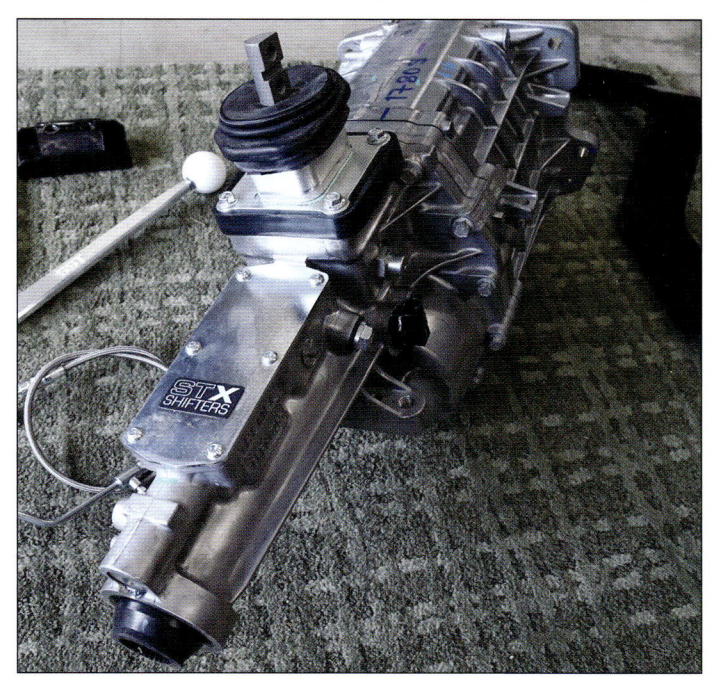

2 The TKX, as delivered from SST, is modified to accept SST's bearing retainer and slave cylinder. This unit is a close-ratio transmission with a 2.87 first gear and a 0.68 overdrive. From SST, this transmission has a 36-month warranty. The STX front-mount shifter is designed to clear a factory bench seat in a C10 cab.

3 This is SST's Advance Friction LS steel 6-bolt flywheel. It's a 12-inch unit specific for LS use. Along with its clutch disc and pressure plate, it's rated for 550 ft-lbs of torque. It needs to be temporarily mounted to measure for proper alignment with the bellhousing. Hand-tight will do.

4 Next up is SST's Super Duty 621-style bellhousing for LS engines that bolts in place using supplied Allen-head hardware. Note the dial indicator, which is here to measure for any alignment issues between the crankshaft and bellhousing due to casting irregularities. The TKX (and any modern overdrive manual) is very sensitive to proper crankshaft centerline alignment. Runout between them needs to be within 0.005 inch to ensure long transmission life.

CHEVY/GMC TRUCKS 1967–1972: HOW TO BUILD & MODIFY

CHAPTER 9

Setting up a TKX from Silver Sport Transmissions in a C10 *continued*

5 The idea is to determine how well the crankshaft centerline matches up with the bellhousing centerline. That's done by positioning the dial indicator base flat on the flywheel and the dial itself on the bellhousing's center register. After adjusting just a little preload into the dial, pick a starting point on the bellhousing, mark it, and zero the dial before having a friend turn the engine over slowly. Mark the most positive number with a permanent marker. In this case, it was +0.024 at about the 6 o'clock mark. Zero the indicator on that mark and run the engine over 180 degrees, mark that reading, and divide that number in half to get the runout. In this case, it was 0.012 inch and outside the 0.005 tolerance.

6 How can it be fixed? SST has some of the best offset dowel pins in the business. They easily slide into place, feature wrench flats for easy adjustment, have the high sides marked for easy reference, and feature locking nuts to snug them into place. These are offset 0.014, which is enough to get this setup back into spec. The only challenge is tapping out the old pins, which requires a punch and a hammer.

7 With the pins installed, double-check the runout in the same way as before and verify that you're within spec. Here, the number is 0.009 inch. When cut in half, it is within spec. The installation can continue.

8 SST ships its flywheels with new bolts, and now's the time to torque them to spec. In this case, it's 74 ft-lbs with a good drop of thread-lock compound on each of them.

TRANSMISSIONS

9 An impact socket that has the same outer diameter as the pilot bearing is the best tool for installation. A few smacks with a hammer seats it in place. Be sure that you have the orientation and style correct for the transmission you're using.

10 The clutch disc, alignment tool, and pressure plate are installed next—but only after cleaning all of the flywheel and pressure-plate surfaces to be sure there's no oil or greasy fingerprints because they will cause clutch chatter. The pressure plate bolts in place using hardware from the kit with a torque spec of 52 ft-lbs.

11 Next, check the clearance of the concentric slave cylinder (CSC). The goal is to achieve between 1/8 and 3/8 inch of cushion beyond the 1/2 inch of compression that the bearing will have at rest when installed. This is done by measuring the compressed bearing distance from the transmission face and comparing that to the measurement from the clutch fingers to the transmission mounting surface at the bellhousing. Adjustments can be made using spacers that mount between the bearing and the transmission.

12 SST supplies a combination hard and braided steel line for the clutch hydraulics. It needs to be fitted to the CSC after the bellhousing is loosely fitted to the front of the TKX transmission. Be careful, as the bearing has aluminum threads that are easy to cross-thread. Then, the bellhousing can be removed from the front of the transmission (with the bearing hanging inside it) and installed on the back of the engine.

CHEVY/GMC TRUCKS 1967–1972: HOW TO BUILD & MODIFY

CHAPTER 9

Setting up a TKX from Silver Sport Transmission in a C10 *continued*

13 Finally, the transmission can be slid into place through the bearing and into the clutch disc and pilot bearing. This can be a bit of a job, so it helps to have a spare set of hands to wiggle, shake, and jostle the transmission into place. Avoid using bolts to pull the transmission to the engine using the mounting ears, as they break easily.

14 The hard work is done. SST provides fabricated covers for either side of the bellhousing at the starter and behind the oil filter. The transmission bellhousing-to-engine bolts take 37 ft-lbs of torque, while the transmission-to-bellhousing bolts get 50 ft-lbs. SST provides a special socket-head bolt for the upper-left transmission-to-bellhousing location, as access is tight there.

15 The TKX is a low-profile transmission, and to make it easier to service, install a high-hump transmission tunnel prior to installing the engine and transmission in the truck. This one is from Classic Industries and was manufactured to fit like an original after you mark and cut the floor.

16 After fitting the new tunnel in place and marking where it sits on the floor, installing it is as easy as cutting an inch or so inboard of its outer measurements and drilling holes in the proper mounting locations. Use something round that fits in the channel at the rear (such as an AA battery) to align the new panel properly before marking your cuts.

TRANSMISSIONS

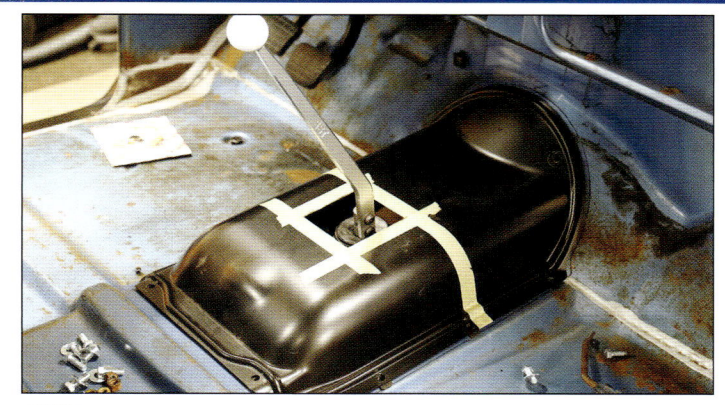

17 Next, mark the shifter location and cut out the center of the new tunnel to match. Leave enough room for the shifter to function but not too much, as to leave a hole you'll have to fill later. The new panel can bolt in place using captured nut clips and hardware-store bolts. Use seam sealer or a similar insulation between the panel and the floor to keep out fumes and moisture. You'll need to swap the carpet to a high-hump floor panel set because low-hump carpet won't fit properly.

18 The transmission crossmember can be installed one of two ways, but if you're using long-tube headers, the angular sections need to be pointed back toward the rear axle to create clearance for the exhaust. Note the OEM-style transmission mount used here, which was provided with the Silver Sport kit.

Hydraulic Clutches

If you chose to upgrade to a modern manual overdrive transmission and you've swapped to an LS or LT engine, chances are good that you'll be looking to upgrade to a modern-style hydraulic clutch too. You can technically run a manual clutch with a TKX if you source the proper bellhousing, but note that different LS swap engine brackets place the engine in different places relative to the frame, which means your original clutch Z-bar won't necessarily be in the proper place to operate the clutch. Swapping to a hydraulic clutch makes sense here because it completely avoids the problem while also giving a better, modern clutch pedal feel.

Here's the thing: all clutches from the 1967–1972 era were manual, so your only choice is to cobble together something using factory GM parts from other cars or to go with an aftermarket kit where the manufacturer already worked out where to mount the master cylinder and other components.

Installing a Hydraulic Clutch from Silver Sport in a C10

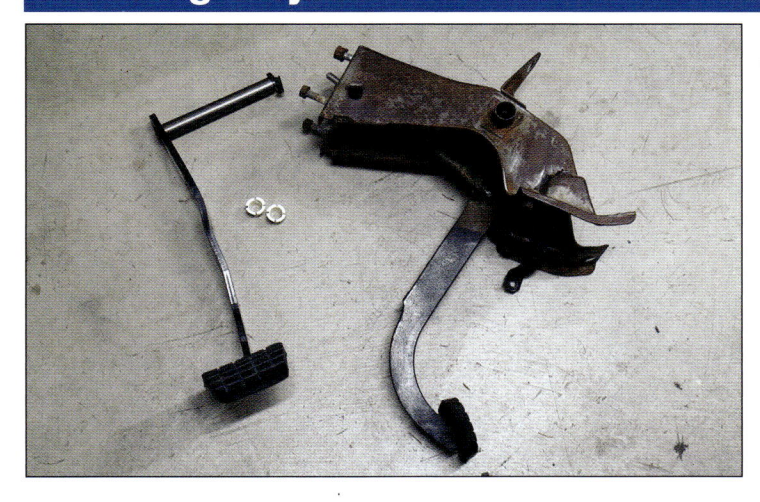

1 SST's 1967–1972 GM truck TKX kit comes complete with all the components needed to run a hydraulic clutch pedal in your truck, including the pedal itself and new pivot bushings to make it function like a new unit. After removing the pedal box from the truck, installation is a snap. It pays to do this, even in a factory manual truck, as the new clutch pedal is drilled in the proper place for use with SST's hydro clutch setup. If you want to drill your own pedal, aim for a 6:1 pedal ratio. For a 15¾-long pedal, drill the hole 2⅝ inches down from the fulcrum. Remove the original clutch return spring, which was part of the original clutch pedal setup.

CHEVY/GMC TRUCKS 1967–1972: HOW TO BUILD & MODIFY

CHAPTER 9

Installing a Hydraulic Clutch from Silver Sport in a C10 continued

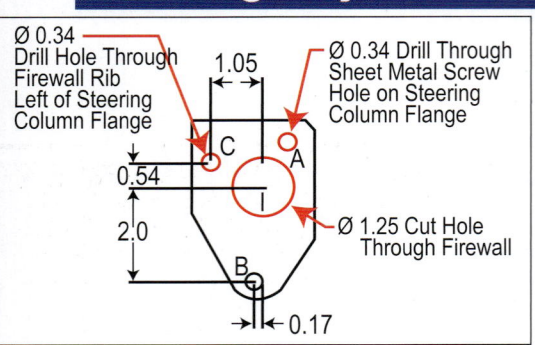

2 *This template is a handy tool for locating all the proper holes in the firewall for the new hydraulic-clutch assembly, including a 1.25-inch main hole that will be used for the new clutch rod. Several holes already exist in the firewall, which helps to index everything properly. (Diagram Courtesy Silver Sport Transmissions)*

3 *This kit comes with a template to show you where to drill. After that, the hydraulic system can be mocked up using the hardware from the kit. The new master cylinder is fixed to the firewall to limit potential flexing thanks to its installation over a double-walled section. Everything lines up well under the hood, with the master tucked up close to the inner fender liner but not touching it. This is a good time to mock up and drill the holes for the reservoir as well. I prefer mounting it as close as possible to the master itself.*

4 *With the pedal assembly back in place, the only thing left is to assemble the clutch rod to the pedal and master cylinder. SST's kit comes with this adjustable unit that features a Heim joint on the pedal end to make both assembly and later adjustment a snap. Make sure the master cylinder rod is fully extended before attaching the pedal. Failing to do so will cause issues with bleeding and can damage the CSC.*

Driveline

GM built its trucks with both one- and two-piece drivelines from the factory. What you received depended on how the truck was configured. For instance, many 6-cylinder rigs came with one-piece drivelines, while most V-8 trucks had two-piece units with a carrier bearing in the middle.

If you're looking to shorten your truck or you'd like to simplify things regarding power delivery, consider swapping over to a one-piece driveline in your C10. Many modern suspension kits, including the one I installed in my project truck, delete the carrier-bearing mount. In that case, the choice is made for you.

A good two-piece unit, if properly set up, will take a lot of abuse and last a long time. After all, GM installed them in trucks for a reason. They're strong.

For any driveshaft, quality U-joints are key, as are the setup and balance job. Get this wrong and you'll have a truck that shakes at speed no matter what you do. It pays to do this once and do it right, preferably via a shop that specializes in driveshafts.

Measuring for the proper driveline length is critical, and various shops have different methods that they like to use. Generally, the method is to measure from the output-shaft housing of the transmission to the U-joint mounting surface on the differential yoke. Shops often have variations on this method, so check with the shop before you climb under your truck. Note that you must measure with the truck at ride height to get a proper reading.

CHAPTER 10

REAR AXLE

Making power in your C10 is great, but it takes a good axle assembly to get that power to the ground. From the factory, every C- and K-series GM truck had a live axle underneath the bed. Depending on the year of your truck and the configuration it had from the factory, there are several different axles that could be underneath it.

There's a good degree of interchangeability, and the aftermarket has created many upgrade and complete bolt-in solutions for owners of 1967–1972 Chevrolet and GMC trucks that can solve many headaches for builders who aren't worried about originality.

Axle Identification

Before you decide on what you'd like to do with the axle under the bed of your truck, look at what's actually under there, identify it, and figure out what your options are.

1/2-ton Axles

If you have a 1/2-ton truck, this should be easy, as most 1/2-tons from 1967 to 1972 came with GM's truck version of the 12-bolt axle, either in trailing-arm or leaf-spring configuration. Looking at the rear axle from the tailgate side of the truck, you should be able to count 12 bolts around the cover. The cover itself is rounded with flat spots on the top and bottom. There's also a noticeable bump in the cover for the ring gear that is offset to the driver's side.

Some earlier 1/2-ton trucks came with a Dana 44 in the rear, which has a different, more squared-off cover. This was known as option code J04 on the service parts identification (SPID) label or Spicer 44. If your SPID is missing or illegible and you think you have one of these units, there should be a "44" cast into the housing below the cover to help you identify it. These will be 6-lug only, and they were most often found in GMCs in 1967 and 1968.

Some trucks came with the heavier-duty Dana 60, even in a 1/2-ton 6-lug configuration. These have the same shape cover as the 44s but are a lot larger overall. They

Most half-ton trucks from this era came with the 12-bolt axle as standard. These are easy to spot, as they have 12 bolts that hold the rear cover to the axle housing.

have a casting mark below the cover that helps identify them as 60s, but note that they are different than the heavier-duty Dana 60s used in 3/4- and 1-ton trucks. These axles are semi-floaters, known as the Dana 60-35s. The code for this on the SPID is J07, and they were only available in leaf-spring applications.

Heavy-Duty Axles

If you have a heavier-duty truck, there were more options from the factory. For 3/4-ton trucks, you either got a GM Corporate (Eaton) HO52 axle or a full-floater Dana 60. One-tons had the Eaton HO72 or the Dana 60. All of these axles are 8-lug versus the lighter-duty 6- and 5-lug options above.

Just like the 12-bolt, the HO52 and Dana 60 came in either leaf-spring or coil-spring axle configurations for 3/4-ton applications. The HO72 was leaf spring only.

The Eaton axles look very similar. Both have a removable cast-iron center section and a round removable rear cover that's held in place with 10 bolts. The main difference between the HO52 and the HO72 is the housing itself and the brakes used. The center sections are interchangeable between the two axles.

The Eatons are known for being extremely durable, but parts supply is an issue due to many components being out of production, including brake parts. On top of that, the lowest factory ratio available in the Eaton series is a 4.10. Keep in mind these axles were made for hard work, so freeway cruising wasn't a consideration. Some aftermarket 3.90-ratio ring and pinions were made at one time, but they're extremely rare today, so that won't gain you much in terms of freeway-cruising abilities.

The good news on the Eaton axles is that they're basically bulletproof, so if you have one that's in good, operable condition, there's no need to worry about it unless you'd like to change gear ratios. In that case, eBay and truck forums are likely your only sources for parts.

The 12-Bolt

The vast majority of C10 owners have the 12-bolt truck axle, which was offered in two different widths from 1967 to 1972. Internally, other than the axle shafts themselves, all parts interchange among 1967 and 1972 units and well into the end of the 12-bolt's run in the early 1980s. That makes parts sourcing a breeze.

The 12-bolt has a good reputation among GM muscle-car enthusiasts, but the truck version is different from the muscle-car versions that were used under Impalas, Chevelles, and

Just about any 12-bolt from 1967–1980 will fit under the back of a C10, but you'll need to use the proper perches for your suspension type. These reproduction trailing-arm units are available from CPP (part number 6072RAS) and must be welded into place. (Photo Courtesy Summit Racing)

Camaros. Those use a beefier pinion bearing and shaft diameter, which helped earn the 12-bolt its reputation as a stout axle assembly, but the truck units are arguably just as good when built correctly.

As mentioned above, the 12-bolt is easy to identify. Interestingly enough, while the rear cover does have 12 bolts, the name "12-bolt" comes from the ring gear that uses 12 bolts to secure it to the carrier. The fact that there are 12 cover bolts is a nice way to verify what you're looking at without being able to see inside.

The 12-bolt was introduced in 1963. In trucks, it's fitted with an 8.875-inch ring gear and a 1.438-inch pinion shaft with 30-spline axles, although 1963 trucks had 17-spline axles. All 12-bolts use C-clips from the factory to retain the two axle shafts inside the housing, and all of them came with drum brakes standard. Positraction units were optional in trucks in this era, and the aftermarket has a range of options available, depending on your goals.

In terms of ratios, GM offered everything from a 3.08 highway gear to a 4.57 stump puller over the years in the 12-bolt.

Not all 12-bolts are created equal. First off, there are two different suspension options to consider: leaf spring and coil spring. Swapping from one style to the other is as easy as cutting off and replacing the axle perches, but this is a process best left to a professional welder, as you don't want a lack of welding penetration to lead to an axle housing failure.

Narrow versus Wide Housings

From 1964 to 1970, GM used a narrower housing in trucks that measures $62^{1}/_{8}$ inches from wheel

REAR AXLE

Not all 12-bolts are created equal. You have to be careful and make sure you get the proper year range for your truck. This is a 1973–1987 rear axle housing, which has wider axle-perch spacing than the 1967–1972 leaf-spring rear axle. Installing this axle in a 1967–1972 requires cutting and moving the leaf-spring perches inboard.

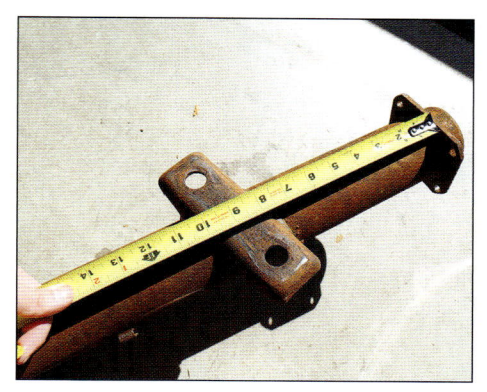

If you find a trailing-arm 12-bolt in a wrecking yard and want a quick reference to determine if it's a 1967–1970 narrow or a 1970–1972 wide, measure from the flange to the centerline of the perch. A 1970–1972 wide axle is about 9 inches. A 1967–1970 narrow is 8¼ inches.

mounting surface to wheel mounting surface. In 1970, partway through the year, GM started to use a wider housing that measures 63½ inches from face to face. That was the standard length through the end of 12-bolt production in the 1980s.

The narrower housings (1964–1970) take a 30½-inch-long axle shaft, while the later housings (1970–1972) take a 31 5/16-inch-long axle shaft. Running a later axle shaft in an earlier housing is technically possible, but it's dangerous because the added length of the axle compared to the shorter width of the earlier housing pushes the brake drum out away from the brake shoes and minimizes the brake's contact patch.

You can swap complete axle housing assemblies from an early (narrow) truck to a later (wide) one, as the mounts are all located in the same spots relative to the frame of the truck. You can also swap 1973–1987 squarebody axle shafts into the wide 1970–1972 housings because the squarebody shafts are the same length as the stock 1970–1972 shafts and they have the same spline count (30).

Complete squarebody axle assemblies can also fit under the earlier trucks if you relocate the later axle's spring perches. All of the 1973–1987 trucks were fitted with leaf springs in the rear, and these axle assemblies are not bolt-in, even with a factory leaf-spring 1967–1972 truck, as the earlier 1967–1972 trucks have narrower frame rails than the later squarebodies. You would need to cut and move the spring perches to match, and if you're going to that much trouble, you can just as easily swap in a 9-inch Ford or similar.

5-Lug versus 6-Lug

Complicating the matter further is that by 1971, GM ceased to build two-wheel drive trucks with 6-lug wheels and went to a 5-on-5-inch bolt pattern. Many builders like the idea of swapping over to the 5-on-5 setup for greater wheel-fitment options, but

Five-lug conversions open the door to many aftermarket-wheel options for a C10, which explains why they've become so popular over the years. This kit from Classic Performance includes everything you need to convert your C10's axle over to a 5-lug setup, including new brake drums and axle shafts. (Photo Courtesy Summit Racing)

CHEVY/GMC TRUCKS 1967–1972: HOW TO BUILD & MODIFY   131

you need to verify which axle housing you have prior to hunting replacement axle shafts. GM never made the shorter axles for the shorter housings in a 5-on-5 pattern, so if you have the shorter housing, you'll need aftermarket axles for this swap. They are available in complete kit form from a few different manufacturers, some complete with brakes.

Checking Gears

Many GM trucks came from the factory with yawn-worthy 3.07:1 rear gears and open differentials, which isn't exactly ideal for the kind of performance that most enthusiasts are looking for today.

However, not all of them were that way, and in terms of the 12-bolt, ratios were available that ranged from that freeway-friendly set all the way up to 4.11s and 4.57s. It's up to you to figure out what you have or what's in the greasy axle housing you're about to buy from a junkyard or Facebook Marketplace.

There are a few places to check to see what might be inside an axle. The first stop should always be the SPID, as it may help you determine the gear ratio and whether or not the truck came with a limited-slip axle from the factory. Look for RPO code G80 for the limited slip.

Another item to check is the axle tube itself. GM stamped either two- or three-letter codes on the upper section of the passenger-side axle tube which will decode both the year of the axle and the gear ratio it would have had from the factory.

Of course, that doesn't always tell the whole story. If you're looking to swap an entire axle assembly anyway, it's a good idea to pull the cover to check on the internals and

Determining Gear Ratio

If you want to figure out a truck's gear ratio without making a mess and draining your axle, this method can help.

1. Park your truck on a level surface and chock the front wheels. Leave the truck in neutral, then jack up the rear axle in the center with a floor jack until both wheels are off the ground. Make sure the parking brake is not set.
2. Spin one tire while watching the wheel on the opposite side. If the other wheel spins the opposite direction of the one you're spinning, you have an open differential. If both wheels spin together in the same direction, you have a Positraction (or limited-slip) differential.
3. If you have an open differential, let the jack down and reposition it under one side so you can lift one tire off the ground while leaving the other side in contact with the pavement. If you have a Positraction, you can continue with both wheels off the ground.
4. With a piece of tape or a piece of chalk, mark a spot on your tire and on the pinion yoke of the rear axle.
5. With both the pinion and the tire marked, spin the tire one full revolution from 12 o'clock to 12 o'clock using your tape mark while counting the number of revolutions of the yoke. The resulting numbers should be your rear-axle ratio. For example, if one revolution of the wheel results in just slightly more than three turns of the yoke, you have a 3.08:1 rear gear. If it's one to 3¾ turns, you have a 3.73:1 ratio. ∎

Don't rely on the stamped numbers or the SPID to tell you what axle ratio you have, but you don't have to pull the rear cover and drain your axle to get a good idea of the ratio that's installed either. The turn/count method can give you a good idea of what you're running without making a mess.

REAR AXLE

count the teeth on both the ring and pinion gears so you can guarantee what you're getting is really what you think it is. Remember that these trucks lived hard lives, and swapping an entire axle assembly has always been easier than pulling a carrier and setting up a new set of gears. Don't simply trust what the SPID or the stampings tell you.

Just because swapping an axle housing is easier than setting up gears, don't be intimidated by a gear swap project in a 12-bolt. With the right tools and a little time, installing any gear ratio you want (there are a lot of them in the aftermarket today) is a relatively simple process.

Two-Tire Fire

The last thing most hot-rodders want is a single tire going up in smoke under power. Unfortunately, that's probably what you're going to get when you stomp on the loud pedal in your stock C10. If you want both rear tires to get in on the action, you need a way to send power to both wheels, and that means you need a limited-slip unit, locker, or spool.

Limited Slip

GM used clutch-operated limited-slip units from the factory because they're strong, quiet, and reliable. The aftermarket has several options for builders today. Generally speaking, they all operate the same with clutch packs or clutch cones that grab under power and force both axle shafts to apply power to the ground. When one wheel starts turning at a different rate than the other, as they would in a corner, the clutches slip to allow for smooth operation. That is, until the driver nails the throttle again and both wheels try to push

The clutch-type Positraction unit is a strong, effective way of transmitting power to both wheels. This is Summit Racing's own 3-series unit (part number SUM-730954) that uses plate-style clutches for reliable operation. It's also fitted with forged-steel internals and is completely rebuildable using Eaton or Yukon Gear–style parts.

together, corner or not. Donuts, anyone?

Both Eaton and Auburn make great options for 12-bolt buyers in the market for a limited-slip unit. The Eaton Posi Performance differential is a clutch-plate-type that's user-rebuildable and tunable via different friction materials or stronger or lighter spring tension. I've found these units to be downright bulletproof, even in a heavy drag car, which makes them ideal for a C10 build that might see anything from hauling yard debris or furniture to drag racing on a given weekend.

The Auburn Gear High Performance Series differential operates in a similar way but with cone-style clutches instead of plates. These units have great grip thanks to increased capacity of the cone versus plates, quick operation, and less chance of clutch chatter under load.

The Auburn Positraction unit works much like the Summit or Eaton plate-style unit but with cone-style clutches instead of flat clutch packs. It's a great option for street-driven trucks that see some performance use. (Photo Courtesy Summit Racing)

They're known for long service life too. The only downside is that the Auburn can't be rebuilt as easily as the Eaton, so take that into consideration. Either option is a great choice for a street/strip truck, and both are available for the truck-spec 12-bolt.

Beyond those, Summit Racing has its own in-house 12-bolt truck limited-slip unit that's just as strong as the Eaton or the Auburn. It's a rebuildable clutch-plate-style unit that offers easy setup and long life. Other options include Yukon Gear's Dura-Grip Positraction and Spicer's clutch-type units.

In any case, be sure you use the proper fluid and proper limited-slip additive with any clutch-type rear axle you choose. Failing to do so will mean burned-up clutches, a lighter wallet, and a return to the dreaded one-tire fire.

Lockers

A locking differential locks both rear wheels together mechanically, electronically, or with compressed air for 100-percent power delivery to both sides of the truck. These remain locked in most situations but can allow for different wheel speeds when going around corners.

CHEVY/GMC TRUCKS 1967–1972: HOW TO BUILD & MODIFY

CHAPTER 10

The Detroit Locker is one of the toughest differentials available and is a great option for big-power applications. These work like a spool until you turn into a corner, when they unlock enough to allow different wheel speeds. (Photo Courtesy Summit Racing)

The main downside to a locker is the price. These tend to be more expensive than the comparable limited-slip unit, but they offset that price by having a longer service life. There are no clutches to wear out, and they tend to be very strong. The only other downside is in usability. Units such as Detroit Lockers tend to be noisy when operating around corners. They usually click or clunk, and sometimes the clunking can be felt via a jerking motion when the rear wheels are turning at different speeds.

A locker allows the outer tire in a corner to spin faster than the differential, but neither tire can spin slower than the differential. That can create some strange handling characteristics. Both sides will lock together instantly mid-corner if you apply throttle, which can be hair-raising in a truck with no weight in the bed or on a wet road. If traction is what you want and you can live with some quirks in handling, especially around corners, consider putting a locker, such as a Detroit Locker, in the back of your C10.

Other Options

Another differential worth considering is the Detroit TrueTrac differential that uses parallel-axis helical gears to provide automatic splitting of torque between the right and left axles. There are no clutches to wear out, and they're street friendly in that they operate like an open differential most of the time. However, they send power to the wheel with the most grip, which is opposite of how an open differential tends to operate. These are available for the 12-bolt. The only downside is price over a comparable clutch style with Positraction.

Beware the Gov Bomb

The factory also offered a version of a locking rear axle in later 12-bolts called the Gov Lock. It's best to avoid it as it has some of the worst characteristics of a locker and an open differential in one unit. The Gov Lock acts like an open rear axle until a certain differential RPM is reached between the left and right wheels. Then, it suddenly wakes up and locks both axles together like Positraction, often with explosive results after 40 or 50 weary years on the job.

These units only apply power to both wheels in slow-speed situations (up to about 25 mph), and they work fine in normal driving. However, they're known for failure in high-power applications and often take out gears, axles, bearings, and differential housings when they let go. GM continues to use them to this day. They work fine when not overpowered, but they aren't well suited for the kind of driving most custom C10 builders are looking to do.

Gov Locks were offered starting in 1973 and became option code G80 after 1974, which is the same code as the Positraction units in the earlier trucks, so be careful if you're planning on swapping in a later axle in your 1967–1972. If you have a line on a G80 axle, the best bet is to pull the rear axle cover and look inside to see what's in there before buying.

Spools

A spool is by far the simplest traction tool available in that it locks both the right and left axle shafts together 100 percent of the time with a steel collar. These allow for no differential action between the right and left wheels in a corner, which can cause tire wear, hopping, questionable handling, and understeer situations that quickly turn to snap oversteer when throttle is applied.

If straight-line traction is your only concern, a spool (or mini spool that only replaces the spider gears and is not as strong) may make sense, but know that these are best left to the track due to their lack of differential action.

Selecting the Right Parts

If you're not concerned about performance, it may make sense to keep an open differential and save some cash. If street performance is your goal, that changes things, and you have some decisions to make on what upgrades you should add.

Regardless of the type of driving you plan to do, I've found the best bet is to plan to build a stronger axle than you think you'll need. Power tends to be addictive, and you're more likely to swap out an engine at a later date than you might think. It's best to aim for overkill so that you'll only have to do the work and spend the money once.

REAR AXLE

12-Bolt Upgrades

While the truck's 12-bolt has a good reputation in stock form, the two carrier bearing caps are a weak point within the stock housing. When large amounts of torque are applied to the axle, the force applied tries to push the carrier out the back of the housing, which puts stress on the bearing caps and their bolts in the process.

Replacement billet aluminum main caps are available and a lot stronger than the original cast units, but they require competent machine work for installation.

Another fix is to add main studs in place of the original bolts, such as those offered by Summit Racing. They're a lot stronger and less likely to yield under big power. Another smart upgrade is to add a reinforced girdle-type rear cover, which has adjustable stops that can be snugged up against the main cap surfaces to support them from the rear and keep them from deflecting under power.

All of these options are smart upgrades for your otherwise-stock 12-bolt, especially if you're adding more power than the truck had from the factory, and I'm willing to bet you are.

One weak spot in 12-bolt Chevrolet axles is the main-cap bolts, which fight the tendency of the third member to push backward out of the axle housing under power. Summit sells replacement main-cap studs (part number SME-85102-1) that are made from 8740 chromoly and are much stronger than stock, which helps limit deflection.

Should You Ditch C-Clips?

Anyone who has used a 12-bolt in the drag-racing or off-road racing world will tell you that the first thing you should add to your GM axle is a set of C-clip eliminators. In high-horsepower situations, axle shafts can break. Since the C-clip retains the axle all the way at the inside of the differential, any break in the axle anywhere along the shaft means that the axle can and will exit the vehicle, take the wheel with it, and usually create mechanical carnage when it leaves.

The C-clip eliminator solves this problem by utilizing a pressed-on bearing at the wheel side of the axle, which then bolts to the housing and keeps the axle in place more or less the same way a 9-inch Ford does.

Here's the thing. The C-clips don't often fail in street use, and the eliminators are generally best suited for drag-racing applications where side loads are kept to a minimum. Traditionally, eliminators are known for being leaky, which can cause other problems. They're not well suited for street use, and you might consider them unnecessary if the factory C-clips, axles, cross-shaft, and other parts don't show excessive play under inspection.

What makes more sense for street trucks is to add a set of aftermarket alloy axles, such as those offered by Moser or Strange Engineering. Aftermarket shafts are much stronger than stock carbon-steel units and greatly limit the chances of breakage. Add in a set of new C-clips and a rear disc-brake kit, and you have an axle shaft that's not going to leak fluid and/or go anywhere, even if it does break.

If drag racing is your plan, consider a set of eliminators to be on the safe side. After a certain ET threshold (10.99 or faster), the NHRA requires them anyway. ■

C-clip eliminators are great insurance against carnage caused by axle breakage in C-clip housing. These press into place at the wheel side of the axle and retain it to the housing much the same way that a 9-inch Ford does. This one is from Moser Engineering. (Photo Courtesy Summit Racing)

Selecting Gears

Before selecting a set of rear gears, look at all the aspects of your build from the camshaft and the engine's resulting torque curve to the type of transmission that will be bolted behind it. All of these things come into play with rear gear selection, as you'll want to be able to use the power band that your engine combination creates.

There are a few online gear-ratio calculators that can help determine your engine RPM with different final gear ratios, which is a pretty valuable step as it can help you visualize how your truck will behave with a variety of different ratios, tire sizes, etc.

Cars and trucks that have a lopey cam with big overlap and high compression tend to be happier with numerically higher (functionally lower or shorter) gear ratios in the 3.73 to 4.56:1 range. Gears like these allow for quick acceleration off the line, but they make for screaming-high cruising RPM unless the truck is fitted with some kind of overdrive transmission, such as a 4L80E, 6L80E, 700R4, TKX 5-speed, or T56 6-speed.

On the other hand, cars and trucks with stock engines can benefit from numerically lower (functionally higher or taller) gears ranging from 2.73 to 3.42:1. These gears allow for lower engine speeds at higher wheel speeds, which makes for less frantic freeway cruising, lower engine temperatures, and better fuel mileage when cruising on the highway. They also work great with the TH350s, TH400s, and Powerglides that came stock in C10s and C20s of this vintage.

The downside here is in the holeshot. Taller gears feel lazy off the line compared to shorter gears, but those shorter gears are a lot harder to live with when sustained speeds creep up to the 55-mph level.

This 12-bolt is running a 3-series carrier with a thicker 4-series conversion ring gear. This is a smart setup because it allows an owner to swap to numerically lower 3-series gears at a later date without having to swap out an expensive limited-slip carrier.

GM offered several different carrier styles for the 12-bolt rear axle based upon the gears used. These are referred to as 2-series, 3-series, and 4-series carriers. The 2-series carriers work with gearsets ranging from 2.29:1 to 2:73:1, 3-series carriers work with gearsets from 3.07:1 to 3.73:1, and 4-series work with 4.10:1 to 4.88:1.

The reasoning for this is simple. The lower numerical (functionally higher) ratios require a larger-diameter pinion gear, which requires the ring gear to be placed farther away from the centerline of the pinion shaft to make room for that larger pinion gear. The 2-series carrier places the ring gear farthest away from the pinion centerline, while the 4-series is closest. The takeaway is that you can't buy a 4.11 gearset and swap it in place of a 2.73. For that you need a new carrier too.

There is an exception to that rule. You can buy thicker gearsets to run 4-series ratios in 3-series carriers. These sets use a thicker ring gear to mesh properly with the smaller pinion and the spaced-away 3-series carrier. The benefit here is flexibility. If you want to run 4:11s now for drag-racing fun and keep the option to run 3:55s later, a 3-series carrier with thicker 4-series gears designed to fit it is the way to go.

As for what parts to use, that's up to you, but it's always smart to spend more on better parts when it comes to something as important as your rear axle assembly. I prefer to do this once and do it right.

Once you pick the perfect ratio for your C10 build, installing and setting it up properly is not the complicated science that you might think it is. Here's how to do it.

REAR AXLE

Building Your Axle

1 If you hunt around, you can find 12-bolt 1/2-ton axle housings for C10 pickups fairly easily. Don't let a little rust turn you off from a good deal. This housing looks toasted after years sitting outside with no cover on it, but it was $50 at a local wrecking yard and is the longer, later 1970–1972 axle for trailing-arm trucks. This will easily take the place of the HO52 after it's cleaned up and built. Keep in mind that you don't need a complete axle if you intend on installing upgraded parts. You won't use most of the factory stuff anyway.

2 There are several options for cleaning a rusty housing, but the best bet is to either have it sandblasted or chemical dipped. The nice thing about having it dipped by a specialist shop is that its processes remove rust and paint from inside and out and doesn't leave sandy residue behind. It's hard to imagine this was the same rusty housing as seen before.

3 One of the more challenging aspects of building an axle is getting it off the floor and retained properly so that you can work effectively. The Auto Dolly axle adapter for engine stands is a good option, as it retains the axle while you're working on it and allows access to the pinion and carrier sides without making you work on the floor. Summit Racing sells this under part number M998084.

4 Starting with a clean housing is key to any axle setup. Blast out the internals with brake cleaner and wipe everything down with a clean rag after you've disassembled it and remove any old seals, bearings, and races. This is also a good time to inspect your housing and chase each threaded hole with a tap or thread chaser to clean out the threads.

CHEVY/GMC TRUCKS 1967–1972: HOW TO BUILD & MODIFY

CHAPTER 10

Building Your Axle continued

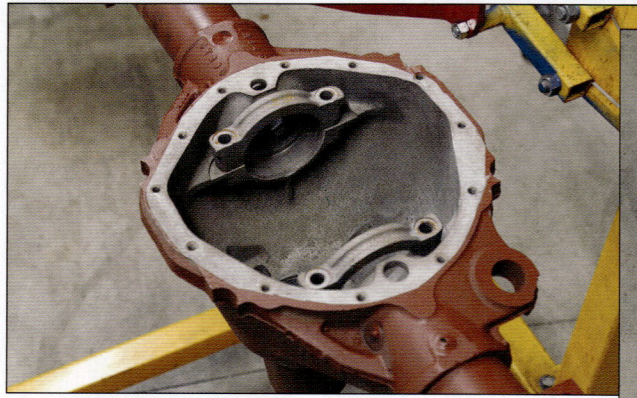

5 A 12-bolt rear axle's main caps aren't interchangeable. If you mix up the left and right sides, your readings will be off when you set up your new ring and pinion. Be sure to mark which one is which before you lose track of where they came from.

6 Overkill is the name of the game here, which is why I chose to add Moser's reinforced housing cover (Summit part number MSR-7111) with a set of bearing cap studs (part number SME-85102-1) to beef up this 12-bolt. I also went with Summit Racing's 12-bolt 3-series Positraction carrier (part number SUM-730954), a set of Richmond 3.73 gears (part number RMG-12BT373T), new C-clips from Yukon Gear (part number YGA-33083), and a complete install kit from Ratech (part number RAT-3005K) that includes axle bearings, inner and outer pinion bearings, carrier bearings, ring-gear bolts, carrier shims, pinion shims, a new crush sleeve, and all the proper seals to do this job correctly.

7 The other overkill piece here is a set of Moser axles for the wider 1970–1972 housing (Summit part number A30-70GMT2). These are made of 1541H alloy steel and feature a 5-on-5-inch bolt pattern with 1/2-inch press-in wheel studs. These are much stronger than stock but are direct replacements for stock axles. If you have a narrow housing built from 1967–1970, look for 30.5-inch versions sold as Summit part number A30-65GMT5.

8 Once your axle is clean, the first step is to install the front and rear pinion bearing races. The best way to handle this is with an aluminum bearing and race installation tool that are inexpensive and can be found online with various-sized drivers that won't damage the bearing race surfaces. Use a big hammer and drive each race home. Be careful and make sure that they're going into their bores straight. The "ping" sound will change tone when each is fully seated.

9 Next, remove the ring and pinion and carrier unit from their packaging and carefully clean and inspect them. This is a good time to make sure that the ring gear's mounting surface is straight and true. Remove any burrs with a file before you mount it to the carrier.

REAR AXLE

10 The ring gear is a tight fit to a new carrier, so be prepared to use the ring-gear bolts to help pull it snug. Some builders use an oven to heat the ring gear slightly so that it will drop into place. Tighten the ring-gear bolts in a crisscross pattern to 55 ft-lbs and be sure to use thread-locking compound. A bench vise is a good tool to help hold the carrier in place while you torque the ring-gear bolts.

11 Once the ring gear is mounted and tight, use a shop press (or go to a shop that has a press) to seat the carrier bearings on the new carrier. No shims are needed. Just drive each of the bearings onto the carrier until they bottom out.

12 The 12-bolt uses a shim behind the pinion gear's inner bearing to set its depth in the housing. GM typically used a 0.030-inch shim in 12-bolts, but if you have the piece that came out of the housing, measure it and match it as close as possible with a new shim. I did this using a shim from the Ratech kit. In my case, the factory shim was 0.028 inch, so I found a new one with the same thickness.

13 If you're feeling lucky, you can drop your pinion shim in place and then proceed to press the new inner pinion bearing onto the pinion. But if you need to adjust pinion depth later, it's going to be a hassle to press the bearing back off to swap shims. Instead, make a setup bearing out of a spare or used unit by opening up its inner surface with a grinding wheel. This allows it to slide in place on the pinion without a press, which makes setup way easier.

CHEVY/GMC TRUCKS 1967–1972: HOW TO BUILD & MODIFY 139

CHAPTER 10

Building Your Axle continued

14 With the inner pinion shim and setup bearing in place, the next step is to drop the pinion into place within the housing. From there, slide the outer pinion bearing into place along with the yoke and pinion nut. Note that we've left out the crush sleeve and the front seal, as we're only mocking up the pinion at this point. Tighten the pinion nut until there's zero play in the pinion bearings. The idea is to get the bearings pulled up to their races without putting them in a bind.

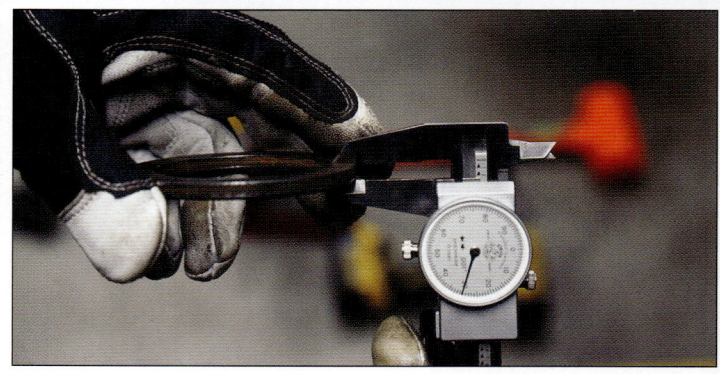

15 Another helpful tip is to retain the two carrier shims that came in the housing because they'll give you an idea of what to start with in terms of shims for the new setup. In my case, I had a 0.230-inch shim on one side and a 0.250 shim on the other, with the thicker one to the opposite of the ring gear. Original shims are one-piece cast-iron units that can be reused if they're in good shape.

16 With the pinion in place, drop the carrier into the housing with the carrier bearing races and shims together as one piece. This should be a very tight fit. The goal here is to get as much preload on the carrier bearings as you can, and it's done via the shims between the carrier bearings and axle housing. It can be a bit of a challenge to get everything lined up, so take your time.

17 How much preload is too much? The rule of thumb is that if you can drive the carrier into the housing with some taps from a big dead-blow mallet, you're on the right track. If the hammer doesn't move the carrier, it's too tight and you need to use smaller or fewer shims on both sides. If the carrier drops into place, it's too loose and you need to add shims. The overall goal is a carrier that doesn't have any left-to-right play once it's in the housing.

18 Next, install and tighten the bearing caps to their specified torque. Here, I've installed Summit Racing's bearing-cap stud kit, which takes 10 ft-lbs to install into the housing. The nuts take 70 ft-lbs to tighten over the original bearing caps. For factory bolts, the torque spec is 60 ft-lbs.

REAR AXLE

19 Before checking your gear's contact patch, first check backlash, which is the amount of play between the pinion and ring gear. Your gearset should come etched with a number on the ring gear. Mine was 0.008 inch. The factory specification is 0.006 inch to 0.010 inch. The only way to check this is with a dial indicator. With the indicator in line with the ring gear and zeroed out, immobilize the pinion and rock the ring gear back and forth. In this case, I had about 0.016 inch. Correcting this means changing out the carrier's shim pack to move the ring gear closer to the pinion.

20 Getting the carrier back out can be a challenge, but a long screwdriver and a long pry bar can make quick work of it. Be careful of the gears themselves and go slowly, working out each side a little at a time. Once it's out, adjust the shim packs accordingly. I used all new shims from the Ratech kit, centered up the carrier at 0.240 inch on both sides, and then reinstalled to bring the backlash to 0.008 inch—right on spec.

21 Check the gear's contact patch. The Ratech setup kit comes with bearing-marking compound and a brush, which is used to paint on the ring-gear teeth to check the contact patch with the pinion gear. Once you've painted five or six teeth, run the gears around a few times, both backward and forward, and then read the pattern to see if adjustment is needed.

22 Ideally, there's a centered pattern on the drive side and the coast side of the gear teeth. Adding or subtracting shims moves the pattern from the root to the crown of the gear (bottom to top), but a little goes a long way. If you elect to change the pinion shim at this point, recheck the backlash and adjust as required to get within spec once again. This pattern is about as good as it gets, so no changes are needed.

CHEVY/GMC TRUCKS 1967–1972: HOW TO BUILD & MODIFY

Building Your Axle continued

23 With the axle torn back down again, remove the setup bearings and press on the ones you intend to run using the same shim pack as before. A press is the only tool for this job.

24 Next, slide the crush sleeve over the pinion. It's good to have a couple of these on hand, as getting one set up to spec can be a bit of a challenge. Once you've torqued one too far, it's not usable again. This sleeve crushes when the pinion nut is tightened, thereby setting up the proper preload on the inner and outer pinion bearings and maintaining that reading.

25 The outer pinion bearing drops in place, followed by the new front seal, both from the Ratech kit. Here, I applied RTV sealant around the seal where it makes contact with the housing. Once that is in place, the pinion can be fed through from the rear of the housing. You may need to use the pinion nut, washer, and yoke to seat the outer pinion bearing on the pinion shaft, as it's a tight fit.

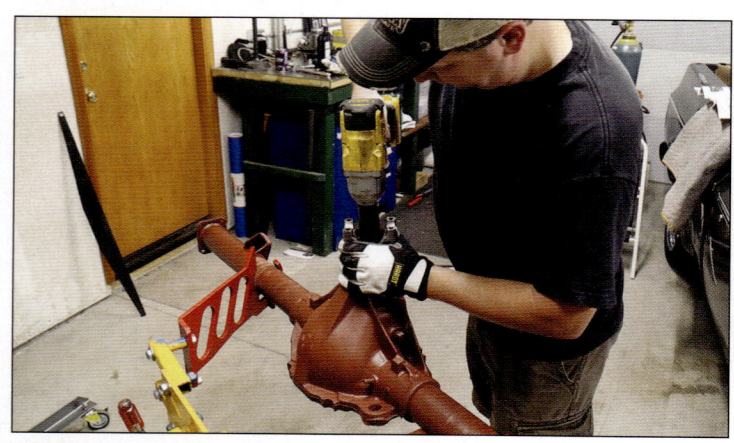

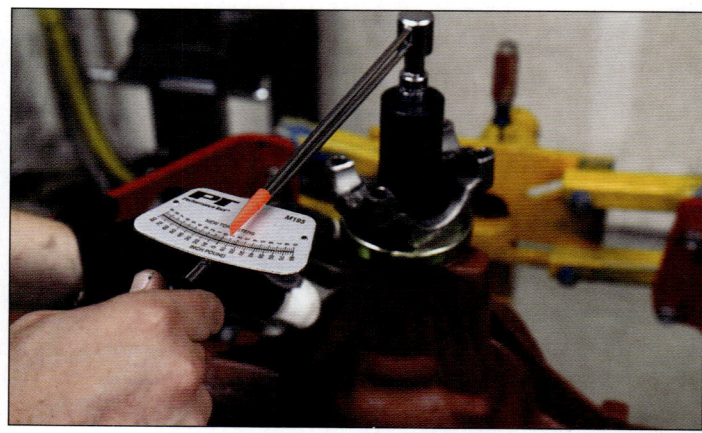

26 The tricky part of 12-bolt setup is adjusting the pinion-bearing preload, as the crush sleeve can take up to 300 ft-lbs of torque to start crushing. A heavy-duty 1/2-inch drive impact is a good tool for the job. The Ratech kit comes with a new pinion nut, which needs a bit of thread-lock compound. I installed a new 1350-style yoke in place of the original 1310-style unit, and I put a little RTV sealant inside the yoke on the splines to help stop any possible leaks. The key is to sneak up on the proper spec, which is 14 to 19 in-lbs of rotational torque for new bearings. Stop frequently and check the reading, as it doesn't take much to overshoot and ruin the crush sleeve.

REAR AXLE

27 With the pinion set, reinstall the carrier and torque the bearing caps to spec. Double-check the backlash and gear pattern to be sure that nothing changed with the setup. Here, my pattern stayed the same as it was before, so this axle is nearly complete.

28 The Ratech kit comes with new axle bearings and new axle seals that need to be tapped into place. A bearing and seal driver works wonders here for both. With just a few taps, the bearings and seals are home. From there, some grease on each wheel bearing is good insurance for the first few revolutions of the axles.

29 Installing axles requires removing the differential's cross-shaft bolt and the cross-shaft itself, which takes a 5/16-inch wrench or socket. With the shaft out of the way, the axles can slide into the housing far enough to fit the C-clips that retain them.

30 With the axles in place, the C-clips then go in. Each sits in a groove that is machined in the end of each axle. After the C-clip is placed on each axle, pulling the axles away from the center of the housing seats the clips in the differential. Then, the cross-shaft and bolt can be reinstalled, locking them in place. Be sure to use thread-lock compound on the threads of the cross-shaft bolt when reinstalling it.

CHEVY/GMC TRUCKS 1967–1972: HOW TO BUILD & MODIFY

CHAPTER 10

Building Your Axle continued

31 The differential housing cover is the final piece of the puzzle. In this case, it's a heavy-duty Moser piece with two load bolts that contact the carrier's caps and help keep it from moving under load. The included gasket goes on first, followed by the perimeter bolts that are torqued to 25 ft-lbs (max). The load bolts can be snugged to 5 ft-lbs before tightening the jamb nuts that hold them in place.

32 After a quick cleanup and some masking, a good coat of black paint finishes off this job. All that's left is to fill the differential with the proper gear oil and limited-slip additive before installing it in the truck. Break in the gears properly before heading off to smoke the tires.

Breaking in New Gears

Once you've installed a new set of gears in your 12-bolt, you can't just head off down the road with the tires smoking. It's important to first break in your new gears appropriately. Otherwise, you risk damaging the gears and voiding any warranty you may have on the parts. Run through a break-in procedure as specified by your gear's manufacturer.

For the first 15 or 20 miles, drive between 15 and 55 mph, and then stop to let the differential cool before continuing. Heat is a killer, so this helps to limit it while allowing the gear surfaces to mate together properly without breaking down.

Don't run over 60 mph for the first 100 miles if possible. After 500 miles, drain and refill the differential to remove any metallic contaminants from the oil.

Don't tow anything until after you've crossed the 500-mile mark. Stop every 15 miles or so in those first 45 miles of towing to keep heat down.

Listen for any odd noises and watch for leaks, particularly from the rear cover and the front seal, as those are common with 12-bolt Chevrolet axles. Once you've done all that and have run through the break-in procedures, you're free to melt some tires.

CHAPTER 11

INTERIOR AND AIR CONDITIONING

The way a truck looks and how it handles are some of the most important parts of any build, but it's also important to make the interior into a place where you actually want to spend time. Vinyl, carpet, and interior paint can age well or terribly, depending on the region where the truck was used and how it was used. However, there are many things you can do to make your truck's interior better than new.

Seats

Chevrolet offered four styles of seats for trucks in this era. The first is the standard bench seat, which was hinged at the back and featured a thin foam base and coil-spring back for 1967 and 1968. By 1969, the folding portion was bolted in place and the seat cover was adjusted to delete the ability to flop the seatback forward.

There was a full-depth foam version of the bench seat offered from 1969 to 1970, as well as a deluxe seat in 1971 and 1972, which came in some higher-spec trucks from the factory. The deluxe seat featured more padding than the basic bench seat, and it's more comfortable for longer-distance use. It takes a different seat cover than the basic bench and the 1969 and 1970 seat, as the seat foam is thicker. This is the rule of thumb: if you intend to use an original seat, source a seat cover that matches the year of the seat that you're going to use to be sure it will fit properly.

The cabs didn't change with regard to the seat-mounting locations in the floor, so you can install a Deluxe 1972 seat in a 1967 cab if you so choose. The seat brackets are year specific, so be sure that any bench seat you source has the mounting brackets attached to it before you buy.

The rarest seat option is the bench-seat option, referred to as "Buddy Bucket" seats, which was offered from 1967 through the end of 1968. These featured an integrated frame with a folding center section that could be used as a third seat.

Your truck's seat likely lived a hard life, but crispy vinyl, missing foam, and broken springs shouldn't stop you from bringing a stock bench seat back to life. However, you might find that an aftermarket seat with some added side bolstering might make more sense for your intended use.

These tend to go for a pretty penny and require the proper mount, which can be hard to find if not already with the seat.

From 1969 forward, GM offered a standard set of bucket seats, typically with a console mounted between them. Both sets of buckets are hard to come by today because they're coveted by the restoration crowd.

Other Seats

If you're interested in using a more modern seat, many options are available for a C10, starting with later-model GM seats. Many builders have swapped OBS/GMT400 (1988–1994) seats into their trucks with good results, as they're more comfortable than originals and are typically easy to find. They're generally a direct bolt-in, although they do require some seat-bracket modification to fit the contours of the 1967–1972 floor.

Later GM truck seats tend to get thicker and more cushy, which can be a benefit in terms of comfort (if not in terms of space), but mounting becomes more complicated, especially when dealing with seats that have integrated seat belts as part of the package. Simply drilling holes and bolting this style of seat to the factory floor isn't exactly safe because the floor wasn't braced for that type of duty. GM NBS/GMT800 (1999–2007) seats are a good option (particularly second-row Suburban and Tahoe seats) that cover up the factory fuel tank but don't have a provision to slide.

Considering that just about any modern seat sticks out in an otherwise-old truck interior, it's a better bet to source a new custom bench or set of buckets from an aftermarket company (such as TMI) to swap directly into your truck. The nice thing about these seats is the variety of colors and options available and the bracketry that's been designed to work with your truck's original seat mounting locations. Even though they're new seats, you have the option to make them look like they're supposed to be there.

Another added bonus is the fact that aftermarket seats typically come with larger side bolsters, which are a significant plus in a truck that's been modified with better suspension and brakes. If you've ever tried to autocross or sprint up a curvy road while sitting on a stock bench, you've worn yourself out trying to stay in one place on the bench by holding on to the wheel. A modern bench or set of buckets will help solve this problem and will look good too.

Sound

There's no getting around the fact that these trucks feature many metal surfaces in the interior, and metal surfaces amplify noise.

GM trucks came from the factory either with carpeting or rubber mats. Those with carpeting tended to also have tar-based sound-deadening materials installed at the factory. You can get reproductions of these from most of the restoration parts houses, but there is better technology to help keep sound levels down. The stock stuff only works so well.

Dynamat has been a mainstay for years, and now many different options are available on the market to help eliminate unwanted noise. Note that most of them are butyl-based and sticky by nature. As such, they can be difficult to remove once placed, but they all do a good job to help reduce vibration and noise.

Once applied, Dynamat needs to be secured in place with a roller to remove any wrinkles. A heat gun works wonders here. To do this right, you'll need a good amount of time, a warm day, and about 50 square feet of whatever material you plan to use, which will provide more than enough for the floor, back of the cab, and inside the doors.

You don't need complete coverage for a good solution. The idea is to eliminate vibration, which can be accomplished with deadener applied to the center of each side of the floorboard both ahead and under

A modern aftermarket seat offers better bolstering and more comfort than any factory C10 seat. Seats such as this custom bench from TMI are customizable to match your paint and interior.

INTERIOR AND AIR CONDITIONING

the seat. With that being said, most of us cover everything with product, which works too.

Weatherstripping

When it comes to sound, something that's often overlooked is factory-style weatherstripping, most of which is long dead by now and probably whistling air through cracks and shrunken areas. Keeping water out of the cab is a priority, and that likely means installing new rubber, particularly if you bought a truck from somewhere sunny and dry.

Windshield weatherstripping can be replaced in your own garage if you have a spare set of hands to help. Not every aftermarket weatherstrip is equal, particularly when it comes to the windshield. Source a Precision piece, which is carried by most of the reproduction parts houses because it's the go-to brand among truck builders today, at least those using stock-style seals.

The rope method is the best here, and there isn't much to it. The idea is to install the new seal on the glass and stuff a small-diameter rope into the channel in the rubber that pinches over the truck cab's metal flange. With the windshield set in place and a corner of the seal started, pull on the rope from the inside of the truck. This action will pull the windshield seal over the flange in the truck and secure the glass in place.

The OEM-style door weatherstrips on 1967–1972 GM trucks were originally glued in place using weatherstrip adhesive, which can be a real pain to work with. If you're looking to replace leaky door seals, the aftermarket has a solution in press-on-style seals that fit over the pinch weld and require no adhesive to stay in place.

There's no reason to mess with original glue-on door seals for your C10. These push-on seals are from Precision and were sourced from Classic Industries. They are a fantastic upgrade over stock.

Other Interior Components

Cleaning up your interior is a basic project. You'd be amazed what a quick carpet, dash pad, and seat cover install can do to the look and feel of your truck's interior. For a thorough and detailed look at installing your interior, order a copy of CarTech's *Automotive Upholstery & Interior Restoration* by Fred Mattson.

Dash Pad

You may not think of a dash pad as something that takes much abuse, but the sun has likely baked your original piece to a crisp, so an upgrade will be worth your time.

Scan this QR code with your smartphone to buy Automotive Upholstery & Interior Restoration *(SA393) by Fred Mattson.*

TECH TIP: Alternative Door Seals

If you're heading to the junkyard and have a need for new door seals for your truck, look for a late-model two-door Honda Civic (2006–2011). The door seals on these cars are very close to the proper length for a GM truck. They pinch on over the cab pinch weld, which makes them easy to remove and install. They tend to fit quite well and don't require door slamming, which is a notorious problem with new door weatherstripping. You can also substitute 1987–1997 Dodge Dakota seals, which work great in this application.

CHAPTER 11

Good dash pads—not plastic covers—are not expensive, considering the impact that they bring to your truck's interior cosmetics.

The most challenging part of the entire process is gaining access. To swap out a dash pad, which is likely the roughest component in any C10 interior due to solar damage, you have to remove the glove box, which is a lot easier to do with the gauge cluster and radio out of the way. It's not impossible to work around these things, but it will take longer, and you'll spend more time standing on your head trying to reach the hardware that holds the dash pad in place than if you tear everything apart for better access.

The key here is the order of operations. If you intend on swapping a dash pad, do it as part of a larger dash project, and make sure you install the dash pad before reinstalling everything else.

Carpet

C10 trucks came with either carpet or rubber mats from the factory, and both are available in the aftermarket today to provide plenty of options for whatever you're looking to build.

You'll need a different carpet set for a high-hump floor over a low-hump floor, as they're molded differently and not interchangeable. Beyond that, installing a carpet kit in a C10 from this era is very straightforward, as they have a sewn edge on all the corners. Unlike later trucks that need to have their carpet cut to fit and installed under pieces of interior trim, carpet in these trucks basically lays in place. There's no cutting required beyond marking the location of the seat-mount and seat-belt bolts. It does, however, pinch in place under the door sill plate that's mounted to the rocker panel on either side.

Reviving a C10 Interior

1 This is a Just Dashes dash pad in light blue from Classic Industries. This piece is identical to a factory unit, complete with the proper grain and padding. It's a simple install but requires some access into the dash that's best found by removing the radio, glove box, and gauge cluster.

2 If you plan to use the original bench seat, the first step is to tackle the teardown and inspection of the seat frame and foam under the original seat cover. If the foam is crumbly or flattened, you can make or buy reproduction replacements.

3 The factory often used these spring clips to hold the seat covers in place. If you try to reuse them, you'll rip the new seat cover. Removing them is best done with a standard screwdriver. Place them directly into the trash can.

INTERIOR AND AIR CONDITIONING

Reviving a C10 Interior continued

4 Before you attempt to install the seat cover, lay it out flat to work out any wrinkles. It's best to lay it in the sun if you can, as the heat will help loosen the material and work out any packaging kinks. This seat cover is from Classic Industries.

5 Measure and mark the center of both the new seat cover and the seat frame, particularly with covers that have pleats from the factory. This way, you can be sure the cover is installed straight and that the pleats sit where they're supposed to sit.

6 Don't be surprised if your seat cover is a tight fit. Professional installers usually use steam to stretch the covers slightly for a better fit, and they're very hands-on while installing. If it's way off, double-check that you have the proper year of seat cover. Don't be afraid to slap and push the cover around to get it to sit properly.

7 Most aftermarket covers are installed with hog rings, but plastic zip ties are a huge help. These allow you to snug up the cover as you go and allow more adjustment as you work. Once you're happy with the fitment, hog ring the cover into place. Most seat cover kits come with the proper hog-ring tool.

CHEVY/GMC TRUCKS 1967–1972: HOW TO BUILD & MODIFY

Reviving a C10 Interior *continued*

8 Selecting a hot day to do the work or using steam (if available) and zip ties to assist in stretching the cover into place will pay off in a tight-fitting cover and a better-finished product.

9 The carpet kit is placed on top of the floor and any sound-deadening material that you've installed. It's helpful to thread your seat bolts into place at this point before fixing the carpet in place. This is Classic Industries' molded carpet kit for high-hump C10 floors. The company offers every stock color for both high- and low-hump applications.

10 Here's why I like to install the bolts first. You can use the bolt heads to mark where to slice the carpet for the bolt to pass through. I like to cut an X over the head of the bolt before removing it, as that will allow the threads to pass through without unraveling and winding up the carpet.

11 With the bolts loosely threaded through the carpet, and the carpet placed properly in the truck with no gaps at the kick panels on either side, the seat can slide into place and be bolted solid along with the door seals, seatbelts, and sill plates.

12 If you have a floor shifter, the best time to install its shift boot is after the seat has been bolted in place. The seat works to lock down the carpet that may otherwise shift while you're working. This is Silver Sport Transmissions' STX front-mount shifter for Tremec TXK 5-speeds, which is designed to clear the factory bench seat.

INTERIOR AND AIR CONDITIONING

Gauges

Your C10, depending on the year and options, came with one of two styles of gauge clusters. The first, basic version featured little more than a speedometer, fuel gauge, and a host of warning lights. The majority of trucks featured a full host of gauges, including an ammeter, temperature gauge, and oil-pressure gauge. Some trucks had tachometers from the factory, while others had a vacuum gauge or both, which made it a very rare setup. Medium-duty trucks often came with an air-pressure gauge for air-brake systems, which is a nice touch on an airbagged truck.

Keep in mind that while the medium-duty trucks often featured tachometers, those tachometers are typically low-RPM units. Even more important to note is that the big truck clusters don't simply swap over to the C10 and C20 line because the steering-column mounts are different. However, you can move the gauges between housings if you find a big truck dash that has the gauges you want.

Swapping between an idiot-light dash and a gauge dash requires some wiring modifications because the harnesses were slightly different to support idiot lights versus sending units for actual gauges. To swap, you must re-pin the connector that plugs into the back of the dash using a factory wiring diagram as a guide.

Adding a tachometer is a common upgrade, and doing so is straightforward. It's important to get a functional tachometer that's calibrated to the type of engine in your truck: inline six or V-8.

If you're looking for a modern spin on your truck's OEM gauges, check out Dakota Digital's RTX series of instruments. These are all-new units designed to bring modern functionality with classic looks. They feature LED back lighting, dual digital message centers, and late-model drivetrain compatibility. This is a subtle but worthwhile upgrade, especially if you intend on using your truck regularly. (Photo Courtesy Dakota Digital)

Swapping to a Tachometer Dash

1 *This 1967 dash is typical of a simple gauge-style setup with no tachometer. Adding one is easy and is a good excuse to clean up years of dirt and grime from all of the components.*

2 *With the cluster flipped onto its face, the printed circuit can come off, and the gauges can come out. It's all held in place with small hex-head screws.*

CHEVY/GMC TRUCKS 1967–1972: HOW TO BUILD & MODIFY   151

Swapping to a Tachometer Dash *continued*

3 You can try to source a used tachometer, but it's better to go with an aftermarket kit that has all of the parts required for the swap. This is Classic Industries' tachometer conversion kit (part number CW1008), which comes with an 8,000-rpm tachometer and gauge face, the proper backing, and the proper printed circuit and wiring.

4 To install a tachometer, change to a tachometer-style gauge backing plate. This means moving the gauges from your original plate over to the reproduction piece. Be very careful when cleaning gauge faces, as the original paint is very sensitive to even light scrubbing.

5 With the tachometer bolted in place, the conversion is nearly complete. If faded orange indicators are a concern, address it now with some orange paint. This is best sprayed versus brushed, and it's easy to do with some newspaper masking.

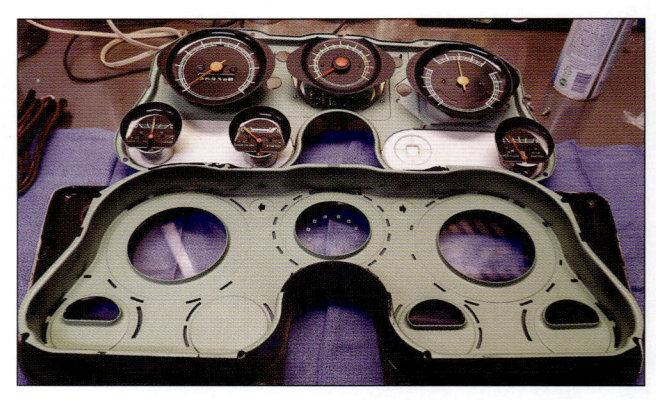

6 With the new plastic face pressed into the original bezel, all that's left is to start reassembly.

7 The final step is to install the reproduction tachometer-dash printed circuit, which has a provision for the tachometer wiring to pass through it. Note that the tachometer isn't powered off the circuit but instead uses a harness that comes with the kit. One wire goes to keyed ignition power at the fuse box, while the other goes to the coil's negative terminal or to the ECU's tachometer output wire.

8 In this case, a little cleaning while the cluster was apart went a long way on my patina truck build. It's a lot easier to do while the dash is disassembled for a tachometer conversion.

INTERIOR AND AIR CONDITIONING

Sending Units

Here are some things to keep in mind. First, the fuel-tank sending unit is a 90-ohm unit. It's wise to check the resistance of any replacement sending unit you get prior to installing it in a tank, which is easy enough with a multimeter that's set up to measure ohms. The gauge will sweep from 0 to 90 ohms (empty to full).

It's also important to consider the remaining gauges. This era of truck uses a large coolant-temperature sending unit that was mounted in the cylinder head from the factory. There are many similar units on the market today that are sized the same but have a different resistance range from stock for gauge-equipped trucks. For an accurate gauge, be sure to source the proper sending unit with the proper resistance. The GM part number is 1513321.

To adapt one of these to an LS engine, drill and tap the top of the water pump or buy an adapter that threads into the passenger-side coolant port to the rear of the cylinder head (12-mm threads) that accepts the large sending unit's 1/2 NPT threads. ICT Billet sells one as part number 551149.

Every oil-pressure gauge in this era of truck is mechanical, which means you'll need to run a steel line from the back of the factory gauge to an oil gallery in whatever engine you've chosen to use. In an LS, a good spot is the oil-cooler line block-off plate that can be drilled and tapped to accept a brass fitting. Keep in mind that you'll need the proper style of fitting for the gauge. If yours is missing or damaged, Classic Industries sells a complete line assembly as part number 14193.

Air Conditioning

Air was an option on trucks from 1967 through 1972, but it wasn't as common as you might think. While you can adapt an original unit to run the more modern R134a refrigerant, it's almost easier these days to install a modern A/C and heating system from Vintage Air.

In terms of looks and functionality, Vintage Air has the original system beat. The new units really clean up the firewall on the engine side. They also tuck up nicely under the dash and offer an optional wired control panel that eliminates the need for bulky cable actuators under the dash, which makes other under-dash work much easier.

Installing Vintage Air in a Non-A/C truck

1 Vintage Air's SureFit system (part number 751170 for trucks without factory air) is a complete self-contained unit that tucks almost completely under the dash. It replaces all of the OEM factory heater assembly, including the fan, wiring, heater core, ducting, and engine-compartment heater box.

2 With the battery disconnected and the cooling system drained, remove all the factory components from under the dash and inside the engine compartment. None of this will be reused. Note that the inner fender is off the truck to give better access to remove the under-hood heater box.

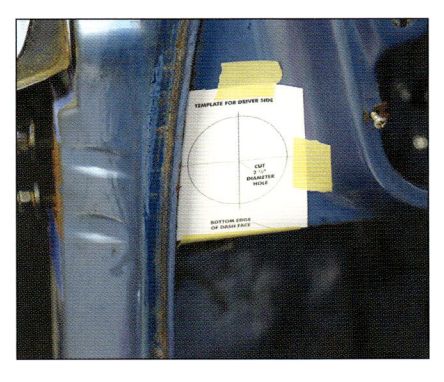

3 The Vintage Air kit comes with new dash vents. Non-A/C trucks will need to have holes cut for them. The kit provides templates for proper placement. All that's needed is to center-punch on the cross mark and use a 2.5-inch hole saw to make your holes.

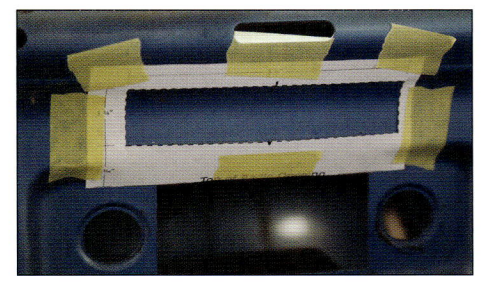

4 The kit uses a factory-style center A/C vent, which needs to be marked and cut using the original radio hole as a reference point. This is best done with a small cutting wheel.

CHAPTER 11

Installing Vintage Air in a Non-A/C truck *continued*

5 The new round vents thread into place with keepers that secure them to the dash from behind. The center vent uses speed nuts that fix it in place from the back. It's best installed with the radio out of the truck.

6 The kit comes with sheet-metal panels designed to bolt in place and cover the factory holes for the original heater box and blower motor. In both cases, Vintage Air suggests using RTV to seal them in place, or you could use seam sealer, as I did here.

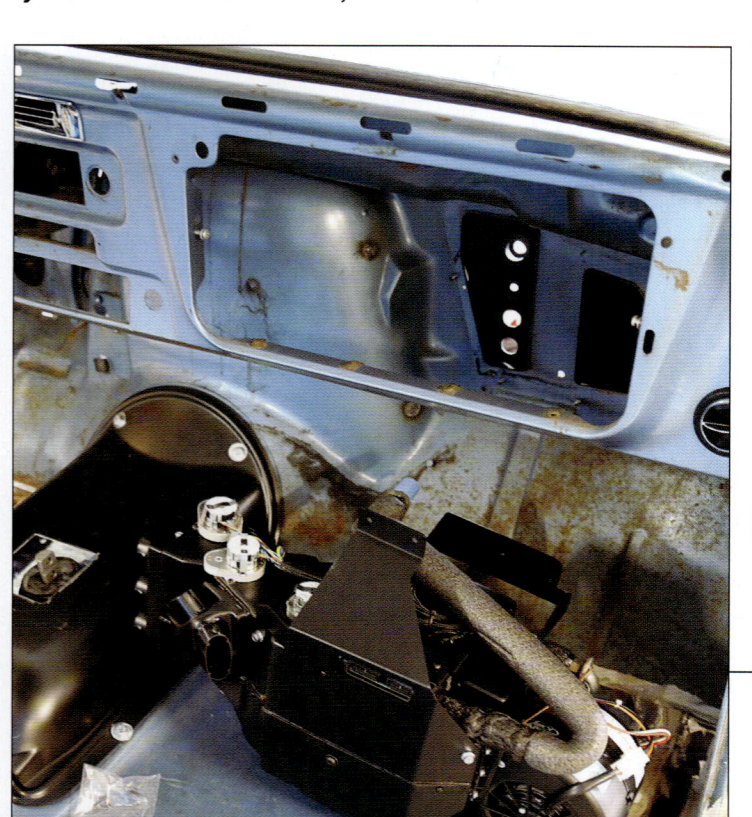

7 The heart of this kit is the Gen IV three-vent evaporator case that tucks neatly behind the dash and provides excellent heating and cooling while minimizing the need to drill, cut, or otherwise modify the truck's cab. The system is microprocessor controlled, so no vacuum lines or cables are required. Before installation, several brackets need to be fixed to the case as well as the hard liquid and suction lines, which are supplied in the kit. Be sure to lubricate the green R134a-spec O-rings with the proper (supplied) oil to prevent damage.

8 The most challenging part of this install is lifting the unit into place under the dash, feeding the hard lines through the firewall plate and grommets, and starting the mounting nuts and bolts to hold it all in place.

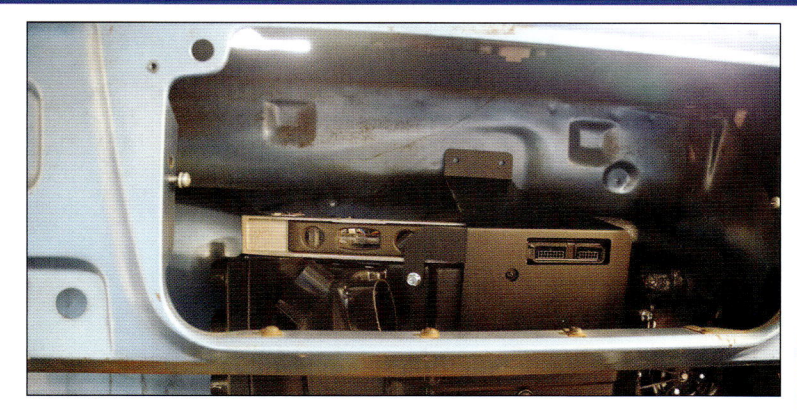

INTERIOR AND AIR CONDITIONING

9 For proper drainage, it's important to make sure the evaporator case is generally level before drilling the last two mounting holes, which are visible just below the windshield. Once it's level, mounting it is a simple process, as is wiring. It features several plugs and requires a keyed power source, dash-light wire, and a few under-hood connections. Power must go directly to the battery for the best performance.

10 The final hole that needs to be drilled is for the drain tube, which is situated just below the case where the floorboard curves up to the firewall. It is 5/8 inch in diameter and needs to sit about an inch below the drain. This is a great time to run the supplied ducting hoses. Two of them go to the defroster vents, and the remaining three go to the two round dash vents and the center dash vent. The supplied hose needs to be cut to fit, but once it's the proper length, simply push it in place.

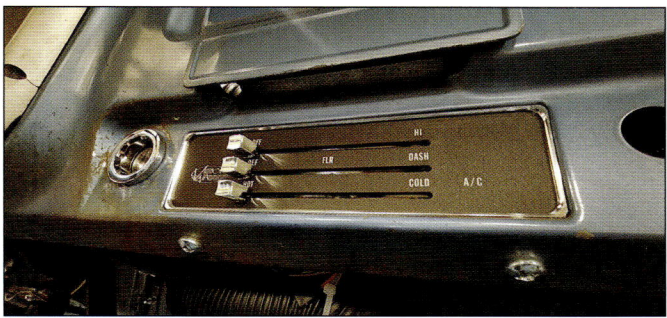

11 One of the coolest parts of this unit is the available SureFit control panel (part number 473080) that removes all of the original control cables from the equation and replaces them with a slick, compact, and smooth-sliding set of controls that interface directly with the computer inside the evaporator case. This system frees up a lot of space under the dash, as there are no cables to deal with. It bolts in place of the original using the supplied hardware and plugs into the controller on the evaporator.

12 Next is the condenser and drier assembly, which is designed to mount directly under the hood-latch assembly and ahead of the radiator. The hard lines for both run through a 1¼-inch hole drilled in the core support. This AMD core support had the inner side hole already in place, which made the process of locating and drilling the outer side easy. Assembly is straightforward. Several small steel brackets are clearly marked and pre-drilled for installation using the supplied hardware.

13 The standard kit comes with a binary-type safety switch (installed) that acts as a safety switch to shut down the system in case pressure is too high or low. The trinary switch (not yet installed) is used when electric fans are utilized as it will activate the fans when pressures climb high enough to require greater airflow through the condenser.

CHEVY/GMC TRUCKS 1967–1972: HOW TO BUILD & MODIFY

CHAPTER 11

Installing Vintage Air in a Non-A/C truck *continued*

14 The Vintage Air kit comes complete with pre-crimped suction, liquid, and discharge hoses but only on one end. Every installation is different, and the kit provides enough hose for just about any type of situation. The key is cutting to length and getting a good, clean, straight cut on the ends that need to be crimped. Any generic hose-cutting tool makes quick work of it.

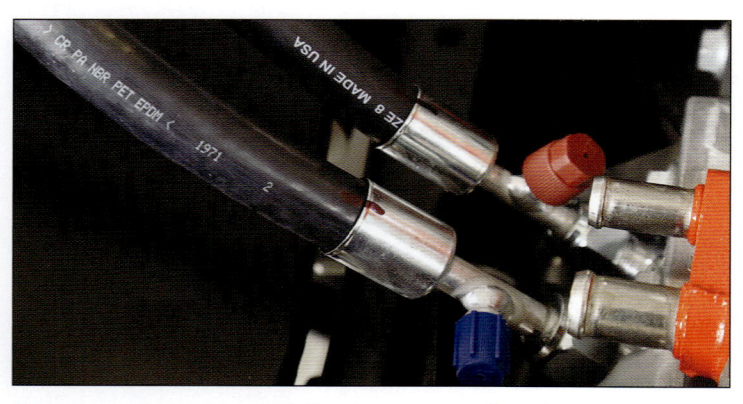

15 Most Vintage Air kits come with a compressor, and most mount high enough on the engine to use the supplied extreme-bend hose ends. In this case, I'm using a Holley low-mount Sanden compressor that requires straight ends to clear the frame. Note how they're clocked to clear the heater hoses and marked to be crimped off-site. Your local radiator shop should have the proper tools to crimp these lines.

16 The heater hoses are next. Both of them run from the water pump to the lower two tubes that pass through the firewall. Fitting these is best done with a spare set of hands to hold the tubes firm under the dash. Note the heater control valve (supplied in the kit) that cuts hot coolant flow to the heater core when the A/C system is functioning.

17 The final step in the process is to connect all the wiring and then calibrate the Gen VI system's controls via grounding a program plug on the harness with a jumper wire and running through both the upper and lower limits of the control levers. All that's left is to have the system charged by a qualified A/C shop.

156   CHEVY/GMC TRUCKS 1967–1972: HOW TO BUILD & MODIFY

CHAPTER 12

WIRING AND LIGHTING

Wiring may not be glamorous, but upgrading your truck's electrical system to match the modern components you've swapped under the hood is important. The original wiring in your truck was built 50 years ago in a GM factory to a design that was created on a budget. None of it was built to operate with any kind of power-hungry modern components in mind. If you added modern computer controls or a bigger alternator than stock, address the rest of your truck's wiring before it becomes an issue.

Alternator

The heart of any good charging system is the alternator. Most of the 1967–1972 GM trucks were fundamentally basic in nature, which meant there was little need for huge-capacity alternators. Many put out just 63 amps, and some made even less, which was plenty to power the few basic systems that these trucks had from the factory. It didn't take much juice to run an AM radio and a heater.

Once you start adding modern stereos, cooling fans, and ECUs, you can start to see the problem. If you've ever been in a truck on a rainy day and stopped at a light with the headlights on, turn signals clicking away, defroster running, windshield wipers going, and brake lights illuminated, you already understand how this can go. Your average stock alternator works hard to keep up with all the stock systems with a resulting dim output and slow speed when the system is stressed.

This 10SI-style alternator is set up as a one-wire unit, which means that it's been fitted with a self-exciting voltage regulator that initiates a charge when the alternator pulley starts to turn. These tend to require some RPM to start charging, and they don't sense remote voltage within the system, which can be a drawback.

Adding more things, as every custom builder will do, is going to make the problem worse and will lead to issues with the charging system. That's the long way of saying an alternator upgrade is vital, particularly if you intend on installing anything other than stock-style components in your C10.

There are two main upgrades to consider when looking at alternators.

CHEVY/GMC TRUCKS 1967–1972: HOW TO BUILD & MODIFY   157

The first is an increased-output 10SI style. The SI stands for systems integrated or internally regulated. Prior to 1969, GM alternators were externally regulated with a regulator mounted to the core support. These are often eliminated by builders when switching to modern alternator power, but this is not always the case. If yours is still plugged into your wiring harness, chances are good that it's still on the job.

The SI units are good, but there are limitations, particularly in low-RPM performance. The main plus here is fit, particularly if you're still running a small-block or big-block. These bolt in place, and since they're internally regulated, installation is simple. A simple conversion harness from any of the restoration parts houses is all you need to make a modern internally regulated unit plug and play for your C10 application.

The second option is an upgraded 12SI alternator. These units hit the scene in 1983, right as computerized electronics were being added to cars and trucks. They have better output (up to 94 amps) than the OEM alternators that GM used from the factory in these trucks. While they have different cases with additional cooling fins over the smaller 10SI units, they tend to bolt right in place.

Stock units are good upgrades, but the aftermarket is full of both 10SI and 12SI alternators that can push out big power. However, they are limited by their design. Alternators get hot when used, and these designs can only push so much cooling air through their cases.

The best bet, and what you'll find on every LS engine from the factory, is the CS-style alternator that was designed from the start for power-hungry computer-controlled engines with electric fans, fuel pumps, PCMs, and more. The first CS unit (the CS130) hit the scene in 1986 with much larger cooling fins than the SI units and more stable power output at idle. An upgraded CS130D came out in 1994 with outputs of 100 amps and more.

If you want to run a CS-style unit on a small- or big-block engine, look for one from a 1986-or-newer truck with mounting ears that are 180 degrees apart. It will mount up using several metric 8x1.25-mm bolts and some bracket clearance work.

If you've swapped to an LS engine, plan for a CS alternator. They came stock on every LS engine from the factory, and there's no reason to run anything else.

Adding Big Power

Adding a high-output alternator to your original C10 is a good idea, but it's just one step in a process. What do you think your original wiring is going to do with 105 amps of power? Can you smell the smoke already?

At the very least, if you've upgraded your alternator, you'll need to modify the wiring harness to accept a larger-than-stock charging wire that's directed straight from the alternator to a main power lug that connects to the battery. Run that charging wire through either a main fuse or a fusible link to protect the truck's wiring from meltdown.

If you added power-hungry components to your truck, pull power for them from that power lug you've created, which keeps them from sucking their power through the fuse box and potentially overloading the original wiring. From the factory, GM trucks used smaller 10-gauge wire and a handful of fusible links to deliver power to the fuse box. That's not beefy enough for alternators that produce anything more than the original output.

The rule of thumb on charging wires is this: 8-gauge wire for alternators up to 60 amps, and 6-gauge wire for alternators up to 105 amps. When it comes to fusible links, the key is to run at least a 6-inch-long section, and it needs to be sized four sizes smaller than the wire it's protecting. For example, a 6-gauge charge wire would get a 6-inch-long 10-gauge section of fusible link. The link is there to break

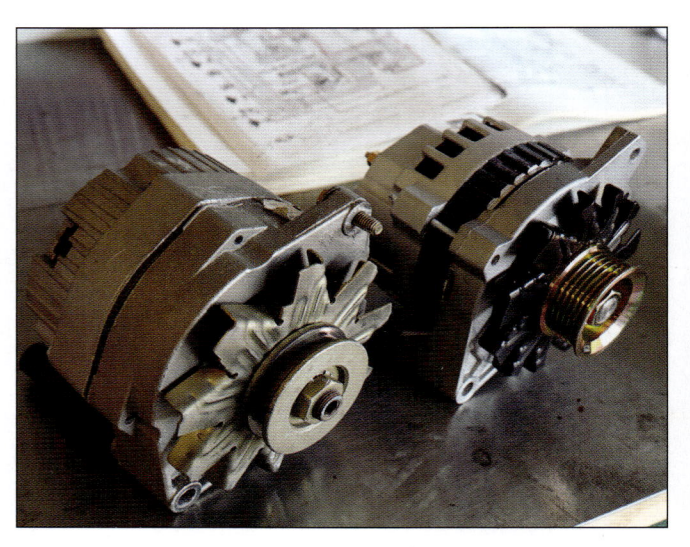

The CS130-style alternator on the right is physically smaller than the 10SI-based one-wire on the left, but its mounts are in the same places, which means it will work with classic C10 applications. All of the original brackets work. This CS130-style 105-amp unit is from AC Delco (part number ADO-335-1014).

WIRING AND LIGHTING

Alternator: How Much is Too Much?

When it comes to powering a classic C10, many choices are available from both the aftermarket and salvage yards. More-capable modern alternators offer much-improved charging over stock, particularly at low RPM, where your truck needs it most. But how big should you go?

Your truck's alternator, if working properly, will only output what the truck's charging system requires. If you have a 200-amp alternator and the truck only calls for 40 amps of power, the alternator will output only 40 amps. In that sense, no alternator is too big. The problem is when you try to funnel more power than you should to new, hungry components through old, original, small-gauge wiring. If you're adding power-hungry components to your truck, use heavy-gauge wiring on items that demand greater amperage, and don't pull that power from the original fuse box. ∎

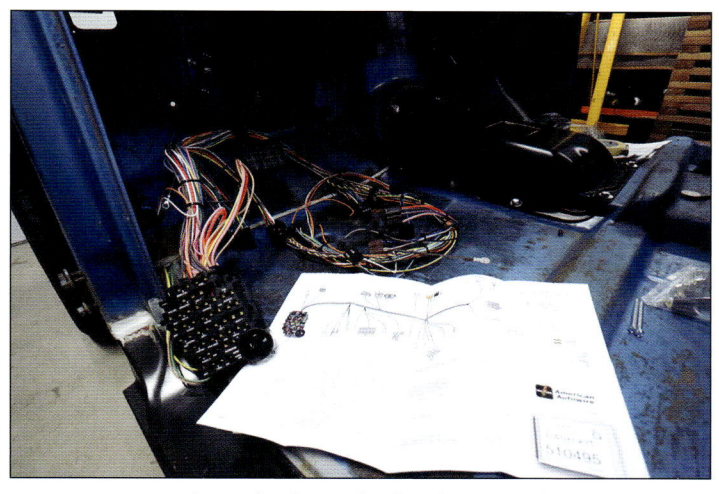

This is American Autowire's Classic Update kit for 1967 and 1968 C10 pickups. It comes with everything you need to completely rewire your C10. This system uses modern blade-type fuses and OEM-style Packard crimp connectors and stock plugs. It also has provisions for several add-on circuits, both keyed and 12V constant hot. This is part number 510333.

If you're going to go to the trouble to rewire your truck, plan on sourcing a good set of proper Packard-style crimpers. These offer OEM-style crimps and are vital for kits, such as those sold by American Autowire.

Autowire are available in direct-fit configurations, complete with well-marked wires and in-depth instructions to walk you through the entire installation. It's an added cost, but it is insurance against electrical problems that can easily lead to breakdown, fire, or both.

As an added benefit, the American Autowire and Painless Performance kits are set up for larger-than-stock alternators. They've been designed to handle the increased demands of modern add-on components. Both systems have great reputations, but I've found the American Autowire kit to be easier to install. In either case, the expense and time it takes to install will be worth it in the long run.

Lighting

One of the easiest and probably most frequently overlooked areas of improvement for your C10 or C20 is in its lighting. Seeing and being seen is vital to safety, and your truck's original lighting has likely seen better days.

Originally, these trucks used incandescent bulbs throughout—from the then-standard sealed-beam headlights to the 1156 and 1157 taillight and turn-signal bulbs and the little 194-series dash lights that illuminate your fuel gauge and speedometer. All of these are easy to replace, except for some of the 194s under the dash. Using OEM-style stock replacements won't make your truck any more visible than it would have been from the factory.

Headlights: Sealed-Beam and Halogen

Every C10 built in this era came with sealed-beam headlamps from the factory. These were named due to the fact that the bulb and reflector were sealed in place inside the headlight as a single, replaceable unit.

the connection in case of a short to ground and kill power before your wiring can melt or catch fire.

If your budget allows, it's wise to consider ditching the original 50-year-old wiring altogether for a modern replacement wiring harness. Kits from Painless or American

CHEVY/GMC TRUCKS 1967–1972: HOW TO BUILD & MODIFY

CHAPTER 12

Sealed-beam lights hit the scene way back in 1939 and stuck around well into the 1980s. It's likely that your truck still has one or two twin 7-inch round units with dual filaments for both high beam and low beam for Chevrolet folks, and quad 5-inch units for the GMC people.

The next step up from the original sealed-beam lights were halogen lights, which got their start in Europe in the 1960s. Halogen sealed-beam units are brighter than the original sealed-beam headlights thanks to the addition of halogen gas and a revised internal reflector assembly, both of which increase output. These became legal and ubiquitous in the U.S. in 1978, so it's likely that your C10 has been fitted with a set already.

Sealed-beam and halogen lights were more than capable for their time, but the world has become brighter over the years thanks to the addition of high-intensity discharge (HID) and light-emitting diode (LED) power in other cars on the road. Heck, even the streetlights have more oomph than they used to. What that means for you is that your old sealed-beam units are not as effective as they once were. When it comes to upgrades, a few options are available.

The Relay Mod

It may seem odd, but when discussing headlight upgrades, the first thing you should look at is your truck's wiring and not the lights themselves.

From the factory, GM didn't use a headlight relay to control power to the bulbs themselves. Instead, power traveled from the battery and alternator through the wiring harness, into the headlight switch, through the high-beam switch on the floor, and out to the headlights. That's a lot of wire to pass through, and the resulting voltage drop from that length of wire, the switches, and all the connections results in significantly less power at the headlight plug than you'll find at the battery. It's not uncommon to see only 10.5 volts at the lights themselves when the battery is resting at 12.5 volts, and that much voltage drop is a huge factor in headlamp brightness.

Adding a modern relay into your original headlight wiring harness is an inexpensive and effective upgrade, and doing the work is simple. It requires a pair of 30-amp relays, two 20-amp circuit breakers, some 14-gauge wire, assorted shrink tube, and a few wiring terminals.

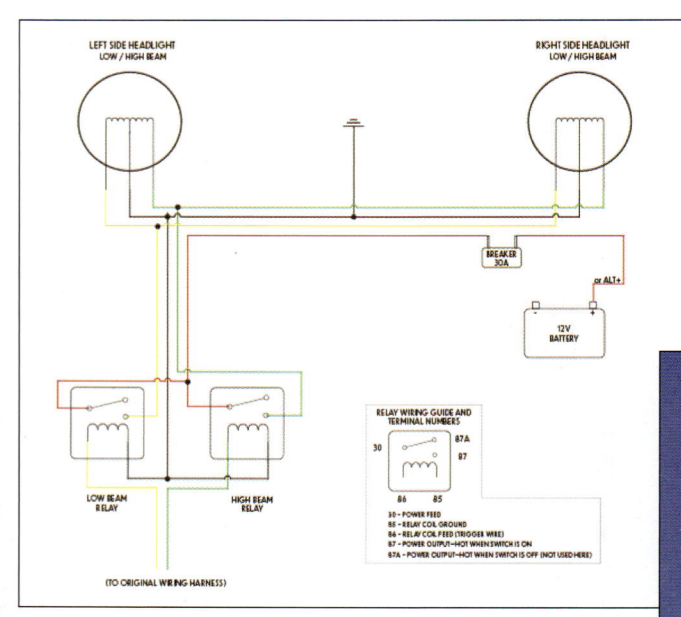

The sealed-beam headlight was a mainstay for years, but the world has moved past it in terms of output, longevity, and reliability. The only real benefit here is in the OEM look they provide. You can get more performance out of this type of light by installing headlight relays in your circuit.

Adding headlight relays is a simple process that isn't expensive and provides a huge benefit to halogen-style headlamps. As seen in this diagram, the relays install in-line between the factory headlight switch and the headlights themselves using the original wiring to trigger the relays rather than power the lights. The load of the circuit is removed from the headlight switch and comes directly from the battery or alternator via a much shorter run of heavier-gauge wire. The result is 14 volts at the bulb rather than 12 (or less) and brighter lights.

160   CHEVY/GMC TRUCKS 1967–1972: HOW TO BUILD & MODIFY

WIRING AND LIGHTING

Inexpensive Euro Upgrades

In Europe, the rules surrounding automotive lighting are much different than in the U.S. Starting in 1983, Ford took a step in the Euro direction by adding replaceable bulb–style headlamps to its vehicles, which is something that had been the norm overseas for years prior.

For you, that's good news, as your C10 uses basic 7-inch (or 5-inch) round headlamps that were universal for their era. This means there are already replaceable-style-bulb headlamp housings available that can fit in your C10's headlight buckets using H4-style headlight bulbs.

Companies such as United Pacific Industries offer the round housings that accept the H4-style bulbs. Keep in mind that true Euro H4 bulbs are not DOT compliant here because they're too bright. If you're looking for a DOT-approved H4-style setup, source some HB2-9003 bulbs. They fit as well.

The nice thing about this modification is that the H4-style bulb shares the same style of connector as the old sealed-beam units, so they'll plug in where the original headlights did. Once you've done the relay mod, installing a set of these can represent a pretty big boost in lighting output. Many H4-style bulbs are available in a variety of color tones and temperatures.

The idea is to use the original headlight wiring to trigger a relay rather than to power the headlamps. The relay draws power through heavier-gauge wiring on a shorter run direct from the battery. Doing this eliminates the voltage drop inherent in the system, and therefore creates brighter lights (stock or not). It also preserves all the stock headlight harness functions, such as the high-beam indicator, etc.

Just about any modern headlight swap will benefit from increased voltage supply over stock, so in terms of headlight upgrades, this is the first thing to do.

Lighting Upgrades

Once you've ensured that your lights are operating at full voltage, the next thing to do is to swap out the original sealed-beam units for something a little more modern. There are any number of inexpensive upgraded halogen units on the market today from places such as Summit Racing, Rock Auto, United Pacific, and others. High-output sealed-beam units are a great upgrade here, and installation is plug-and-play. They're DOT legal for use on US roads, which can be a concern with overseas-sourced replacements. Note that Euro-spec lights tend to output more light than US-spec versions, and they're not always local law compliant.

HID Lights

HID lights became available in OEM applications in the 2000s and hit the aftermarket soon thereafter. The HID bulb operates by creating an electronic arc that passes from one tungsten electrode to another inside a fused quartz or alumina tube that's filled with a noble gas or some other metals and/or salts.

The resulting light is very bright (much brighter than a halogen light) and requires a special kind of lens to help to reflect it properly. HID kits tend to come with a bulb and a lens housing as well as a ballast to power the system.

The main benefit is increased light output and visibility of objects both on the road and in the periphery. Note that one of the hallmarks of HID lighting is an abrupt cutoff point in the light due to the lens required to focus the light properly. That's not exactly a bad thing, but it can take some getting used to. HIDs also come in different intensity levels, which produce different colors from blue to white to purple, depending on the kit you choose.

Keep in mind that not every kit is DOT compliant. If you attempt to use HID bulbs in standard H4-style housings, you'll scatter light all over the place and be a blinding nuisance to other drivers.

High-intensity discharge (HID) is a much brighter solution than what you'll find with a standard halogen conversion, but it requires more components to work properly, including a ballast to start and maintain the light's arc and a lens to focus the light properly. These are available as kits, but LED lighting is now just as effective and typically easier to install.

CHEVY/GMC TRUCKS 1967–1972: HOW TO BUILD & MODIFY

CHAPTER 12

Many 7-inch LED light conversions are available today. The key is to look for a kit that features a glass lens and has a good track record of performance. Dapper Lighting's OE7 LED lights are solid, made-in-US units that are built with OEM-style quality and bolt in place with minor headlight bucket modifications. These are plug and play with your truck's OEM wiring. No relays are needed. They're much brighter than any halogen/relay conversion.

Another option comes from United Pacific. These LED units are called "ULTRALIT" and feature five high-power LEDs that provide a bright, white light. They only draw 1.7 amps at low beam and 2.6 amps at high beam. Like the OE7s, these bolt into place and plug into your original harness. No other modifications are needed.

LEDs

The best solution these days is to convert your truck's lighting to LEDs. While HID is still a brighter technology, LED has a number of benefits to consider.

An LED is basically a semiconductor that emits light upon a flow of current through it. They don't take much power to run. That, along with long service life and superior output, make them the ideal upgrade solution for everything from marker lights to sealed-beam or halogen headlights—but only if you use quality parts.

LEDs are easy to spot, as they don't ramp up to full power the same way a regular bulb does. They're either all the way on or all the way off. They turn on quickly compared to the HID's several-second warm-up time.

A lot of modern stoplights are LED powered these days, as are city-bus taillights. In both cases, they've been chosen because of their bright output and long service life, which are typically much longer than the average halogen-style filament bulb. They're also smaller and easier to package.

When it comes to LED headlamps, several options are available for a C10. The first is to source an H4-style light housing as you would for an H4-style headlight conversion. Simply install an H4-style LED bulb inside it. This works, but it isn't ideal because it doesn't allow for proper focusing of the light source.

The second method is to source a complete LED unit (housing and all) that bolts in place of a stock headlight bulb. The main consideration here is to source a set that is high quality from a reputable manufacturer.

The key here is in an LED's power consumption compared to its output. With an LED, all you need is the LED. No wiring mods or relays are required. They'll draw less power than the original bulbs they're replacing, so the entire OEM wiring system can remain intact.

Holley has just entered the LED headlight market with its Retrobright LED lights. Dapper Lighting makes some of the best LED conversions in the business, and its OE7 setup is designed to look stock and perform better than any H4-style LED swap thanks to its integrated LED projectors. The Dapper units are built in the US and come with a 5-year warranty.

WIRING AND LIGHTING

Installing OE7 Lights in a C10

1 Installing a set of OE7 lights in a C10 is a straightforward process that begins with removing the OEM setup down to the headlight bucket. Some clearance needs to be added, as the OE7 includes a 194-style running light that needs clearance and an access point to be able to service the plug and bulb with the light assembly installed. A set of tin snips is all that's required to make the bucket's opening slightly bigger.

2 The OE7 is slightly deeper than a stock halogen or sealed beam, and the wiring is self-explanatory. This is a plug-and-play solution other than the running-light bulb, which can be wired into the park-lamp circuit. OE7s come in several options, including with halogen, if preferred.

3 The nice thing about the OE7, aside from the heavy-duty construction and OEM quality, is the fact it doesn't look that different than a stock setup. This won't stand out as much as some overseas LED conversions, but it does bring a modern look and modern lighting to your C10 and removes some of the load from the original headlight circuit.

Turn Signals and Brake Lights

When it comes to taillights, turn signals, and running lights, LEDs tend to be the industry favorite from conversion bulbs to complete LED panels.

If you're determined to use your original taillight sockets, you can source LED bulbs to replace the 1156- and 1157-style bulbs your truck used from the factory. The only downside is regarding size. Only so many LEDs can fit on a standard-swap LED bulb, which means you're

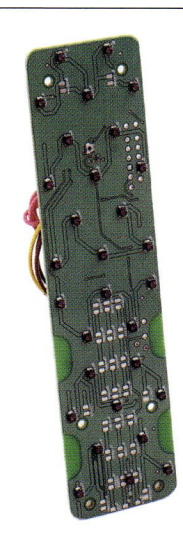

If ultimate visibility is your goal, it's hard to go wrong with an LED panel installed inside the rear taillight housings. These take the place of your original bulbs, replacing them with LEDs, which are significantly brighter than stock. This is Dapper Lighting's Advanced Sequential setup, which can be configured to illuminate in many different patterns. (Photo Courtesy Dapper Lighting)

CHEVY/GMC TRUCKS 1967–1972: HOW TO BUILD & MODIFY   163

CHAPTER 12

The simplest LED solution is to use 1156 and 1157-style conversion bulbs in your original housings. These are Dapper Lighting's Revive LED bulbs, which feature metal bodies that act as heat sinks. LED life is extended when heat is eliminated. These are direct swaps that were offered in white, red, and amber and are much brighter than the bulbs they replace.

leaving some brightness on the table by going this route. It is, however, the simplest solution.

LED panels are a favorite of most builders, even if they're more expensive than standard LED replacement bulbs.

The main reason for this is simple output. Using a conversion bulb works just fine, but a larger panel with integrated LEDs puts out more light by design. In most cases, that setup allows for a range of sequential options as well.

For example, Dapper Lighting's sequential taillight kit for 1967–1972 GM trucks tucks inside the original taillight housing, but it's made up of a panel of LEDs that allows them to illuminate in a variety of patterns. You get the added brightness and reliability of LEDs with the custom touch of adjustable pattern illumination. In the case of the Dapper kit, it's plug and play with your stock wiring, it only requires a low-current flasher module, and it will fit behind the stock taillight lens.

Note that every LED light that's connected to your truck's thermal flasher won't operate properly without a special low-current or LED-style electronic flasher in place of the stock unit. Be sure you source one at the same time you source your LED lights. LEDs don't place enough of a load on the circuit for a thermal flasher to operate properly.

All the restoration parts houses have their own versions of LED taillamps, as does Digi-Tails. What you choose is up to you, but note that you get what you pay for. I think we can all agree that the bolder the brake light, the better.

Dash Lights

Your C10's dash gauges are illuminated via a handful of small incandescent bulbs, all of which twist into place using plastic retainers that clip into the back of the gauge cluster and make contact with the printed circuit. Over the years, these can burn out, and either the sockets or the printed circuit itself can wear out enough to break contact and eventually kill a bulb's power supply.

Unfortunately, the best time to replace these bulbs is when the cluster is out of the truck because trying to get to them all with the gauges in the truck is a chore. You'll need to lie on the floor to see them, and you'll likely miss a few because they aren't all clearly marked. Both the idiot lights and the dash lights use the same kind of twist socket, and when you're standing on your head looking up at them, it's hard to sort out what's what.

You can install 194-style LED bulbs in your truck's dash, but they tend to be almost too bright, and you'll likely lose your ability to dim them via the headlight dimmer switch, as it's designed for incandescent bulbs only. If you go this route, try to find LEDs without forward-facing diodes to help spread out the light and eliminate bright spots in the dash.

CHAPTER 13

FINISHING TOUCHES

Many builders say that how your truck looks is just as important as how it drives, and there's a lot of truth to that. Curb appeal is key to any hot rod or custom, and it's no different for your C10. The goal is to build something that you turn to look at every time you park it—and not because of the things that bother you about it. Selecting the proper wheels, paint, and trim pieces are all a part of that curb appeal.

Common Body Modifications

Truck people, particularly 1967–1972 GM truck people, will tell you that GM got it right with the design of these rigs. Of course, that doesn't mean that you can't make yours better or stand out by using some of what the aftermarket has to offer.

Glass

When it comes to glass upgrades, there are two main options. The first is one-piece side glass, as you'd find in an old bodystyle (OBS) or newer truck. The second is flush-mount glass at the windshield and back light.

One-piece glass has become all the rage among truck builders over the past few years—and for good reason. One-piece side glass ditches the wing windows and provides a clean and simple side profile that lends itself well to the roofline of the C10.

Brother's Trucks, One Piece Products, and Classic Industries offer complete kits for the C10, which basically consist of a new front window channel, associated weatherstripping, and the larger-than-stock one-piece side glass with an option of tint.

Installation is not too challenging, as it only requires slight modification to the inside of the door frame. There's a reinforcing plate just below the wing window that needs to be cut away, and some work with the door stop mechanism so that it can clear the one-piece glass panel.

Who needs wing windows? One-piece side glass gives a modern, clean look to any C10 and eliminates those leaky wing windows that are hard to rebuild. A kit such as this installs in about a day with some light internal door structure modification required.

CHEVY/GMC TRUCKS 1967–1972: HOW TO BUILD & MODIFY

CHAPTER 13

Flush-mount glass glues in place like a modern windshield in a late-model car and uses no exterior trim. Several companies offer kits, but Fesler's glass is known for fitting well with usually little-to-no bodywork required for a good fit. It's also Department of Transportation (DOT) approved. Fesler offers both front and rear glass.

Flush-mount glass is available for both the windshield and back light from Fesler (for both the small 1967 glass and the larger, later rear glass). These kits eliminate the original weatherstripping completely and replace it with modern urethane to fix the glass in place, as you'd find in a modern car or truck.

In general, these kits don't require any special bodywork to install properly, but it may be required for perfect gaps. In either case, all of the above will make your C10's greenhouse look a lot more modern in a very subtle way, which is probably why the kits have become so popular.

You'll also need to grind a few other areas for clearance and drill some holes on the inside of the door frame for bolt access. It's important to note that this is one modification that you can't easily reverse, so keep that in mind before you dive in.

Roll Pans and Bumpers

Another option for a clean look is to ditch your factory bumpers for roll pans in the front and rear. Roll pans install in place of the original bumpers but are aligned to the body like an additional body panel. They're available in steel or fiberglass, but paint work will be required regardless of the material you choose.

With the current popularity of a stock look with modern low suspension and big wheels, it may make more sense to install a new set of reproduction bumpers, either in painted steel or in chrome, or use the originals.

There are both good and bad reproductions, so beware. I've had great luck with both AMD and Classic Industries when it comes to quality reproduction units and their assorted mounting brackets. Classic Industries also has reproduction painted bumpers for 1967–1968 and 1969–1972, which can be hard to find for these trucks.

DIY Smooth Bumpers

1 *Building a set of smooth, painted bumpers starts with sourcing a good starting point. These are Classic Industries' painted bumpers for a 1967 and 1968 C10. The company offers both front and rear bumpers in basic black.*

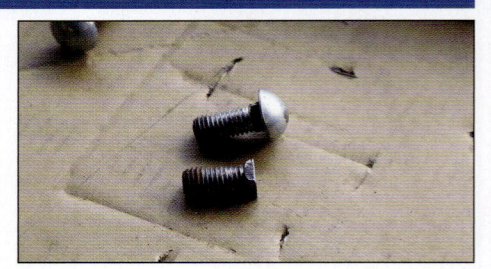

2 *GM bumper bolts tend to have a big, round crown over the top of a square shank that sits down inside the bumper itself. That's what makes all of this possible. The first step is to pry off any chrome or stainless cover on the crown of the bolt, chuck it up in a vise, and cut off the head of the bolt with a hacksaw. For a front bumper, you'll do this to two bolts.*

FINISHING TOUCHES

DIY Smooth Bumpers continued

3 With a grinder or a file, chamfer the edges of the square shanks of these two bolts to prep for welding them into the outermost bolt holes in the bumper. I did this with a pedestal-mounted sander, but a handheld grinder works just as well.

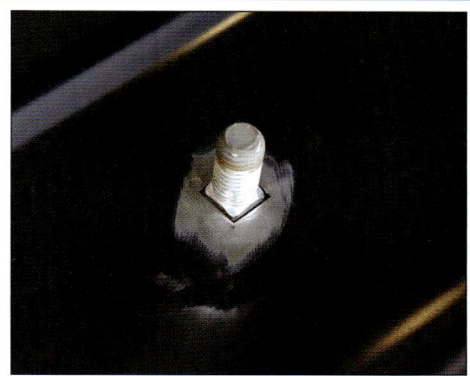

4 The view from the inside of the bumper is similar. The trick is to use a flat magnet to hold the bolt flush to the exterior face of the bumper and weld it in place from the back. Be sure to remove any paint first.

5 Once the back is welded, it's time to weld the face too. These don't need to be pretty, as they're going to be ground flush to the bumper surface. You do want good penetration on the front and rear welds, as this is what will hold your bumper in place.

6 Next, move to the four innermost bolts that are not flush-mounted to the face of the bumper. Grinding most of the bolt head off (but not all of it) helps fill in the indentation in the bumper and gives you more to weld to. Double-nutting them and using Vise-Grips to hold them makes this job easy using a bench grinder.

7 A straightedge can give you a good idea when to stop grinding down the head of the bolt. Once it's complete, burn them in from behind and weld up the face as well.

8 Once welded and ground down flush, this is what is left. If you're a fantastic welder, you may not need much body filler to hide the work, but don't bet on it. Welding even a thick bumper can cause some warping, and you'll need the heat to be sure that there's good penetration in your welds. You don't want these coming loose.

CHEVY/GMC TRUCKS 1967–1972: HOW TO BUILD & MODIFY

CHAPTER 13

DIY Smooth Bumpers *continued*

9 I prefer to use Evercoat finishing compound for things such as this because it's harder than standard body filler and provides good results after it's sanded down and primed. Once all six bolt faces are smoothed out with a skim coat of body filler over the welded areas and sanded down flush with 400- and 1,000-grit paper, it's hard to tell that the holes were ever there, especially after primer.

10 When fitted with base-level equipment, GM trucks of this era used Cameo White for their bumpers, grilles, and headlight buckets. I used paint from AutomotiveTouchUp.com. Three spray cans of primer, three of Cameo White, and three of clear were more than enough to tackle both the front and rear bumpers, grille, and headlight buckets. The end result is subtle and improved over a bumper with visible bumper bolts.

Cleaning Up and Matching Original Paint

Love it or hate it, the patina movement continues to be one of the biggest trends in the truck world. This is where traditionalists who like shiny things and modern builders who covet originality clash, and it happens in the truck world more often than just about anywhere else.

At one time, scruffy paint with worn-through spots was grounds for a respray. Leaving the truck like that made others think the builder ran out of money or was lazy with the build. These days, it's a different story. If you have a rig that shows its years, it may be a smart move to leave it that way, as popular opinion has embraced the aged look. After all, it's only original once, even if the only original component on your truck is the body and paint.

Cleaning up original paint is a generally straightforward process, but it all depends on the condition of the finish in question. I've had great luck with Meguiar's Ultimate Compound on a foam pad and a dual-action polisher. That setup is strong enough to remove overspray but gentle enough to put a polish into remaining OEM finishes without removing them. If there's any shine left in your paint, that kind of compound will bring it out. As an added benefit, if your truck has been touched up over the years to hide thin spots, that method of cleaning will bring them out, and the patina crowd loves the way it looks.

Really rough paint, particularly if it's showing surface rust, can benefit from a dose of household CLR cleaner to remove the rust staining, followed by a scrub with a scouring sponge and a gritty household cleaner, such as Bon Ami or Comet. The best method is to start in a small section and see how it looks before you continue. Remember that it's easy to go too far here, so proceed with caution.

The bigger challenge is matching the patina, particularly if you have to replace a bedside, rocker panel, door, or fender due to damage; or if you

168 CHEVY/GMC TRUCKS 1967–1972: HOW TO BUILD & MODIFY

buy a truck that's already had some of its parts swapped. All paint ages relative to the truck, which means that sourcing another door with the same level of fade isn't easy. A better solution is to match the patina yourself, and there are many ways to handle that process. If you're looking for in-depth guidance, check out Kevin Tetz's CarTech book *Patina: How to Create and Preserve*.

Scan this QR code with your smartphone to buy *Patina: How to Create & Preserve* (SA447) by Kevin Tetz.

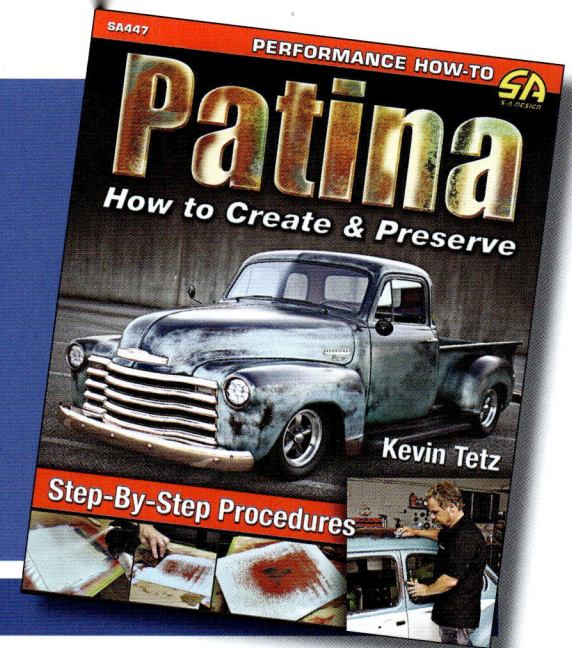

Matching Original Patina

1 The first step in creating patina is research (not sanding or spraying). That research includes looking at other trucks (or your own). In my case, this truck had one white fender due to damage, and the other fender had a light respray over OEM paint that needed to be buffed off before I could match it. Study how other components have weathered and then come up with your plan to match it.

2 For this project, I used automotivetouchup.com's products. The company has a great reputation for matching factory GM truck colors, and the products come ready to spray and right to your door. AutomotiveTouchup has everything you need to get the job done from masking to sanding, and the ready-to-spray paint comes in spray cans or quart or gallon containers.

3 Once you've completed the body work or rust repair, prime the panel to prepare it for paint. In this case, we started with several coats of primer and wet sanding with 1,000-grit paper between coats to level out the surface.

4 Here's where the research pays off. In this era, GM truck factories used black primer on beds and front-end components. To match, apply a black base coat between the primer and the color. Work with a test panel to be sure that your paint products won't react. A better idea is to source the color that you intend to use from the same source as the rest of your paint.

CHEVY/GMC TRUCKS 1967–1972: HOW TO BUILD & MODIFY

CHAPTER 13

Matching Original Patina continued

5 Pro painter Alistair Case laid down a decent coat of AutomotiveTouchup code 506 Medium Blue Metallic over the black on this fender without any blocking prior to application. Note the thinner spray pattern in the areas where the paint is thin on your reference piece.

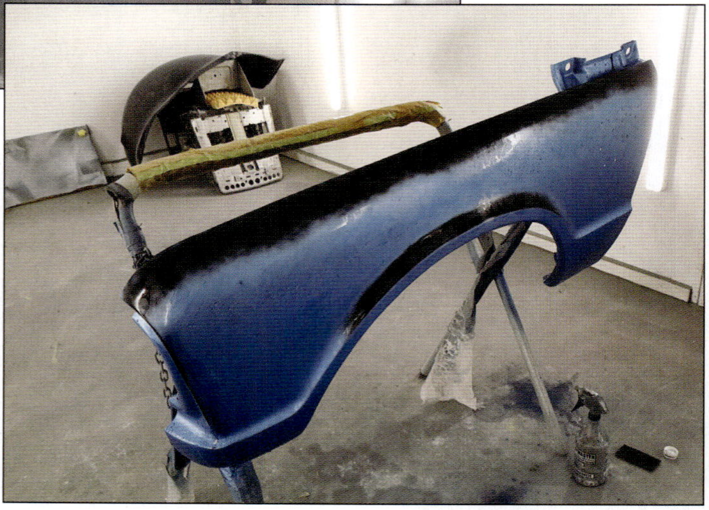

7 It's easy to go overboard, but you can always come back and reshoot the base color if you don't like the result. The goal should be slightly inconsistent lines between the black and the color, and that's accomplished by lighter rubbing as you approach the end of the fade line. Once you have it where you like it, let the fender dry, clean it off with wax and grease remover or a paint prep cloth, and apply the clear to finish the panel.

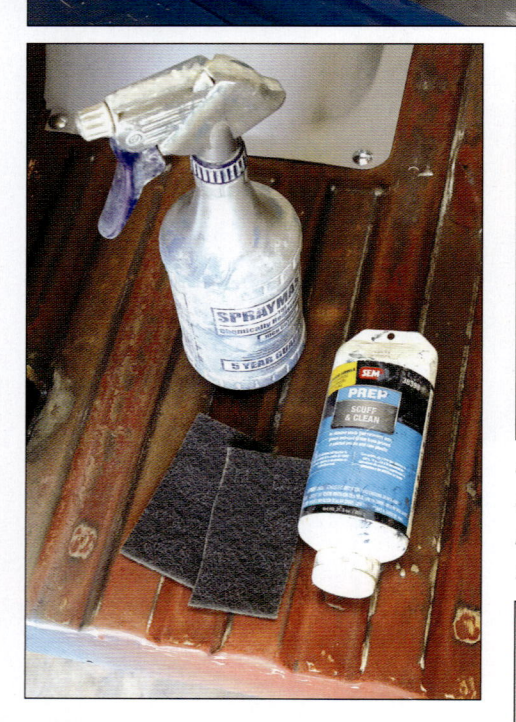

6 Here's a trick developed by Case. Use a gray Scotch-Brite ultra-fine pad, some SEM Scuff & Clean, and a spray bottle filled with water to achieve rapid aging. With the pad loaded with Scuff & Clean and lubed with water, rub through the color coat in the areas where you'd like to create sun fade. The Scuff & Clean and water mix offers just enough grit to help the pad break through but is not as aggressive as sandpaper. The result is a more natural sun-faded look.

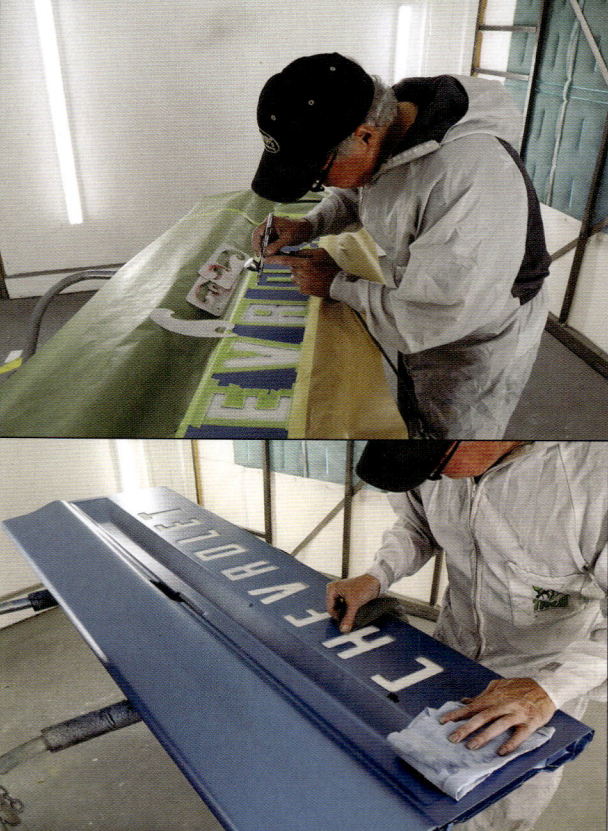

8 This same process works well on new replacement panels too. Here, Case is deliberately aging a new AMD tailgate. He used an airbrush to paint the white Chevrolet letters over the blue prior to aging, as the factory used templates that created a soft edge on the letters from the factory. An airbrush, along with masking that hangs over each letter indent (flush with the stamp line) makes the same effect.

FINISHING TOUCHES

9 Case applied these same basic methods to the bed, which you may have noted was originally red. First bodywork, primer, and a black base coat prior to base color. AutomotiveTouchup's base color gives great coverage and lays down smooth, even when it's a lighter color that's applied lightly in an effort to look thin. That helps immensely in recreating the wear seen on factory-original trucks. The result is paint that looks thin from age rather than paint that looks like it was sprayed to be thin.

10 Another effective method Case used is to run a buffer to thin out the paint on the larger, flatter areas along with some compound to help cut through the paint. Note that compound can react with the base coat, so be careful. In this case, the reaction that we achieved just added to the aged look, particularly at the tailgate.

Reassembly Tricks

Generally speaking, when it comes to reassembling your truck's body, the best method is to start in the middle and work your way out. That means, if you've taken your truck down to its bare frame, reinstall the cab first, then the doors, and then move on to the core support, fenders, hood, tailgate, etc.

The reason for this is ease of adjustment. The door gaps are easiest to set with the front fenders off the truck. Once the fenders are installed, you lose access to some of the bolts that provide the door adjustment. Getting proper gaps from the back of the cab forward starts with the door at the door striker and moves toward the nose of the truck from there. The fenders need to be fit to the doors, and you might find you need body shims to make it all look right.

C10s tended to have consistent gaps from the factory, and all of the panels have plenty of adjustment. The goal is to take your time. When it comes to things like the core support, don't cinch things down completely until after all the body panels are installed, as wiggling things for proper fitment is part of the process.

The time to fit replacement or reproduction panels is prior to any paint work. Don't be lulled into thinking that your excellently rated reproduction doors will fit like a glove without testing them first. Every panel that didn't come on your truck from the factory needs to be fit to the truck before the shine or color is added.

Bed Installation

When it comes to reinstalling a truck bed, it's wise to call on a few extra pairs of hands for help. Two people can pick up a short-bed without the tailgate attached, and I've

CHAPTER 13

Tech Tip

Rear Bed Bolts and Rear Gas Tanks

If you've installed a Blazer tank in your C10, you've likely created a problem for yourself that you won't find until it's time to reinstall the bed. The bed bolts pass down from the inside of the bed through the top of the frame channel, and a Blazer tank will obstruct your access to install or tighten the rearmost nuts.

Some builders solve this by welding nuts to the underside of the frame and installing modern-style Torx-head bolts, but there's a better solution.

All you need to do is measure the diameter of your trusty 9/16-inch socket and drill a hole in the bottom of the frame (right under the bed bolts in the rear) so that the socket can pass through. Then, you can install or remove the bed nuts. This can be done with the tank in place, but note that you may need to loosen its mounting straps and shift it around to gain the proper access. ∎

Blazer tank swappers: drilling two holes in the frame just below the rearmost bed mount bolts will save you a lot of time and swear words. All you need to do is to locate the holes under the proper bed mount and drill them large enough to accommodate a socket and extension. Feed the nut up from the bottom versus fishing it in from the back or the front.

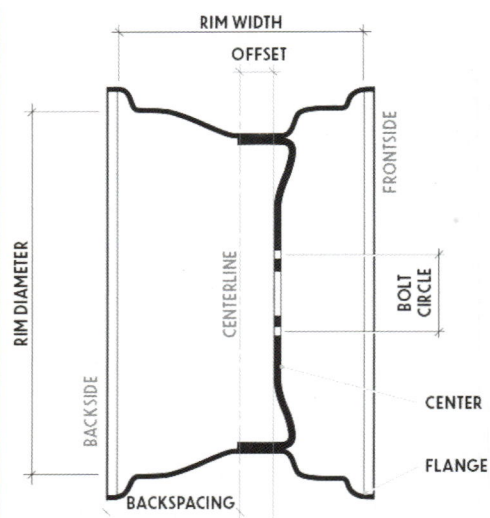

The terms of the trade help visualize what to look for when measuring for wheel fitment. For your C10, the key points are width, diameter, backspace, and bolt circle. Playing with the backspacing measurement can help center the wide rubber under the C10's cavernous rear wheel tubs.

done a long-bed with three without too much trouble. The key is having a plan in place and moving on a count of three.

Pulling the rear wheels off the truck helps in a big way. Otherwise, the only special tool needed here is a long screwdriver for aligning the bed to the mounting plates on the frame. It's also wise to install rubber isolators between the bed and the frame (thin sections of rubber will do) to help eliminate any squeaking. Simply insert and tighten the bed-mount bolts. Be sure to stand back and eyeball the bed's alignment with the cab before you snug the bolts down, as there is some adjustment that can be made.

Wheels

One of the most important decisions in any build comes down to wheel style and size. Thousands of options are available when it comes to wheels alone—from stock-style steel rims to era-correct mags and all the way to today's 20-inch-plus rolling stock.

The look of your truck will change dramatically depending on what wheels and tires you choose, but getting the sizing sorted out properly is vital, as custom wheels are generally hard to return if measured out incorrectly. Little details, such as backspace adjustment to fill the available space without rubbing, can really make all the difference in your truck's curb appeal. You'll want to get the right setup the first time, which takes some measuring, but you also need to know how to measure as well as the terminology involved.

Overall diameter is the measurement of the tire bead seat to the tire bead seat across the rim. For most

172 CHEVY/GMC TRUCKS 1967–1972: HOW TO BUILD & MODIFY

FINISHING TOUCHES

A Stock Look

GM trucks look great on just about any wheel and tire combination, but there's a lot to be said for a stock-style wheel, especially when it's configured to fill up the wheel well on a lowered truck.

GM's standard dog-dish hubcaps from this era came in several configurations. Originals from this era were chrome-plated steel or painted steel that feature a blue bowtie on a convex face for Chevrolet applications and measure 10.5 inches for 1/2-ton applications and 12 inches for 3/4-ton trucks.

From 1973–1975, GM used a similar design but in stainless. It featured a yellow bowtie on a concave face. The later ones are easier to find today, as they didn't rust the same way that the earlier chrome versions did. However, they're all getting harder to come by, so if you find a set for sale at a good price, buy them!

The Wheel Vintiques "62 Series O.E." wheels are very close in design to the factory steel window wheels these trucks ran from the factory, but these new rims are available in a variety of size options. For a truck that still has factory brakes in place, a 15x8 in front and a 15x10 in the back is about right with a 4-inch backspace up front and a 5-inch backspace out back. ■

You can easily modify a later GM hubcap to look like an earlier one by painting the bowtie the proper color of blue. The only other change is in how the cap was stamped, particularly around the bowtie itself.

GM trucks from this era, the stock size is either 14-inch or 15-inch units in 1/2-ton configurations, and 16.5-inch in 3/4-ton and 1-ton applications.

Wheel width is just as simple. Measure across the rim from the inner bead seat to the outer bead seat. Factory 1/2-ton rims were generally 6 inches wide, but optional wheels and just about any aftermarket or later swaps were wider.

Wheel offset is more complex. This is a measurement from the mounting surface of the wheel to the wheel's centerline. Today's aftermarket wheel companies tend to measure this in millimeters, and it can either be a positive or a negative number, depending on how far in or out from the hub that you want the centerline of your tire to sit. Some companies use the term "backspacing," which is a measurement of the mounting surface of the rim to the rear bead seat of the tire. It's generally the same idea but measured in a different way.

Changing your wheel offset or backspacing can really make a difference in how a set of rims can tuck inside the wheel well of a C10. The wheel wells are big enough to pack some serious rubber without rubbing, depending on how far you've lowered your rig. Generally speaking, the less backspacing you have, the less tucked-in your wheels will look. It also allows you to have more of a dished wheel, which makes everything look beefier and wider. A small backspace will push the centerline of the tire out toward the body and potentially cause rubbing issues, so it's a fine line. It just goes to show how important measuring is in this process.

Depending on the year of your truck, you may be looking for either 5-lug or 6-lug wheels (or 8-lug in 3/4-ton applications), but none of that is much of a problem, as the aftermarket has been making wheels for these trucks for decades. One thing to note is that the 5-lug setup that started in 1971 on C10s is not the same as the car setup. Trucks use a 5-on-5-inch pattern with 1/2-inch wheel studs, while cars use the smaller 5-on-4.75 bolt pattern with smaller 7/16-inch wheel studs. The exception to this rule is 1971–1976 GM full-size cars and the 9C1 Caprice/Impala that use the larger truck pattern. Measure any custom rims before you buy to be sure that they'll fit.

CHAPTER 13

Tires

Once you know the wheels that you intend to run, the next step is to pick the appropriate rubber. This is important, as it's the only component of your truck that's ever in contact with the ground. You'll want to select tires that reflect the actual use of your truck and are sized appropriately for both the gearing of your rear axle and the amount of space you have on hand.

Tire diameter impacts the overall rear gearing in a seat-of-the-pants kind of way. Larger tires tend to tame more aggressive gear ratios. This is why you'll see lifted trucks with large wheels and tires running 4.11 and steeper gear ratios. That same large tire on a truck with a 3.08 rear gear ratio will make acceleration sluggish in comparison, so keep that in mind when selecting your tire combination. I've found that an overall diameter of 28 to 30 inches with a 3.73 rear gear ratio makes for a great street combination in a car or truck with a 1:1 final gear ratio in the transmission, and a 3.42 or 3.55 works better for highway driving.

A taller tire will make that 3.73 ratio feel more like the 3.55 ratio, but keep in mind that you'll likely have to recalibrate your speedometer for larger tires. Depending on your transmission, that requires a different speedometer drive gear or a calibration setting inside your transmission's electronic control unit.

With regard to sizing, everything you need to know about a tire is written in code on the side. For example, a P235/70 R15 tire is a passenger car tire (P). The width is 235 mm across the tread (235), (70) is the aspect ratio of the sidewall compared to the tread surface, and it's a radial (R) for a 15-inch rim (15). The letters and numbers that come after are the load rating (two digits). The higher the number, the higher the load rating, which is important if you intend on towing or hauling with your truck. There's also a speed rating and an indicator of whether or not the tire is suitable for all weather conditions.

A tire's speed rating is an important consideration, especially for those running plus-sized rims and low-profile tires. High-performance rubber tends to be expensive, and the higher the speed rating, the higher the price. Remember that even with a host of speed parts onboard, you're still building a truck, so you probably won't need tires that are designed for 150-plus mph. You might be better off with H- or V-rated rubber instead of softer, quick-wearing Z-rated units. At the very least, you'll save some money and won't feel like you're burning dollar bills when you drop the hammer and smoke up the neighborhood.

Maximum Tire Speed Ratings	
Letter	Speed
L	75 mph
Q	99 mph
R	106 mph
S	112 mph
T	118 mph
U	124 mph
H	130 mph
V	149 mph
Z	149-plus mph
W	168 mph
Y	186 mph

Then again, those softer-compound tires, while more expensive and faster wearing, do offer better cornering and stopping abilities, so take that into account before making a decision.

It's important to note that every truck, while similar, is different based on the parts that were used to build it. To be sure a wheel and tire combo is going to fit, you first have to measure, even if your truck is completely stock.

Measuring for Proper Tire Fitment

1 The main consideration for wheel and tire measurement is in assembly. Before you know what kind of clearance is needed, assemble the truck to near completion with the inner fenders, brakes, suspension, and more in place.

2 You don't need a special tool to measure for proper wheel size, but it helps to have one. This is the Wheelrite from Percy's. It mounts to the wheel hub and allows you to adjust wheel and tire settings for a visual on the truck.

Measuring for Proper Tire Fitment continued

3 Setting up the Wheelrite is simple. It just bolts in place on the hub. From there, you can set up your preferred wheel diameter and width. Then, you can play with backspacing to get everything centered where you want it. This needs to be checked at ride height, so it's best to use a floor jack on the lower control arm to lift the truck. Note the wire used to mock up the tire cross-section.

4 The Wheelrite is marked for easy reference. All that you have to do is loosen a screw and slide the tool to the overall diameter of the rim you want to run. In this case, I'm looking at a 20-inch wheel to clear the Baer brakes. It's a similar story for wheel width. Loosen, adjust, tighten, and visualize what will fit. Check for interference when turning, particularly on the front wheels.

5 Up front, I found that an 8-inch wheel with a 4.5-inch backspacing will clear and provide enough room under the OEM inner fenders for a tire with an approximate section width of 9.75 inches and a sidewall height of 4 inches. I chose to run a set of US Mag Bullets (U130) in 20x8 with 4.5-inch backspacing fitted with a 245/40R20 tire to match the sidewall height and section width that I mocked up. Measuring out back brought me to a 20x9.5 rim with a 285/35R20 tire.

6 The truck's wheels and tires are set, but don't be surprised if you find yourself needing a small 1/8- or 1/4-inch spacer for hub-to-wheel clearance issues due to differences in machining. This setup allows the truck to be usable even when dropped fairly low on its coilovers while keeping the stock inner fenders intact.

Source Guide

Alistair Case
503-348-4624

Auburn Gear
400 East Auburn Dr.
Auburn, IN 46706
260-925-3200
auburngear.com

Auto Metal Direct
3348 Gateway Centre Pkwy.
Gainesville, GA 30507
833-404-4777
autometaldirect.com

AutomotiveTouchup Microfinish LLC
208 Plauche Ct.
New Orleans, LA 70123
888-710-5192
automotivetouchup.com

Baer Brakes
2222 West Peoria Ave.
Phoenix, AZ 85029
602-233-1411
baer.com

Borgeson
9 Krieger Dr.
Travelers Rest, SC 29690
860-482-8283
borgeson.com

Carolina Kustoms
6600 NE Columbia Blvd.
Portland, OR 97218
503-954-1369
carolinakustoms.com

Carolina Truck Shop
4056 Anderson Mill Rd.
Spartanburg, SC 29301
864-285-4513
carolinatruckshop.com

CarTech Books, Inc.
6118 Main St.
North Branch, MN 55056
651-277-1233
1-800-551-4754
cartechbooks.com

Classic Industries
18460 Gothard St.
Huntington Beach, CA 92648
1-800-854-1280
classicindustries.com

Classic Performance Products
175 E Freedom Ave.
Anaheim, CA 92801
714-522-2000
classicperform.com

Dakota Digital
4510 W. 61st St. N.
Sioux Falls, SD 57107
605-332-6513
dakotadigital.com

Dapper Lighting
833-327-7371
dapperlighting.com

Dirty Dingo Motorsports
506 E Juanita Ave., Suite 3
Mesa, AZ 85204
480-824-1968
dirtydingo.com

Eastwood
263 Shoemaker Rd.
Pottstown, PA 19464
800-343-9353
eastwood.com

Eaton Performance Aftermarket
800-328-3850
eaton.com

Edelbrock, LLC
2700 California St.
Torrance, CA 90503
800-416-8628
edelbrock.com

Fesler Built
866-553-1856
shopfesler.com

Flaming River Industries
800 Poertner Dr.
Berea, OH 44017
440-826-4488
flamingriver.com

Gearstar Performance Transmissions
132 N. Howard St.
Akron, OH 44308
330-434-5216
gearstar.com

Holley Performance Products
1801 Russellville Rd.
Bowling Green, KY 42101
270-782-2900
holley.com

Hooker Headers
1801 Russellville Rd.
Bowling Green, KY 42101
270-782-2900
holley.com

Hughes Performance
2244 W. McDowell Rd.
Phoenix, AZ 85009
602-257-9591
hughesperformance.com

Metalox Fab LLC
8615 W. Kelton Ln., Suite 305
Peoria, AZ 85382
623-308-1170
metaloxfab.com

MSD
1801 Russellville Rd.
Bowling Green, KY 42101
270-782-2900
holley.com

Pertronix LLC
440 E. Arrow Hwy.
San Dimas, CA 91773
909-599-5955
pertronixbrands.com

Premier Street Rod
1100 N. Lake Havasu Ave.
Lake Havasu City, AZ 86403
800-447-5000
premierstreetrod.com

Ratech
11110 Adwood Dr.
Cincinnati, OH 45240
ratechmfg.com

Ridetech
350 S. St. Charles St.
Jasper, IN 47546
812-481-4787
ridetech.com

Rydman Ranch
701 NE Peters Rd., Suite 3
Prineville, OR 97754
541-527-4777
rydmanranch.com

Silver Sport Transmissions
2250 Stock Creek Blvd.
Rockford, TN 37853
865-609-8187
shiftsst.com

Snap-on, Inc.
877-762-7664
snapon.com

Summit Racing Equipment
P.O. Box 909
Akron, OH 44309
1-800-230-3030
summitracing.com

US Mags
5347 S Valentia Way
Greenwood Village, CO 80111
831-290-6514
us-mags.com

Vintage Air
18865 Goll St.
San Antonio, TX 78266
800-862-6658
vintageair.com